Marx, Engels, and Marxisms

Series Editors
Marcello Musto, York University, Toronto, ON, Canada
Terrell Carver, University of Bristol, Bristol, UK

The Marx renaissance is underway on a global scale. Wherever the critique of capitalism re-emerges, there is an intellectual and political demand for new, critical engagements with Marxism. The peer-reviewed series Marx, Engels and Marxisms (edited by Marcello Musto & Terrell Carver, with Babak Amini, Francesca Antonini, Paula Rauhala & Kohei Saito as Assistant Editors) publishes monographs, edited volumes, critical editions, reprints of old texts, as well as translations of books already published in other languages. Our volumes come from a wide range of political perspectives, subject matters, academic disciplines and geographical areas, producing an eclectic and informative collection that appeals to a diverse and international audience. Our main areas of focus include: the oeuvre of Marx and Engels, Marxist authors and traditions of the 19th and 20th centuries, labour and social movements, Marxist analyses of contemporary issues, and reception of Marxism in the world.

Paul Raekstad

Karl Marx's Realist Critique of Capitalism

Freedom, Alienation, and Socialism

Paul Raekstad
Social and Behavioral Sciences
University of Amsterdam
Amsterdam, The Netherlands

ISSN 2524-7123　　　　　　　ISSN 2524-7131　(electronic)
Marx, Engels, and Marxisms
ISBN 978-3-031-06352-7　　　ISBN 978-3-031-06353-4　(eBook)
https://doi.org/10.1007/978-3-031-06353-4

© The Editor(s) (if applicable) and The Author(s), under exclusive license to Springer Nature Switzerland AG 2022
This work is subject to copyright. All rights are solely and exclusively licensed by the Publisher, whether the whole or part of the material is concerned, specifically the rights of translation, reprinting, reuse of illustrations, recitation, broadcasting, reproduction on microfilms or in any other physical way, and transmission or information storage and retrieval, electronic adaptation, computer software, or by similar or dissimilar methodology now known or hereafter developed.
The use of general descriptive names, registered names, trademarks, service marks, etc. in this publication does not imply, even in the absence of a specific statement, that such names are exempt from the relevant protective laws and regulations and therefore free for general use.
The publisher, the authors and the editors are safe to assume that the advice and information in this book are believed to be true and accurate at the date of publication. Neither the publisher nor the authors or the editors give a warranty, expressed or implied, with respect to the material contained herein or for any errors or omissions that may have been made. The publisher remains neutral with regard to jurisdictional claims in published maps and institutional affiliations.

Cover image: © duncan1890/E+/Getty Image

This Palgrave Macmillan imprint is published by the registered company Springer Nature Switzerland AG
The registered company address is: Gewerbestrasse 11, 6330 Cham, Switzerland

Acknowledgements

I owe a great thanks to my Ph.D. supervisors Raymond Geuss and Lorna "LoLo" Finlayson, who were a vital help during the research that this book is based on. Their abilities and efforts are beyond anything that anyone can reasonably demand or expect. Many other friends and colleagues have been kind enough to listen to, read, and comment on various parts of this work at different stages. For that, I would like to thank professor Akshath Jitendranath, Al Campbell, Annelien De Dijn, Ammar Ali Jan, Ben Cross, Dan Swain, David Bates, Enzo Rossi, Erik Van Ree, Janosch Prinz, Jules Townshend, Mahvish Ahmad, Nicholas Vrousalis, Mathias Thaler, Nina Rismal, Paul "OP" Giladi, Rachel "The Malkinator" Malkin, Ragnhild Faller, Uğur Aytaç, and Zoe Baker.

Among those not already mentioned, I also owe a great deal to the friends who have supported me, you know who you are.

I will always owe a special debt of gratitude to my mother, Evelyn Melanie Rækstad, without whose incomparable efforts and devotion I would never have been able to do any of this, and would most likely not be around at all.

I have presented the research that's gone in this book at various conferences and workshops throughout the last handful of years. I am grateful to all participants of them for their very helpful feedback, and in particular Catarina Neves for inviting me to present at the reading group on "The predistributive politics of a property-owning democracy" and Enzo Rossi for organising a book workshop at the University of Amsterdam.

A couple of chapters of the book have been previously published. Parts of Part I have appeared as Raekstad, P. 2018. Human Development and Alienation in the Thought of Karl Marx. *European Journal of Political Theory* 17(3), pp. 300–323. Parts of Part II have appeared as Raekstad, P. 2017. The Democratic Theory of the Early Marx. *Archiv für Geschichte der Philosophie* 99(4), pp. 443–464. In all of these cases, as well as in the case of the anonymous reviewers of the book manuscript for Palgrave, I am grateful to anonymous referees and editors for their comments and insights.

Finally, I'd like to thank Terrell Carver for his faith in the book and for all his help and Uma Vinesh at Palgrave for her patience and help with getting the book published. I'm sure I've forgotten someone, for which I'm sorry.

Naturally, all mistakes remain my own, but realistically if there are any that are too glaring you'd expect some of these people to have spotted them.

Abbreviations

Throughout this book, I provide two references to quotes from Marx and Engels' writings, the first in the most widely available English translation I can find, followed by one in one of the two editions of Marx and Engels' collected works in German, where possible.

The current edition of the *Marx-Engels Gesamtausgabe—Marx, K. and Engels, F. 1975-. Karl Marx, Friedrich Engels Gesamtausgabe. (MEGA$_2$). Berlin: Dietz/ Akademie Verlag*—has been cited by volume such that volume 1:2, page 234, is cited as I:2, p. 234. There are some cases where I reference texts without quoting, in which case I refer to them only as e.g. I:2, p. 234.

In a few cases where I've been unable to get hold of the German original in *MEGA$_2$*, I've also instead cited from *MEGA$_1$*—Marx, K. and Engels, F. 1927–1932, 1935. *Karl Marx-Friedrich Engels-Historische-kritische Gesamtausgabe: Werke, Schriften, Briefe*. Berlin: Marx-Engels Verlag—in the same way, but preceded with MEGA$_1$, such that e.g. volume I:3, page 206 is cited as MEGA$_1$ I:3, p.206.

The English-language collection of Marx and Engels' collected works—Marx, K. and Engels, F. 1975–2004. *Karl Marx, Frederick Engels: collected works*. London: Lawrence and Wishart—are cited by volume and page number, such that volume 6, page 192, is cited as MECW 6, p. 192.

The Marx and Engels selected works in English—Marx, K. and Engels, F. 1969. *Karl Marx and Frederick Engels: Selected Works in Three Volumes*. Moscow: Progress Publishers—have been abbreviated MESW, followed by the volume number, followed by the page number, such that e.g. volume 1, page 502 will be cited as MESW 1, p. 502–503.

All other citations are given by author, date, and page number.

Contents

1	Introduction	1
Part I	**Human Development and Freedom**	
2	Human Development	21
3	Freedom	49
Part II	**Alienation and Democracy**	
4	The First Theory of Alienation	79
5	Democracy	91
6	From Realisation-Oriented to Agent-Centred Political Theory	103
Part III	**Alienation: The Unfreedom of Capitalism**	
7	Alienation and Unfreedom	119
8	The Socialist Alternative	155
9	Radical Theory and Revolutionary Practice	195
10	Towards a New World	213

Appendix: A Brief Overview of the (Other) Principal
          Interpretations of Marx's Normative
          Commitments   221
Bibliography   263
Index   283

CHAPTER 1

Introduction

Marx is a theorist of emancipation, famous as a trailblazing analyst of capitalism, a fierce critic of its alienation and domination, and perhaps the greatest socialist thinker to date. Yet over a century after his death, there's little agreement on what any of these consist in or how they hang together. This book aims to change that, explaining how they combine to form a unified critique of capitalism that remains as powerful and compelling as ever.

This task is rendered all the more important by Marx's influence on the rebirth of radical politics worldwide and the persistent interest in his theory of alienation.[1] Unsurprisingly, the resurgence of radical movements has been accompanied by a number of new studies on Marx.[2] Many of these rightly emphasise Marx's critique of capitalism being one of unfreedom, but display a number of interrelated shortcomings. One of the most prominent ones is that in order to fit Marx's work into popular moulds that define freedom as not being subject to the arbitrary power of

---

[1] For just a small handful of examples, see Dixon (2014), Graeber (2009, 2015), Holloway (1997, 2010), Mészáros (1972, 1995), and Lebowitz (2003, 2010, 2012, 2020).

[2] There are too many to list here, but they include Carver (2018), Heinrich (2012, 2021), Jones (2016), Musto (2020), Roberts (2017), Lebowitz (2010, 2020), and Saito (2017).

another, there's a tendency not to explore the foundational role played by his theory of human development, as well as misunderstand his theory of freedom and saying relatively little about his radically democratic vision of socialism.[3] This in turn leads to underestimating the challenge that Marx's ideas pose to contemporary proposals for free economic institutions. Nobody has so far been able to provide a holistic account of Marx's critique of capitalism that can make sense of the connections between all of these aspects of his thought and explore their implications for a free and democratic socialist society.

These limitations are partly due to the long-standing neglect of Marx's approach to political theorising. Broadly speaking, the form that contemporary Anglo-American political theory has taken since the 1970s, with its reinvigoration in the work of John Rawls,[4] can largely be described as Platonic and Kantian, focusing on the formulation, comparison, and evaluation of abstract principles of justice, and only subsequently looking to their application in the real world.[5] In response to the manifest shortcomings of this approach, thinkers like Bernard Williams and Raymond Geuss have spearheaded a revival of what they call realist approaches to political theory.[6] Realism is based on the idea that political theory should

---

[3] Following many others in the literature, I prefer to speak of "socialism" rather than "communism". Largely, this is done because the term "communism" today is commonly associated with the centrally planned single-party dictatorships of e.g. the USSR, which were very different from the vision Marx himself lays out under that term. For the literature on Marx and republicanism, see Abensour (2011), Fischer (2015), Isaac (1990), Jones (2016), Leipold (2020, 2022), Leopold (2007), Roberts (2017, 2018), Thompson (2019), and Vrousalis (2021). It's worth pointing out that there are two very different senses in which thinkers are labelled "republicans" in contemporary anglophone political theory, including (a) adopting the republican/neo-Roman concept of freedom as not being subject to the will/arbitrary power of another and (b) sharing a broad cluster of concerns about domination, slavery, servitude, and the emancipation of at least some people. In the former sense, Marx is not a republican, but in the latter sense he certainly is in various ways, and there's a growing cottage industry exploring it.

[4] See Rawls (1999, 2001, 2005).

[5] For more on this, see Raekstad (2015, 2020b, and forthcoming b).

[6] For the discussions most relevant to my concerns here, see Baderin (2014), Brinn (2019), Duff (2017), Finlayson (2015), Floyd and Stears (2011), Frazer (2008, 2010), Galston (2010), Geuss (2008, 2010, 2014, 2016, 2020), Hall (2015, 2017), Honig (1993), Menke (2010), Mészáros (2011), Mouffe (2006), Newey (2010), Philp (2012), Prinz (2016), Prinz and Rossi (2017), Raekstad (2015, 2018b, 2020b, 2020c, forthcoming b), Rossi (2010, 2012, 2014, 2019), Rossi and Sleat (2010, 2014), Sangiovanni (2008), Sleat (2013), Valentini (2012), Williams (2008), Wolff (2011), and Wright

above all seek to make sense of and guide real politics.[7] On this view, the tasks of political theory are first and foremost to help make sense of and guide various forms of real politics—such as social and political movements, political parties, and so on. This requires starting from questions of the available forms of agency and their contexts, questions of timing and priority of possible actions, and questions of motivation, justification, and legitimation. Realists typically argue that doing this well entails rejecting what they call the "moralist" or "ethics-first" approaches to political theory of Rawls and others, because they tend not to be very good at fulfilling this vocation. By contrast, realists tend to avoid abstract theories of moral rules and rule-like systems of perfect justice and their application, in favour of more embedded and contextual reflections on political values; understanding and explaining the operations of different forms of real politics; orienting political agents; evaluating achievable alternative institutions, actions, and the like; various forms of genealogy and ideology critique; and conceptual development and innovation.[8] Key realist thinkers like Raymond Geuss explicitly draw on Karl Marx's work as a paradigm case of the approach they advocate, yet nobody has so far produced a detailed realist interpretation thereof.

Reading Marx through a realist lens enables a holistic reconstruction of his critique of capitalism, tying together his normative commitments, diagnosis of capitalist alienation and unfreedom, and positive vision of

---

(2010). Interestingly, these methodological developments are connected with the re-birth of normative approaches focusing on human development—both within Marxist scholarship (see esp. Lebowitz, 2003, 2010, 2012; other writers who have emphasised Marx's critique of capitalism in terms of human development include Booth, 1992; Hamilton, 2003; Mészáros, 1972, 1995, 2011, 2014; Ollman 1976; Sayers 2007a, b) and among political theorists more broadly (see Nussbaum 1992a, b, 2011; Sen, 1984a, b, 1987, 1992, 1999, 2010; Wolff and de-Shalit, 2007). I've previously argued that Sen's human development approach and his methodology connects to Marx's in Raekstad (2015, 2018a). Finally, it's worth noting that Sen himself is an advocate of what he calls a comparative approach to political theory, which I've argued elsewhere (Raekstad 2015) is a kind of realism.

[7] Realism is sometimes confused with non-ideal theory, which focuses more on what the role of feasibility constraints should be in political theory. While they can come apart (one can do e.g. realist ideology critique that makes no use of feasibility constraints) there's a lot of overlap between the two, with thinkers like Adam Smith, Karl Marx, Amartya Sen, and Charles Mills arguably falling into both camps. For a bit more on this, see Raekstad (2015).

[8] Geuss (2008, Part I).

socialism. My reconstruction begins by explaining the normative commitments that Marx's critique builds on. The two most prominent candidates here have long been theories of human development[9] and of positive freedom.[10] Yet nobody has so far been able to explain how these two connect in Marx's work. This book does, starting with developing a more sophisticated interpretation of Marx's conception of human development than any other so far. On the basis of this, I show how Marx develops a positive concept of freedom as self-direction, which is key to understanding the resulting critique of capitalism. With this in hand, I reconstruct what I argue are two methodologically and substantively distinct diagnoses of capitalist unfreedom in two different theories of alienation, one earlier (1842–1843) and one later (from 1844 onwards all the way to *Capital*), along with their corresponding visions of a free future society—democracy and socialism, respectively. One thing that's often missing from the alienation literature is a precise account of what makes alienation undesirable. I, by contrast, reconstruct both theories of alienation as diagnosing how capitalism thwarts human freedom and thereby human development. Against some recent republican readings of Marx, I show how only a positive theory of freedom is able to make sense of these diagnoses of capitalist unfreedom and his radically democratic proposals for how to cure it. This in turn enables me to defend Marx's analysis against its most insightful critics, showing that it remains both compelling and defensible today. Finally, against the widespread misconception that Marx's ideas of capitalist alienation and unfreedom are ill-at-ease with his later theories about human beings, society, and socialist revolution, I show that they in fact provide the core of his later theorising about the driving forces of socialism: the revolutionary contradictions of capitalism.

This should be of interest to anyone concerned with understanding Marx's critique of capitalism, his theories of alienation and socialism, the prospects for radical forms of realism, contemporary debates about the unfreedom of capitalism, and visions of free future economic institutions. To those interested primarily in Marx, what this book offers is the first

---

[9] Esp. Mészáros (1972, 1995), Lebowitz (2010), Leopold (2007), and Sayers (2007a, b, ch. 9).

[10] Esp. Blackledge (2012), Sayers (2007b, 2011), Swain (2019a, b), and Tabak (2020).

reconstruction of how all the main elements of his critique of capitalism fit together and feed into his mature theory of revolution.

To those interested in alternatives to capitalism, this book shows how Marx's ideas continue to pose a powerful challenge to contemporary proposals for economic reform and offer important ideas about how we can democratise economic institutions and why we have reason to do so. Inspired by the republican tradition that Marx was part of and responding to, a number of contemporary thinkers have criticised the personal power of capitalists over workers and the structure of property relations that forces workers to subject themselves to it, recommending things like co-determination, dispersing ownership of the means of production, and democratising individual firms as sufficient to secure economic emancipation.[11] Marx challenges these ideas in a number of ways. He develops a positive concept of freedom that can capture both personal and impersonal forms of domination. He also diagnoses the impersonal domination inherent in capitalist-type competitive markets and how hierarchical divisions of labour entail personal relations of domination in the workplace. Based on this, he shows that economic freedom thus requires not just replacing the power of capitalists with workers' councils, but also replacing competitive markets with democratic planning and abolishing the hierarchical division of labour.

To those primarily interested in realism, this book reconstructs two models of how Marx did it in ways that are both radical and transformative. The first of these is a radical democratic critique of capitalism and the state; the second is his socialist critique of capitalist society. Both of these merge empirical and normative components and seek to make sense of and guide real politics—but this is no obstacle to their radicalness. On Marx's view, the inhabitants of capitalist societies have at our disposal all the potentials we need for a truly free society, one that better enables the development and flourishing of all. What's preventing us from making use of these potentials are the inherently unfree social relations of capitalism. Marx's later political theory aims to make sense of this situation and guide the revolutionary working-class movement to better realise its interest in its own empowerment and emancipation, replacing capitalism with a free society that enables us all to develop our potentials.

---

[11] See e.g. Anderson (2017), Breen (2015), González-Ricoy (2014) Gourevitch (2015), Hsieh (2008, 2012), and White (2011). Naturally, there's a lot more detail to their proposals, and differences among them, than can be discussed here.

Marx is not reading a normative ideal of capitalism off from its existing institutions, nor from the ideas and values of pro-capitalist theoreticians. Instead, he's analysing the inherent potentials and limitations of capitalist societies from the perspective and interests of the oppressed who already are fighting for their self-emancipation. Marx doesn't need some abstract theory of justice to do this, nor impose some enlightening principles on the working-class movement from the outside. Instead, this critique is offered to a (potentially) revolutionary working-class movement that's already perceiving the unfreedom of capitalism and seeking to overthrow it. In this way, Marx is fulfilling the realist vocation of making sense of real politics and contributing to the actions of the agents involved, helping the present give birth to one of the futures it's already pregnant with.

The book is structured as follows. Part I begins by laying out a unified account of the normative commitments that Marx's critique of capitalism builds on, namely a commitment to human development and to a notion of freedom as self-direction as an important aspect thereof. Thus, Chapter 2 develops a more sophisticated interpretation of Marx's conception of human development than others so far. I argue that Marx is committed to a conception of human development as the development of powers, i.e. as real possibilities to do and/or to be, and that these can only be understood through their interaction with human needs in lived human practice/praxis.[12] Chapter 3 builds on this analysis to explicate his concept of freedom and the role it plays in his critiques of capitalism. Here I argue that Marx has a conception of freedom as self-direction, according to which humans have an internal species-specific power for free or self-directed activity. The realisation or exercise of this power is both valuable in itself and valuable because it positively impacts the development of many other humans powers. This view is contrasted with conceptions of

---

[12] Praxis and practice are two different translations for the same German original. The theory of practice is explained in Chapter 2 and in Raekstad and Gradin (2020), so readers of that book may wrongly think that I first figured out the theory of practice and then used it to reconstruct Marx's theory of human development. The reality is the other way around. During my PhD research (specifically during 2012–2013), I first reconstructed Marx theory of human development based on readings in social movement Marxism (which I felt didn't quite nail his theory of needs and its role correctly), work by Bertell Ollman, and Deleuze's first book on Spinoza; then realised that was simultaneously his theory of practice; and then that many historical anarchists also shared that theory and that it was a core component of their political theory and practice, including their views on prefigurative politics.

freedom as non-domination and defended against common misconceived criticisms. At their core, both of Marx's critiques of capitalism consist in a diagnosis of how it thwarts freedom and thereby human development, along with a proposed cure that realises freedom by removing alienation.

Now, although my reading is gaining ground, it is far from the only position on Marx's normative commitments. Since I think these other positions deserve serious discussion, and since any such discussion requires so much space as inevitably to break up the narrative of my argument in a potentially disorienting way, I have added an appendix where the other major positions, along with my objections, are very briefly discussed. There are at least three groups of readers who will likely find this appendix especially valuable: those with strong ideas that Marx is an amoralist who rejects all forms of normative theories; those who think Marx is a moralist with rule-like principles of justice or morality grounding his critique of capitalism; and those highly interested in different kinds and sources of normativity, and how Marx may or may not fit or inform contemporary debates thereon. If this sounds like you, I strongly recommend starting with the appendix, and then moving on to the other chapters in order. For other readers, I'd recommend reading the chapters in order, only diving into the appendix if and when you feel like it.

With an understanding of Marx's normative commitments in place, Parts II and III turn to what I argue are two distinct critiques of capitalism. My realist interpretation allows me to show that each of these critiques consists of an integrated whole that combines his normative commitment to human development and freedom; a diagnosis of how capitalist society thwarts freedom and thereby human development; and a proposed future society to cure these ills. Together, Parts II and III show how some elements of Marx's earliest work carry over to his later work—e.g. his general realist approach to political theorising, his commitment to human development, his basic account of human nature, and his deep commitment to radical participatory democracy. What changes from the former to the latter is his diagnosis of how modern society thwarts human freedom, in particular his expanded analysis of the alien powers and forms of unfreedom inherent in modern capitalism. As a result of this so too does his conception of the cure required.

Thus, the chapters in Part II examine what I term Marx's first theory of alienation, his radical notion of democracy, and the methodological development he undergoes during the years 1843–1844. They argue, *inter alia*, that prior to 1844 Marx has a distinct critique of capitalism from the later, socialist Marx, and that this theory of alienation and his conception of an alternative form of society—democracy—jointly constitute a realist critique of capitalism which is distinct both methodologically and substantively from the one he articulates later on. Once this is understood, we can see how this provides the radical democratic core of Marx's later diagnosis of capitalist unfreedom and vision of socialism.

Chapter 4 presents a novel reading of what I call Marx's first theory of alienation, which he develops during the years 1842–1843. On this view, Marx's first theory of alienation consists in a critical diagnosis of capitalism and the state, according to which they are both alienating on the grounds that they thwart the human species-specific power for participating in deliberation and decision-making on public affairs. This chapter argues for four original theses with respect to the existing literature: that the early Marx did in fact have a developed theory of alienation distinct from the one he developed in the 1844 manuscripts[13]; that this theory is not centred solely on a critique of the modern state, or Hegel's conception thereof[14]; that this theory centred on the suppressing of human species-powers principally by their being subjected to seemingly external power and domination, rather than in any significant way consisting in some sort of "split" between citizen and private person distinctive of the modern society/state complex[15]; and that this in turn means that this early account of alienation applies much wider than merely to capitalist civil society and the state, but also e.g. to feudalism.[16] Already at this stage, Marx critiques how capitalist social relations subject people to alien powers which those subject to them cannot control, driving him to develop a vision of democracy that's significantly more radical than is typically recognised.[17]

---

[13] *Contra* Colletti (1992), Lukács and Livingstone (1974), and Plamenatz (1975).

[14] *Contra* Berki (1990), Breckman (1999), McGovern (1988), and Mészáros (1972). Against this view, and for mine, see Draper (1977).

[15] *Contra* Avineri (1968), Duquette (1989), Hudis (2013), McGovern (1988), and Tucker (1970, 1972).

[16] Although these points have not all been noted and fully explicated together, some authors do come close, esp. McLellan (1970, 1971).

[17] This relates to another controversial issue, namely my choice to distinguish explicitly between two different "theories" of alienation, despite the fact that they have very different structures. What I call Marx's first theory of alienation, and examine in

With the analysis of Marx's first theory of alienation in place, Chapter 5 examines Marx's proposed alternative to capitalism and the modern state: democracy. Here I argue that Marx advocates a vision of radical democracy inspired by the radical enlightenment, seeing democracy as a form of society in which all people participate in deliberation and decision-making on public affairs, replacing both the modern state and capitalism and thereby doing away with alienation. This includes an unwavering commitment to freedoms of speech, press, conviction, and association. This affirms that Marx is, in some important senses, a republican concerned with ideas of popular power and the harms of absolutism. At the same time, it's worth noting that many historical republicans, especially those popular today, were not democrats in any meaningful sense and explicitly said so, frequently explicitly excluding women, people of colour, and the working classes. Marx does not. Finally, by eliminating the separation between state and economy and subjecting the economy to democratic control, Marx's notion of democracy goes far beyond many of his contemporary republicans and prefigures his later socialist ideas.

These two chapters show how Marx's realist approach to political theorising prior to 1844 was what I call "realisation-oriented", in the sense that it focuses on comparing competing achievable alternatives—democracy compared to the modern state and capitalism. Chapter 6 then explores the methodological development that Marx underwent during

---

Chapter 4, basically consists in a familiar Young Hegelian critical concept of "alienation" (Entfremdung), which in Marx's early works refers to the ways in which the human capacity for conscious participation in deliberation and decision-making on public affairs is thwarted by a seemingly external socially generated power. By contrast, the much more familiar theory of alienation that Marx first presents in the *Economic and Philosophical Manuscripts of 1844*, which I call his "second theory" of alienation and discuss in Chapter 7, consists in a much more developed account of how capitalism specifically thwarts the human power for self-directed activity. It may be doubted whether what I call the first "theory" of alienation really merits the term at all, since it is very different in structure from the second one. I cannot properly discuss the issue of whether the first theory truly deserves the label "theory" of alienation in the same way that the second theory clearly does here and I very much recognise that the two "theories" of alienation are very different in structure and the extent to which they are developed. Noting these important differences, however, I will call the first "theory" of alienation a distinct "theory" for three reasons: it is part of an interesting critique of the basic institutions of contemporary society that can be found in Marx's early works; it is clearly distinct from the later theory he develops from 1844 onwards through to the published volumes of *Capital*; and it forms part of a distinct critique of modern society that his later critique develops from in interesting ways, both methodologically and substantively.

the years 1843–4, leading to the second theory of alienation that he begins to develop during 1844. Here I show that Marx's focus on comparing achievable alternatives leads him to investigate which social agents he can find to bring about his envisioned alternative, leading him to the proletariat. Having identified the proletariat as his revolutionary agent, Marx investigates its nature through studying political economy and by making contacts and engaging with groups of socialist workers. Part of this investigation involves coming to grips with how the capitalist economy, and the alien powers it entails, functions in more detail, how it generates different and conflicting classes, and how best a theorist or critic can act to help the process of proletarian agency along its route to revolution. At the end of this process, Marx develops what I call an "agent-centred" approach to political theory. This approach starts from a descriptive account of a particular form of society, draws from this a conception of the available forms of political agency, including their structurally determined capacities and constraints, and focuses on contributing to these forms of agency and their actions. I briefly analyse the implications of this for Marx's later political theorising, focusing on how this shift led him to acquire a different, and much more detailed, diagnosis of how capitalism thwarts human freedom.

With the stage thus set, Part III shows how Marx employs this agent-centred approach in developing his second critique of capitalism. This includes developing a second theory of alienation as a distinct diagnosis of how capitalism thwarts human freedom and thereby human development, a further developed conception of its cure in his vision of socialism, and his understanding of the (best) practice of the political theorist to help bring this about. I also argue that this critique remains both defensible and compelling, by considering and responding to the arguments of two of its most insightful critics: Max Weber and Friedrich Hayek. Together with the foregoing part, it also shows how many components of Marx's thought—his realist approach to political theorising, his commitment to human development, his conception of human nature, and his deep commitment to democracy—are carried over from the one to the other. What changes are the details of his approach to political theorising, his diagnosis of the ills of capitalism, and his corresponding conception of the required cure.

Chapter 7 reconstructs the theory of alienation Marx first develops in his 1844 manuscripts and retains for the rest of his life. The theory of alienation diagnoses how, in capitalist social relations, people produce and reproduce certain forms of power that come to dominate their producers. Marx distinguishes four kinds of alienation: alienation from product; alienation from productive activity; alienation from species-being; and alienation from others. Each of these is examined in turn, with an emphasis on the personal and impersonal forms of domination they show to be inherent in capitalist production. I show in greater detail than has been done before that there are convincing and oft-overlooked connections between the different kinds of alienation that Marx discusses, and that once understood not as an analysis of capitalism's effects, but of its inherent structure, common misunderstandings can be cleared up. At its heart, the second theory of alienation, like the first, is an analysis of how capitalism thwarts human freedom and thereby human development. Throughout this analysis, I show how Marx's ideas about capitalist alienation persist through his later works, all the way to *Capital*. I finish by defending this diagnosis against common criticisms, arguing that it still applies to contemporary capitalism.

With this diagnosis in place, Chapter 8 examines Marx's conception of its cure: socialism. Since the diagnosis of modern society has changed with Marx's increased understanding of political economy, so too must his conception of its cure. However, I argue that Marx's new vision of a future society retains the core idea of his earlier conception of democracy, namely that it must be a full participatory democracy—including freedoms of speech, press, association, etc., as well as, critically, the democratic organisation of all aspects of social life. Overcoming capitalist alienation requires that socialism also feature a democratically planned economy, replace capitalism's hierarchical division of labour, and distribute according to need. I defend this vision of an alternative form of society against prominent Weberian and Hayekian criticisms, showing that Marx's critique of capitalism remains not only compelling, but also defensible. If Marx is right, human emancipation from the tyranny of capitalism requires much more ambitious changes than many recognise.

Chapter 9 delves deeper into Marx's realist understanding of the role of the theorist in bringing about a socialist society. Here I explore how Marx's views on the revolutionary nature of the proletariat shift during 1844 and the implications this has for his political theorising. Chapters 7 and 8 have already shown that Marx retains all the components of the theory of alienation throughout his mature works, especially *Capital*. Chapter 9 goes further to explain how this theory forms the core of his famous doctrine of the revolutionary contradictions of capitalism:

between the productive powers/forces and relations and between workers and capitalists. There's a clear red line through his normative critique of capitalist unfreedom and his understanding of the forces of social struggle that can drive a successful socialist revolution. By the same token, there's no real conflict between Marx's normative critique of capitalism and his later views on dialectical and historical materialism. Quite the contrary, it forms both the developmental root of these mature ideas and the core of their notion of the driving forces of socialist revolution under capitalism. I go on to discuss how Marx seems to de-emphasise normative political theorising largely because he believes it not to be as useful as his more descriptively focused research on the political economy of capitalism for furthering socialist revolution. Against this, I argue that there is good reason to think that normative political theorising can play a significant role in social change, and that therefore, on the grounds of Marx's own realist approach to political theorising, there is good reason to resurrect these ideas today.

Finally, Chapter 10 summarises and concludes with some reflections about the continued importance of Marx's thoughts on human development, freedom, alienation, and socialism today.

REFERENCES

SECONDARY

Anderson, E. (2017). *Private government: How employers rule our lives (and why we don't talk about it)*. Princeton University Press.

Avineri, S. (1968). *The social and political thought of Karl Marx*. Cambridge University Press.

Baderin, A. (2014). Two forms of realism in political theory. *European Journal of Political Theory, 13*(2), 132–153.

Berki, R. N. (1990). Through and through Hegel: Marx road to communism. *Political Studies, 38*(4), 654–671.

Blackledge, P. (2012). *Marxism and ethics: Freedom, desire, and revolution*. State University of New York Press.

Booth, W. J. (1992). Households, markets, and firms. In McCarthy (Ed.), pp. 243–271.

Breen, K. (2015). Freedom, republicanism, and workplace democracy. *Critical Review of International Social and Political Philosophy, 18*(4), 470–485.

Breckman, W. (1999). *Marx, the Young Hegelians, and the origins of radical social theory*. Cambridge University Press.

Brinn, G. (2019). Smashing the state gently: Radical realism and realist anarchism. *European Journal of Political Theory, 19*(2), 206–227.
Carver, T. (2018). *Marx.* Polity.
Colletti, L. (1992). Introduction to Marx 1992, pp. 7–56.
Dixon, C. (2014). *Another politics: Talking across today's transformative movements.* University of California Press.
Draper, H. (1977). *Karl Marx's theory of revolution, Volume I: State and bureaucracy.* Monthly Review Press.
Duff, K. (2017). The criminal is political: Policing politics in real existing liberalism. *Journal of the American Philosophical Association, 3*(4), 485–502.
Duquette, D. A. (1989). Marx's idealist critique of Hegel's theory of society and politics. *Review of Politics, 51*(2), 218–240.
Finlayson, L. (2015). *The political is political: Conformity and the illusion of dissent in contemporary political philosophy.* Rowman & Littlefield International.
Fischer, N. (2015). *Marxist ethics within Marxist ethics within western political theory: A dialogue with republicanism, communitarianism, and liberalism.* Palgrave Macmillan.
Floyd, J., & Stears, M. (Eds.). (2011). *Political philosophy versus history?: Contextualism and real politics in contemporary political thought.* Cambridge University Press.
Frazer, E. (2008). Political theory and the boundaries of politics. In D. Leopold & M. Stears (Eds.), *Political theory: Methods and approaches.* Oxford University Press.
Frazer, E. (2010). What's real in political philosophy? *Contemporary Political Theory, 9*(4), 490–507.
Galston, W. A. (2010). Realism in political theory. *European Journal of Political Theory, 9*(4), 385–411.
Geuss, R. (2008). *Philosophy and real politics.* Princeton University Press.
Geuss, R. (2010). *Politics and the imagination.* Princeton University Press.
Geuss, R. (2014). *A world without why.* Princeton University Press.
Geuss, R. (2016). *Reality and its dreams.* Harvard University Press.
González-Ricoy, I. (2014). The Republican case for workplace democracy. *Social Theory and Practice, 40*(2), 232–254.
Gourevitch, A. (2015). *From slavery to the cooperative commonwealth: Labor and republican liberty in the nineteenth century.* Cambridge University Press.
Graeber, D. (2009). *Direct action: An ethnography.* AK Press.
Graeber, D. (2015). *The Utopia of rules: On technology, stupidity, and the secret joys of bureaucracy.* Melville House.
Hall, E. (2015). Bernard Williams and the basic legitimation demand: A defence. *Political Studies, 63*(2), 466–480.

Hall, E. (2017). How to do realistic political theory (and why you might want to). *European Journal of Political Theory, 16*(3), 283–303.
Hamilton, L. A. (2003). *The political philosophy of needs*. Cambridge University Press.
Heinrich, M. (2021). *How to read Marx's capital: Commentary and explanations on the beginning chapters*. Monthly Review Press.
Holloway, J. (1997). A note on alienation. *Historical Materialism, 1*(1), 146–149.
Holloway, J. (2010). *Crack capitalism*. Pluto Press.
Honig, B. (1993). *Political theory and the displacement of politics*. Cornell University Press.
Hsieh, N.-H. (2008). Workplace democracy, workplace republicanism, and economic democracy. *Revue de Philosophie Economique, 9*, 57–78.
Hsieh, N.-H. (2012). Work, ownership, and productive enfranchisement. In M. O'Neill & T. Williamson (Eds.), *Property-owning democracy: Rawls and beyond* (pp. 149–162). Wiley Blackwell.
Hudis, P. (2013). *Marx concept of the alternative to capitalism*. Haymarket Books.
Isaac, J. C. (1990). The lion's skin of politics: Marx on republicanism. *Polity, 23*(3), 461–488.
Jones, G. S. (2016). *Karl Marx: Greatness and illusion*. Belknap Press.
Lebowitz, M. (2003). *Beyond capital: Marx's political economy of the working class*. Palgrave Macmillan.
Lebowitz, M. (2010). *The socialist alternative: Real human development*. Monthly Review Press.
Lebowitz, M. (2012). *The contradictions of real socialism: The conductor and the conducted*. Monthly Review Press.
Lebowitz, M. (2020). *Between capitalism and community*. Monthly Review Press.
Leipold, B. (2020). Marx's social republic: Radical republicanism and the political institutions of socialism. In K. Nabulsi, S. White, & B. Leipold (Eds.), *Radical republicanism: Recovering the tradition's popular heritage* (pp. 172–193). Oxford University Press.
Leipold, B. (2022). Chains and invisible threads: Liberty and domination in Marx's account of wage-slavery. In A. de Dijn & H. Dawson (Eds.), *Rethinking liberty before liberalism*. Cambridge University Press.
Leopold, D. (2007). *The Young Marx: German philosophy, modern politics, and human flourishing*. Cambridge University Press.
Lukács, G., & Livingstone, R. (trans.). (1974). *History and class consciousness: Studies in Marxist dialectics*. Merlin Press.
McGovern, A. F. (1988). The Young Marx on the state. In Wood (Ed.), pp. 166–193.
McLellan, D. (1970). *Marx before Marxism*. Penguin.
McLellan, D. (1971). *The thought of Karl Marx: An introduction*. Macmillan.

Menke, C. (2010). Neither Rawls Nor Adorno: Raymond Geuss' programme for a 'realist' political philosophy. *European Journal of Philosophy, 18*(1), 139–147.
Mészáros, I. (1972). *Marx's theory of alienation* (3rd ed.). Merlin Press.
Mészáros, I. (1995). *Beyond capital: Towards a theory of transition.* Merlin Press.
Mészáros, I. (2011). *Social structure and forms of consciousness, volume II: The dialectic of structure and history.* Monthly Review Press.
Mészáros, I. (2014). *The necessity of social control.* Monthly Review Press.
Mouffe, C. (2006). *The return of the political.* Verso.
Musto, M. (Ed.) 2020. *The Marx revival: Key concepts and new interpretations.* Cambridge University Press.
Newey, G. (2010). Two dogmas of liberalism. *European Journal of Political Theory, 9*(4), 449–465.
Nussbaum, M. (1992a). Nature, function, and capability: Aristotle on political distribution. In McCarthy (Ed.), pp. 175–212.
Nussbaum, M. (1992b). Human functioning and social justice: In defense of Aristotelian essentialism. *Political Theory, 20*(2), 202–246.
Nussbaum, M. (2011). *Creating capabilities: The human development approach.* Belknap.
Ollman, B. (1976). *Alienation: Marx's conception of man in capitalist society.* Cambridge University Press.
Philp, M. (2012). Realism without illusions. *Political Theory, 40*(5), 629–649.
Plamenatz, J. (1975). *Karl Marx's philosophy of man.* Clarendon Press.
Prinz, J. (2016). Raymond Geuss' radicalization of realism in political theory. *Philosophy & Social Criticism, 42*(8), 77–796.
Prinz, J., & Rossi, E. (2017). Political realism as ideology critique. *Critical Review of International Social and Political Philosophy, 20*(3), 334–348.
Raekstad, P., & Gradin, S. (2020). *Prefigurative politics: Building tomorrow today.* Polity Press.
Raekstad, P. (2015). Two contemporary approaches to political theory. *International Critical Thought, 5*(2), 226–240.
Raekstad, P. (2018a). Human development and alienation in the thought of Karl Marx. *European Journal of Political Theory, 17*(3), 300–323.
Raekstad, P. (2018b). Realism, utopianism, and radical values. *European Journal of Philosophy, 26*(1), 145–168.
Raekstad, P. (2020a). Adam Smith: Radical neo-roman and moderate realist. *Archiv für Geschichte der Philosophie, 103*(1), 70–92.
Raekstad, P. (2020b). Realism, utopianism, and human rights. *Political Studies Review, 18*(4), 542–552.
Raekstad, P. (2020c). The present and future of political realism. *Res Publica, 26*(2), 293–297.
Rawls, J. (1999). *A theory of justice* (Revised Edition). Belknap.
Rawls, J. (2001). *Justice as fairness: A restatement.* Belknap.

Rawls, J. (2005). *Political liberalism* (Expanded Edition). Columbia University Press.
Roberts, W. C. (2017). *Marx's Inferno: the political theory of capital.* Princeton University Press.
Roberts, W. C. (2018). *Marx's social republic: Political not metaphysical* (13 p). (Unpublished Manuscript).
Rossi, E. (2010). Review: Reality and imagination in political theory and practice: On Raymond Geuss's Realism. *European Journal of Political Theory, 9*(4), 504–512.
Rossi, E. (2012). Justice, legitimacy and (normative) authority for political realists. *Critical Review of International Social and Political Philosophy, 15*(2), 149–164.
Rossi, E. (2014). *Facts, principles, and politics* (SSRN Working Paper). Available online: http://papers.ssrn.com/sol3/papers.cfm?abstract_id=2378366
Rossi, E. (2019). Being realistic and demanding the impossible. *Constellations, 26*(4), 638–652.
Saito, K. (2017). *Karl Marx's ecosocialism: Capitalism, nature, and the unfinished critique of political economy.* Monthly Review Press.
Sangiovanni, A. (2008). Justice and the priority of politics to morality. *The Journal of Political Philosophy, 16*(2), 137–164.
Sayers, S. (2007a). Marxism and morality. *Philosophical Researches, 2007*(9), 8–12.
Sayers, S. (2007b). *Marxism and human nature.* Routledge.
Sayers, S. (2011). *Marx and alienation: Essays in Hegelian themes.* Palgrave Macmillan.
Sen, A. (1984a). Well-being, agency and freedom: The Dewey lectures 1984. *The Journal of Philosophy, 82*(4), 169–221.
Sen, A. (1984b). *Resources, values and development.* Basil Blackwell.
Sen, A. (1987). *The standard of living (the Tanner lectures).* Cambridge University Press.
Sen, A. (1992). *Inequality reexamined.* Clarendon Press.
Sen, A. (1999). *Development as freedom.* Oxford University Press.
Sen, A. (2010). *The idea of justice.* Penguin.
Sleat, M. (2010). Bernard Williams and the possibility of a realist political theory. *European Journal of Political Theory, 9*(4), 485–503.
Sleat, M. (2013). *Liberal realism: A realist theory of liberal politics.* Manchester University Press.
Swain, D. (2019a). *None so fit to break the chains: Marx's ethics of self-emancipation.* Brill.
Swain, D. (2019b). Not not but not yet: Present and future in prefigurative politics. *Political Studies, 67*(1), 47–62.

Tabak, M. (2020). *Marx's philosophy of revolution and freedom: A critical reconstruction*. Self-published.
Thompson, M. J. (2019). The radical republican structure of Marx's critique of capitalist society. *Critique, 47*(3), 391–409.
Tucker, R. C. (1970). *The Marxian revolutionary idea*. George Allen & Unwin Ltd.
Tucker, R. C. (1972). *Philosophy and myth in Karl Marx*. Cambridge University Press.
Valentini, L. (2012). Ideal vs. non-ideal theory: A conceptual map. *Philosophy Compass, 7*(9), 654–664.
Vrousalis, N. (2021). The capitalist cage: Structural domination and collective agency in the market. *Journal of Applied Philosophy, 38*(1), 40–54.
White, S. (2011). The Republican critique of capitalism. *Critical Review of International Social and Political Philosophy, 14*(5), 561–579.
Williams, B. (2008). *In the beginning was the deed: Realism and moralism in political argument*. Princeton University Press.
Wolff, J. (2011). *Ethics and public policy: A Philosophical inquiry*. Routledge.
Wolff, J., & de-Shalit, A. (2007). *Disadvantage*. Oxford University Press.
Wright, E. O. (2010). *Envisioning real utopias*. Verso.

PART I

Human Development and Freedom

The core of Marx's thought is his conception of human beings, activity, and society. Viewed from the perspective of Marx's theories of human social structures, history, and social change, we call it his theory of practice or praxis. From the perspective of his critique of capitalism, we call it his theory of human development. Though oft-neglected, it offers the key to unlocking an understanding of the evolving totality of Marx's thought.

Thus, Chapter 2 explains the basics of Marx's conception of human development through his concepts of powers, needs, and their interaction. Chapter 3 then shows how Marx builds upon this to develop a positive concept of freedom and its value. This provides us with the necessary components for exploring how capitalism shackles human development and how socialism can set us free.

CHAPTER 2

Human Development

Marx values human development as the development of powers, as the development of real possibilities to do and/or to be. As we will see, his conception of this is inherently contextual, pluralist, and open-ended in nature. It is also intricately connected to his theory of human needs and his views on consciousness and freedom. To understand this properly, I will first outline the role of Marx's conception of human development in his critique of capitalism. I will then move on to explain how Marx thinks about human development as the development of human powers, his theory of needs, and how powers and needs intertwine. I finish by showing how, despite its openness and pluralism, Marx's theory of human development can still be useful for informing real politics. One way it can do so is by identifying human powers which are particularly valuable in their own right and for the development of many other human powers and using these to compare and evaluate competing institutions. We will then be able to see, in the following chapter, how this furnishes the basis for Marx's understanding of the nature and importance of freedom.

The Basic Structure of Marx's Critique of Capitalism

Marx criticises capitalism for holding back the potentials for human development[1] available in contemporary society. This is a kind of internal critique that criticises something by virtue of how it fails to live up to certain achievable potentials internal to a particular context (for more on which, see the appendix). In other words, Marx thinks that we are in a context where a much greater degree of human development is possible if we replace capitalist with socialist relations. To see this more clearly right from the start, it's worth looking briefly at the bare-bones structure of Marx's later critique of capitalism[2]:

1. It is valuable for human beings to realise their powers of free or self-directed activity, because this promotes their greater development.
2. Capitalism has major shortcomings when it comes to the promoting of human development, due to how it, by its very nature, prevents the realisation of these powers.
3. There is an alternative form of society, a socialist one, which is currently achievable and able to realise these powers.
4. There is an existing social agent capable of and, under the right circumstances (such as being made aware of their interests in doing so), likely to replace capitalism with a socialist society, namely the working class.
5. By 3 and 4, the diagnosis of 2 is one that is curable through a working-class overthrow of capitalism in favour of a socialist society.
6. Thus, by 1, 2, and 5, capitalism is both unable to satisfy certain valuable requirements of further human development and is replaceable by a socialist society, which can satisfy these requirements.

---

[1] See Lebowitz (2003, and esp. 2010) for a similar Marxist account of human development, but with a different specification of socialism/communism's institutional requirements. Other Marxist writers who have emphasised Marx's critique of capitalism in terms of human development include Booth (1992), Hamilton (2003), Leopold (2007), Mészáros (1972, 2011), and Sayers (2007a, b, ch. 9). For well-established non-Marxist approaches see Nussbaum (1992a, b, 2011) and Sen (1984a, b, 1987, 1992, 1999).

[2] This overall view, albeit with modifications of point 1 regarding the details of Marx's normative foundations and without the detailed structure I have laid out, is largely in agreement with Collier (2009), Raekstad (2015), and Wright (2010).

It's important to note the contextual parameters involved in 3 and 4. Whereas Marx holds capitalism to be regressive in the nineteenth century and beyond, he can also hold it to be progressive compared to other social formations at earlier times. If there are earlier social formations where socialism is not an achievable alternative, then this argument would fail to apply. Furthermore, if the development of capitalism is held to clear the way for socialism—e.g. by developing the powers of production to the required level and by developing a potentially revolutionary proletarian class—then capitalism may, in principle, coherently be advocated in different historical contexts by means of the very same considerations as it is critiqued for in the argument just reconstructed. As I'll show in Chapter 9, the revolutionary contradictions of capitalism that Marx emphasises throughout his later work—between the powers and relations of production and between workers and capitalists—are rooted in the way that capitalist social relations restrict the emancipation and thereby human development that it has also helped to make possible.

We can thus see how important Marx's realist approach is in terms of his overall political theory. Recall that realism emphasises the need for theory to help make sense of and guide real politics, especially by helping to guide the actions of real political agents. Since Marx's focus is on comparing different achievable alternatives, only those alternatives which in fact can be brought about by some social force or agent, inherent in a particular social formation, are acceptable candidates for political theorising (of this kind). As a result, the *scope* of this political theory is rightly constrained by its conception of political *agency*. Having laid out the general structure of Marx's critique, I turn now to outline the conception of human development that it's rooted in.

HUMAN DEVELOPMENT AS THE DEVELOPMENT OF POWERS

Many discussions of Marx start from a basic misconception about what Marx thinks is valuable, because they misunderstand what Marx (and many other political economists at the time) mean by "wealth" and "value". Classical political economy featured a standard distinction between two different concepts—wealth and value—which typically have very different connotations to contemporary readers. The concept of "value" refers to the core of a kind of theory (a "theory of value") that attempts to explain changes in equilibrium prices, around which actual prices are thought to fluctuate. This is in turn used to explain and predict the various operations, what Marxists often call the laws of motion, of capitalist economies. "Wealth" refers instead to what the political economist in question takes to be valuable, desirable, worthy, and so on. For obvious reasons, this often trips contemporary readers up.

Marx is clear that, for him, true wealth—i.e. what's really valuable—consists in human development as an end in itself. He writes that:

> [T]he society that is *fully developed* produces man in all the richness of his being, the *rich* man who is *profoundly and abundantly endowed with all the senses*...[3]
>
> [T]he *rich man* and the wealth of *human* need [should or must] take the place of the *wealth* and *poverty* of political economy. The *rich* man is simultaneously the man *in need of* a totality of vital human expression; he is the man in whom his own realisation exists as inner necessity, as *need*.[4]

The same sentiment is echoed in the *Grundrisse*, where Marx writes that:

> [W]hat is wealth other than the universality of individual needs, capacities, pleasures, productive forces etc., created through universal exchange? The full development of human mastery over the forces of nature, those of so-called nature as well as of humanity's own nature? The absolute working-out of his creative potentialities, with no presupposition other than the previous historic development, which makes this totality of development, i.e. the development of all human powers as such the end in itself, not as measured on a *predetermined* yardstick?[5]

Before this, in the same work, Marx describes the production of a human being "as rich as possible in needs, because rich in qualities and relations" and "the cultivation of all the qualities of the social human being" as "the most total and universal possible social product".[6]

---

[3] Marx (1992, p. 354/I:2, p. 271/394), emphases in the original.

[4] Marx (1992, p. 356/I:2, p. 273/397, emphases in the original).

[5] Marx (1993, p. 488/II.1.2, p. 392, emphasis in the original). While I prefer the translation here to be "productive powers" rather than "productive forces" here, for reasons I discuss below, I've retained the original translation here in order not to not confuse the reader at this stage. See also II.1.2, p. 427.

[6] Marx (1993, p. 409/II.1.2, p. 322).

Finally, he returns to this point in Volume 3 of *Capital*, writing of the "true realm of freedom" as the "development of human powers as an end in itself".[7]

These quotations emphasise a number of things. First of all, they express an intimate connection between human development and human powers (Kräfte): a "rich" or well-developed person is one who has acquired a wide range of human powers.

Furthermore, human development as the development of human powers is an end in itself. It's not valuable only by reference to other considerations or insofar as it realises some particular "pre-determined yardstick" of what is supposed to constitute "adequate" or "full" human development. This immediately raises a number of questions. Must we think that all human powers are valuable? Can we make no distinction between who is more or less deserving of having certain powers? How, if at all, do we rank and/or compare different valuable powers? These are all important questions, the answers to which are determined by how different people find it best to use a theory of human development in different contexts.

By avoiding any particular predetermined standards, Marx's conception of human development is inherently open-ended (because it's not evaluated in terms of any predetermined yardsticks), pluralistic (because it acknowledges that there are many different valuable ways to develop, and no particular vision of full or perfect development is imposed upon anyone), and flexible (because, as we will see below, it can be used to evaluate things in a variety of different ways). Marx is an inherently contextual thinker, and is well aware that any appropriate standards for human development that people come up with will rightly vary a great deal with natural, social, and historical context. The ability to fish, sail a boat, and pillage Ireland are likely core aspects of the powers expected of Norwegian would-be raider of the Viking Age, while contemporary Norwegians are much more likely to think it's important to be proficient at assembling IKEA furniture than murdering and enslaving unsuspecting civilians. They are also less likely to think that pillaging powers are valuable to develop, both in themselves and because they harm the development of many others' powers. It's this openness, pluralism, and contextualism that means there's no universal answer to the questions raised in the preceding

---

[7] Marx (1991, p. 959/II:15, p. 795).

paragraph. Instead, particular decisions about which powers to value and how much must be made by particular political agents (including theorists), using a theory of human development to address the problems and opportunities they're concerned with in their particular contexts. We'll see how Marx does so in the last sections of this chapter and beyond.

Human development is not only valuable in itself, it's also the most universal product of political economy[8]—perhaps of all human activity. We can make sense of this idea in the following way: Human economic activity is always a process of *double production*, in which one and the same labour process creates both a given good or service and, at the same time, creates and re-creates the various powers and needs of the human beings (both as individuals and as groups) that partake in it. Since the goods and services produced vary across different branches of production, and since human powers and needs in general are produced and reproduced in any and all such activity, the latter constitutes a more universal product than any of the former. But if human powers are so important, what are they exactly?

Marx's conception of "powers" here is, I propose, best understood as referring to real possibilities to do and/or to be.[9] Drawing on socialist thinkers like Marx, what today are called capabilities in the capabilities approach roughly correspond to what Marx called "powers".[10] To see

---

[8] Marx (1993, p. 409/II.1.2, p. 322).

[9] See esp. Ollman (1976, ch. 7).

[10] I read Marx's "powers" as close to what are called "capabilities" in the capabilities approach – indeed, what today is called the capabilities approach is sometimes explicit about drawing on socialist thinkers like Marx. For discussions of Sen's capabilities approach, which is in many ways close to Marx in both substance and general application (if not specifically to Marx's more radical ends), see Sen (1984a, b, 1987, 1992, 1999, 2010). Sen's capabilities approach has been discussed in Marxist literature in both more general discussions in the context of egalitarian political theory (e.g. Callinicos, 2000, ch 3; 2008, ch. 7) and more specifically to spell out Marx's ideas of human development (Lebowitz, 2010; Raekstad, 2018a). I've argued elsewhere that Marx's approach to human development differs from Sen's in that (a) "Marx pays more attention to the processual and relational aspects of the acquisition of capabilities (though Sen also mentions both), (b) "Marx has a theory of human needs which forms an integral part of his conception of human development", and (c) "Marx develops a conception of freedom or conscious self-direction as a distinctively human internal ability, the exercise of which is particularly important both in its own right and for the development of other capabilities" (Raekstad, 2018a: 306).

how, let's begin with the idea of *functionings*, which consist of "beings"—states like being well-fed, being educated, being literate, and so on—and "doings"—activities we undertake like eating, reading, voting, deliberating, and so on. Often things can be described as either a being or a doing—like a person being housed in a pleasantly warm house and that person consuming a lot of energy to keep their house warm. For Marx, who sees all beings in terms of processes of becoming of various kinds, the two terms are co-extensive. *Powers* or *capabilities*, in turn, are a person's real possibilities for achieving functionings—like having the real possibility of feeding oneself, of reading, and so on. In other words, functionings are beings and doings, and powers are real possibilities to do and/or to be. A functioning is thus the realisation of a power, and a range of powers is a range of really possible functionings.[11]

A power in this sense consists of the right combination of two things. First of all, it consists of a context or set of conditions which enables one to do or be certain things (e.g. a book for learning German and not having a boss forcing me to work so much that I'm prevented from using it). Secondly, it consists of what I shall call internal powers, i.e. the abilities or capacities internal to a person required to take advantage of the relevant context or conditions (e.g. being able to read the instructional language that the book for learning German is in).[12] To have a (full)

---

[11] See Sen (1992, 1993, 1999, 2010).

[12] I use this term synonymously with what is sometimes called "internal capabilities" in the capabilities approach, see e.g. Nussbaum (2003, 2011). Here I use the term "internal powers" instead, in order to make it cohere better with Marx's "powers". One point I would like to make, though, is that Marx's use of the term "power" is vague between two things which are distinguished in the capabilities approach, namely between what the latter calls capabilities and it calls internal capabilities and I call internal powers. Although I've associated it more with capabilities, I think Marx uses "powers" in both senses and that he does not explicitly distinguish between them. The distinction is a relative one, as every internal power is itself a functioning of some sort. For instance, the power of listening to music requires the internal power of hearing; that internal power is itself a functioning, in the sense that it is being in the state of being able to hear; it is thus trivially (since a functioning implies a power) also a power (albeit obviously a different one from the power of listening to music, which also requires additional external conditions). For some of the discussion in the next chapter, however, this distinction is important to bear in mind, since it's central to Marx's argument that human beings have an internal power for conscious self-direction, but that this only becomes a full power under the right circumstances. Calling humans' capacity for conscious self-direction a "power" in the first sense clearly does not, and should not be taken to, entail them also automatically possessing a "power" in the latter sense as well.

power is thus to have the right combination of *both* the requisite external context or conditions *and* the internal powers required to take advantage of them.

We must understand these complexes as an inherently *processual* and *relational* kind of thing.[13] My power to learn German is predicated on access to certain external materials—for instance, books devoted to that purpose. Such access requires me to be in certain relations which enable me to get hold of that book—viz., relations of property, access to a place to purchase or borrow the book, being able to transport myself or the book to a suitable location for pickup, and so on. The particularities of these conditions are only obtained as a result of the continual production and reproduction of complex social relations and institutions in which I must partake.

Secondly, in order to be able to learn German from the book in question, I need certain internal powers to understand the language the book is written in, to see, to read, to write, to learn in some systematic way, and so on. These powers are themselves currently constituted by an ongoing process in which my body (including my brain) continually reproduces itself through time in interaction with the world around it (breathing, drinking, eating, etc.).

Thirdly, any such powers I presently possess are the result of a wider process of maturation and development, of which its current time-slice is a moment. This process of maturation and development, through which I have come to acquire and maintain the internal powers to do things like process natural language, hear, read, and write, etc., is in turn a function of the interplay between my powers and needs at previous moments of development on the one hand, and the context and conditions within which that development has taken place on the other. In this manner, not only do complex powers consist of a conjunction of internal powers and external conditions, these internal powers are, in turn, constituted by a processual unity itself consisting of an interplay between internal powers

---

[13] It might be objected to the following discussion that it really speaks only of the *acquisition* of human powers, or perhaps also of their development and maintenance. This objection only makes sense if we ignore Marx's process ontology and philosophy of internal relations, according to which things are thought of as processes and as partly constituted in and through processes of interaction with other things. I cannot examine this issue here, but for an excellent account see Ollman (2003).

and external conditions, and this process goes, as it were, all the way down.

We should therefore not think of powers, in Marx's usage, merely in terms of an abstract set of possibilities. Instead, we should think of them as the range of options available to an organism constantly engaged in turning (some of) its powers into functionings, in interaction with its wider environment, in order to satisfy its needs.[14] Doing so in turn continually maintains, alters, destroys, and/or creates new powers and needs—hence Marx's comment, in the *Grundrisse*, about a society where one "does not reproduce himself in one specificity, but produces his totality", where one "[s]trives not to remain something he has become, but is in the absolute movement of becoming?".[15]

Finally, the passages quoted earlier in this section express an intimate connection between powers, needs, and the senses. We can now begin to make sense of this. Powers, in Marx's sense, include abilities both to affect things in the world (like being able to hold someone's hand or join them in defending a picket line) and to be affected by things in the world (like transforming the sound waves hitting your ear into the experience of enjoying Beethoven's 9th symphony). On Marx's view, the production of various pleasures and enjoyments, and the drives and desires they are connected to, is an inherent part of his theory of human development. To understand how, we must unpack his theory of needs and see how they're connected with his theory of powers.

NEEDS

For Marx, there is an intimate relationship between what he calls "needs" (Bedürfnisse) and human powers, a relationship that must be understood in order to make sense of his conception of human development. Having already discussed powers, I turn first to discuss Marx's conception of needs and thereafter to the nature of their interaction.

To do this, it's first necessary to dispel a common misunderstanding in what Marx means by "need". Some believe that Marx has what might be

---

[14] This, as well as the importance of the passions, drives, and strivings in Marx is explored further in van Ree (2020).

[15] Marx (1993, p. 488/II.1.2, p. 392).

called a normative theory of needs[16] that's distinct from his commitment to the development of human powers. Such a conception of needs can be spelled out in a few different ways, including in terms of.

(a) something which is a requirement for the avoidance of harm, malfunctioning, or pathology[17]; or
(b) something which is a requirement for full human development.[18]

There are, however, other conceptions of needs which are relevant here, including:

(c) something which is a requirement for someone to do or attain something, thus fitting the general formula "X needs Y in order to Z".

Reading (c) is, then, broader than, and extends over, (a) and (b), in so far as the latter two give, for Z, the avoidance of harm, pathology, or malfunctioning, or full human development and flourishing, respectively.

The two most important alternative ways of interpreting Marx's conception of "needs" include:

(d) the drive or striving of an animal, e.g. a human being[19]; and
(e) the drive or striving of someone or something.[20]

It is evident that (e) is broader than and extends over (d). The sense of "drive" in (e) is to be broadly understood to include not only individuals' conscious intentions and desires, but also something's stated goals, values, or concerns (where the "something" in question might even be a theory or an ideology), as well as the unconscious motivations or tendencies of

---

[16] See esp. Hamilton (2003), Leopold (2007), Soper (1981), and Springborg (1981). The positions of the two former will be discussed below. Those of the latter are too complex to be dealt with here.

[17] Examples of such a theory include Doyal and Gough (1991), Geuss (1981, 2012), and one of the two senses Leopold (2007) takes Marx to have. Note that I am referring to these as instances of a conception of needs of this kind, nor claiming that all of the authors hold this to be an accurate reading of Marx's conception of needs.

[18] Hamilton (2003) and Leopold (2007).

[19] E.g. Chitty (1993), Ollman (1976, ch. 7), and Maslow (1970) and many other psychological theories of need.

[20] See Springborg (1981, ch. 6).

individuals, social institutions, and more besides. It therefore includes all the things included in (d), and more besides.

If Marx's concept of needs is to be held to do any independent normative work in his writings, it needs to be of kinds (a), (b), or (c)—most plausibly one of the two former. However, there are five reasons why only sense (e) is consistent with Marx's usage of the term.[21]

The first thing I wish to point out about Marx's conception of needs is that, since my focus is on Marx's critique of capitalism, the question of Marx's conception of needs here mainly comes down to whether or not, and if so how, that conception of needs plays a normative role in the writings in which this critique is developed. If we look at the early works leading up to and including the *Economic and Philosophical Manuscripts of 1844*—i.e. the works in which Marx first develops his theories of alienation—we find, however, that Marx's conception of needs plays no important normative role whatsoever. Whenever the term "needs" does appear, it can, in each and every instance, be read simply as a term for something somebody desires, or for something that something or someone is driven or striving towards.[22] Moving on to his later works, we see that needs and drives are frequently used synonymously. This alone renders the normatively loaded readings in (a) and (b) implausible.

The second thing we should note with regard to Marx's usage of needs is that he typically does not distinguish between needs and their objects of satisfaction, collapsing any clear-cut distinction between means and ends in this regard.[23] As we saw earlier, readings (a)–(c) all rely on a distinction between ends and means. Since Marx's usage of "needs" collapses a key distinction these readings presuppose, they cannot be accepted as accurate readings of Marx's conception of needs.

The third thing we should note about Marx's employment of needs is that it is extremely broad. He includes needs which might be considered

---

[21] I thus, like Soper (1981), not only refuse to categorically distinguish between wants and needs; I also, unlike Soper, explicitly subsume the former under the latter.

[22] To support the first part of this claim further it would be necessary to discuss each and every instance of the term's usage in the first few volumes of Marx's collected works. Doing so is impossible here. If the empirical premise my argument rests on is not fully demonstrated here, it is at least easily testable: all that is required is to find one, or a significant number of, instances in the early works in which Marx uses "Bedürfniss(e)" in a manner incompatible with the readings I advocate, namely (d) and/or (e).

[23] For more on this see Hamilton (2003, p. 57).

basic physiological needs, like "a human need for sustenance (he talks about 'eating, drinking' and, more generally, 'nourishment'), for warmth and shelter (he lists 'heating' and 'clothing' as well as a 'dwelling'), for certain climatic conditions (he mentions both 'light' and 'air'), for physical exercise (the need 'to move about' and the need for 'physical exercise'), for basic hygiene ('the simplest animal cleanliness'), and for reproduction and (heterosexual) sexual activity (he writes of 'procreation' and describes sexual relationships between women and men as characteristic of the 'species')".[24] Marx's usage also includes needs for things like self-development and community. However, he also mentions a range of other needs which would be difficult to fit into any plausible single, unitary, and predetermined set of criteria of the kind required for (a) or (b). These include a "human need for recreation (to 'go drinking', to 'go dancing', to 'fence', to 'sing'), for culture (to 'go to the theatre'), for education and intellectual exercise (to 'think', to 'theorise', to 'buy books', to engage in 'learning'), for artistic expression (to 'paint'), for emotional fulfilment (to 'love'), and for aesthetic pleasure (Marx identifies 'a musical ear, an eye for the beauty of form' as among our essential human capacities and powers)".[25] It's hard to square this with any other reading than one in terms of (socially and historically mediated) drives. Such uses were common at the time, as when e.g. the anarchist Peter Kropotkin writes that once "material wants are satisfied, other needs, which, generally speaking may be described as of an artistic character, will thrust themselves forward".[26] It might be argued that many of these are mentioned only in passing and that a reconstruction of Marx's views on human needs need not necessarily be bound by the strictures of off-hand remarks and singular mentions in notebooks and letters. This reply is correct, but inadequate. The fact remains there is at least one reading, that of (e) (and, as far as our argument so far has been concerned, also (d)), on which these uses are all made coherent. Consequently, this alternative reading is the most plausible one.

Fourthly, whenever Marx talks about what "needs" are, he clearly takes every instance of a human drive or impulse to constitute a need, including all manner of wants, desires, and preferences, regardless of origin. As a

---

[24] Leopold (2007, p. 228).
[25] Ibid, p. 233–234.
[26] Kropotkin (1995, p. 94).

result, he does not distinguish at all between "true" and "false" needs or between "actual" needs and "imaginary" ones, because these aren't the sort of things that can be true or false—though one can, of course, desire things that are contrary to one's interests. In Volume I of *Capital*, for instance, Marx asserts that a necessary condition for being a commodity is for an object to satisfy a need, regardless of "nature" of these needs, "whether they arise, for example, from the stomach, or the imagination, makes no difference".[27] In an associated footnote, Marx quotes from Nicholas Barbon's *A Discourse on Coining the New Money Lighter. In Answer to Mr Locke's Considerations about Raising the Value of Money*, where Barbon explicitly talks in terms of "Desire" and "appetite" using (as does Marx in his discussions of "needs") the example of hunger.[28] This makes no sense at all from the point of view of the more objective and normatively laden conceptions of needs in (a)–(c). Simply creating a desire does not of itself make it into a requirement for avoiding harm or pathology, a requirement for human development or flourishing, or a requirement for achieving some particular purpose (other than merely the satisfaction of that particular desire). By contrast, all of this fits snugly within readings (d) and (e), since desires clearly and unproblematically fall within the scope of needs conceived of as drives or strivings.

Relatedly, throughout his *oeuvre*, Marx talks about creating wants or demand for commodities in a capitalist marketplace in terms of creating (unsatisfied) needs.[29] As we'll see in Chapter 7, this plays an important role for understanding some of the harms of alienated, unfree labour, as when Marx argues that alienated labour results in that labour becoming undesirable, so it's no longer itself the satisfaction of a "need", i.e. people feel no drive or impulse to do it apart from in order to satisfy needs external to it, like hunger. This clearly supports a reading of needs in terms of drives or strivings.

Finally, in other instances Marx writes about things becoming "needs" only if and when they become actual drives:

---

[27] Marx (1990, p. 125/II:6, p. 69).

[28] As we will see below, Marx does, of course, distinguish natural from historically restricted needs, but, *pace* Springborg 1981, this in no way amounts to an normatively loaded distinction.

[29] See throughout the *Grundrisse*, *Capital*, and other economic works, as discussed in Ollman (1976, ch. 7).

> When communist *workmen* gather together, their immediate aim is instruction, propaganda, etc. But at the same time they acquire a new need – the need for society – and what appears as a means has become an end. This practical development can be most strikingly observed in the gatherings of French socialist workers. Smoking, eating and drinking, etc., are no longer means for creating links between people. Company, association, conversation, which in its turn has society as its goal, is enough for them. The brotherhood of man is not a hollow phrase, it is a reality, and the nobility of man shines forth upon us from their work-worn figures.[30]

Here it is clear that new needs are developed when and only when they become driving forces for concrete living beings, which fits perfectly with how we've just seen that Marx talks about what "needs" are in *Capital*. By contrast, if needs are, as they must be according to readings (a)–(c), the requirements Y for ensuring certain ends Z, and if society is important for human beings, then society becoming a conscious human end cannot plausibly be accepted as an instance of acquiring a new need, since the mere fact of becoming the object of a conscious human end does not, in itself, affect whether or not that particular Y is a requirement for some Z—unless Z is nothing more than e.g. the realisation of ends or satisfaction of desire, in which case it collapses into a version of (d). On the other hand, a reading of needs as drives as per (d) and (e) coheres perfectly with Marx's wording: since conscious ends, desires, and so forth fall under needs, the acquisition of a desire for society is unproblematically the acquisition of a new need which one did not previously possess.

It might be argued that the links Marx makes between needs and desires do not show that he conceives of needs as drives, but instead that he conceives of them as an individual's perceived requirements for the avoidance of harm. This would be a variant of interpretation (a). The connection between desires and needs would then be that if someone has a sufficiently strong and enduring desire for X, then they will come to see the non-satisfaction of X as causing them suffering, which is a kind of harm, they will perceive X as a requirement for them to avoid a harm, and so will come to "need" X in the above sense. If this is the kind of thing Marx has in mind, we would expect him to mention the strength or endurance of a drive for it giving rise to a need. He never does so. Furthermore, we would expect some sort of distinction between

---

[30] Marx (1992, p. 365/I:2, p. 425).

drives and needs, where the latter would be associated with strength and/or endurance, and perhaps also with consciousness (in the sense of self-awareness) and consequent plasticity and variation across contexts—like we see in Hegel.[31] No such distinction appears in Marx. Finally, if "needs" were conceived in terms of strongly felt requirements, we would also expect some sort of distinction to be made between "natural" and "constructed" needs, "real" and "false" or "imaginary" ones, etc., of the kinds we see in writers such as Rousseau and the Frankfurt School. As I've shown, Marx makes no such distinctions with respect to "needs". In short, if Marx held a view of needs as perceived requirements in a sense beyond merely drives, it would be extremely surprising that these kinds of distinctions are never even alluded to, especially since they are made in literature which he was intimately familiar with. If, however, he was in fact construing "needs" differently, as drives, these interpretative difficulties disappear.

One might also worry that a concept of needs as drives risks leaving Marx unable to distinguish the requirements for healthy life and functioning from things like luxuries and mere wants. The answer to this is that Marx already has a concept for this, namely "necessity", and that this enables him to make just such a distinction. While Marx doesn't distinguish "needs" from mere wants, he does write that "[l]uxury is the opposite of the naturally necessary".[32] On this view, "necessities" are requirements for survival, healthy functioning, or the like, and the "naturally necessary" is what we require to survive and function well by virtue of being the kind of animal we are. Of course, what is, and what is considered to be, necessary varies according to natural, social, and historical context, and Marx thinks it is a "tendency of capital" to transform "what was previously superfluous into what is necessary, as a historically created necessity".[33] We see again and again that what once was a luxury—cars,

---

[31] Hegel mentions how "psychology relates and describes these [immediate and naturally given] drives and inclinations and the needs derived from them" (Hegel, 1991, p. 45), and distinguishes between the "universal needs, such as food, drink, clothing, etc." (ibid, p. 227), and the further development of human needs as "taste and utility become criteria of judgement" (ibid, p. 229). This clearly involves a distinction between more instinctive drives and inclinations on the one hand and more socially and historically mediated impulses on the other. By contrast, Marx talks of e.g. hunger and insists that hungers for different things are different hungers.

[32] Marx (1993, p. 528/II.1.2, p. 427).

[33] Ibid.

mobile phones, the internet—in time becomes necessary to function in society.

The fifth and last point I wish to make about Marx's usage of need is that it occasionally occurs in the context of speaking about social relations and institutions. Since reading (d) restricts the concept of needs solely to human beings, or perhaps animals, whereas (e) is wider so as also to include other things (such as institutions), this gives some support to (e) as a reading over (d). However, for my purposes here it does not matter at all which of the two is in fact the correct one, since either will work for the below reconstruction of Marx's account of the interplay between powers and needs.[34]

THE INTERACTION BETWEEN POWERS AND NEEDS

Human needs are highly plastic. They are canalised by our natural, social, and historical contexts, and so vary across these contexts to different degrees and in different ways. A need for a well-insulated house or flat is very real to the contemporary Swede or Norwegian, but less so to an experienced hunter-gatherer with the ability to construct their own suitable habitation.

Of course, the fact that needs vary across contexts does not mean that they can't be said to exhibit certain convergences or similarities. At least some *need forms* develop (barring rare exceptions and pathology) among all human beings—for example, we feel hunger under certain circumstances. However, what people feel hungry for when they feel hungry is something that varies across different contexts. In these cases, we have a general *kind of need* (hunger) which human beings share, which is channelled by and varies across contexts to create *different needs* (e.g. hunger

---

[34] One way of attempting to salvage a properly normative function for Marx's conception of needs is arguing that there are two different senses in which Marx uses that concept: on the one hand, a restrictive normative conception according to which some goals and desires are of particular importance; on the other hand, a more expansive and developmental conception of needs according to which it consists in mere wants or goals of some sort. The problem with this is not only that Marx makes no such distinction; it is also rendered wholly unnecessary on a sufficiently broad specification of "needs" as per (e). If "needs" just refers to all drives and impulses, all goals and desires count without any problems—regardless of their origin, normative value, and so on. In other words, a distinction between different senses of "need" in Marx is neither conceptually necessary nor textually well-founded.

for a medium-rare steak, for strips of raw flesh, for dried fish, and so on). As Marx writes:

> Hunger is hunger, but the hunger gratified by cooked meat eaten with a knife and fork is a different hunger from that which bolts down raw meat with the aid of hand, nail and tooth. Production thus produces not only the object but also the manner of consumption, not only objectively but also subjectively. (...) Production not only supplies a material for the need, but it also supplies a need for the material. As soon as consumption emerges from its initial state of natural crudity and immediacy - and, if it remained at that stage, this would be because production itself had been arrested there - it becomes itself mediated as a drive by the object. The need which consumption feels for the object is created by the perception of it. The object of art - like every other product - creates a public which is sensitive to art and enjoys beauty. Production thus not only creates an object for the subject, but also a subject for the object. Thus production produces consumption (1) by creating the material for it; (2) by determining the manner of consumption; and (3) by creating the products, initially posited by it as objects, in the form of a need felt by the consumer. It thus produces the object of consumption, the manner of consumption and the motive of consumption. Consumption likewise produces the producer's *inclination* by beckoning to him as an aim-determining need.[35]

The connection between needs and powers alluded to in this passage, and in the ones mentioned above, can now be explained. For Marx, the potentials of human nature—including the senses—develop in and only in ongoing interaction with their requisite stimuli. This is easy to see in cases of practical activities such as learning to play an instrument or a sport. But to Marx, as this and other quotations testify, the very same process is believed to take place for the development of the human senses. Since the latter seems harder to grasp, at least prima facie, I will expand on the interplay between needs and powers using an example of this kind. If something as basic as the human senses can be understood in terms of the interplay of needs and powers, it follows trivially that the same will be the case for practical activity, since all human practical activity involves the senses in critical ways. It also follows non-trivially in the sense that if we

---

[35] Marx (1993, p. 92/II.1.1, p. 29 (emphasis in the original), see also 1992, p. 352–6/I:2, p. 269–73/393–7, and p. 391/I:2, p. 409).

can understand the human senses by means of powers then we can likely also understand the other things that human beings do in the same way.

To begin, it is important to understand that Marx has an expansive conception of the human senses. By a sense being expansively conceived, I mean that in the "sense" of, for instance, the ear or hearing, Marx would certainly include not only the external organ (such as the outer ear), but also the full range of auditory stimulation and processing which goes on in a human being in response to the relevant kind of stimuli. Not only is the outer ear thus included, but so too are the inner ear and the relevant cognitive processes taking place in the brain.

Conceived of in this manner, senses are human powers which, like others, develop and flourish within certain contexts and conditions, and in response to their inputs. So having, for instance, a musical ear, means that one has the internal power to partake in musical appreciation and one is in the state of being able to appreciate (at least of some particular kind of) music.[36] Put differently, the internal power of, say, hearing is the power to produce certain kinds of affects or affective experiences in response to certain kinds of stimuli.

The requisite conditions for the development of these senses naturally include the necessary nutrients and other basic requirements for normally healthy physical growth and maintenance; but they also include another set of inputs specific to the sense in question. Without attempting a definition, I shall call this more restricted class a "power-specific" set of inputs. According to Marx, humans' internal powers will either not develop at all, or will develop much less, without their required power-specific inputs. Having a sense of hearing means being able to appreciate (at least certain kinds of) music. It also creates a need—i.e. a drive, in this case a desire—for the person to listen to (at least some kind of) music. If and when this need is satisfied, one's internal power of hearing, expansively conceived, develops in response to these power-specific stimuli. This, in turn, causes the needs associated with the relevant sense to alter, as a result of which new needs emerge (and the old ones may or may not disappear).[37] To be sure, when human beings and other animals use

---

[36] This is of course a state of being, and therefore a functioning. Since functionings are actualised powers, and since something being actual entails (trivially) that it is also really possible, this functioning is also (trivially) a power.

[37] It should by now be clear that Bookchin's (1974, p. 276) charge that "Marxism" has neglected to form a concrete image of sensuous man, while correct about much that

their powers in order to satisfy their needs they are not only using their sensory powers. They are using many of their other individual and social powers as well—such as powers to play instruments, to compose music, to purchase audio equipment, to stand, to walk, to read notes, and many more—and the interaction between their powers and needs is crucial for understanding how humans grow, develop, and flourish in and through our lived activities.

For Marx, this theory of human development also constitutes a framework for making sense of human activity, of lived human experience, of praxis.[38] We can get some sense of how this works by seeing how the theory I've sketched generalises throughout human activities, from gaming to theories of revolution. When you first start playing a new computer game, simply learning the mechanics and completing a few initial tasks or goals is enough. You may have long-term ambitions of completing the game, but in the early stages, your focus tends to be more on learning the basics and making immediate gains in the starting location(s). Having developed your gaming powers and won these initial victories, your needs develop further as well. Simply repeating these same basic tasks is no longer as rewarding and doesn't fill you with the same excitement as it once did, so you set your sights higher—learning more complex mechanics, carrying out more difficult tasks, and so on. Eventually, as your powers grow enough, you shift your focus to winning the game completely, often by facing and defeating one or more final bosses.

The basics of socialist theories of revolution are not so different. Most of them argue that, with or without grander ambitions in mind, you start small and local, bringing people together to develop powers of organising and acting in concert, so that you can use those powers to win small, particular victories that help better satisfy your needs (e.g. for better

---

has gone under the banner of "Marxism", does not touch the thought of Marx himself. In fact, Marx, especially in the *Economic and Philosophical Manuscripts of 1844*, criticises the classical political economists on precisely this point with regard to their conceptions of needs. For more detail on this kind of process-reading of Marx, see esp. Adams (1991), Lebowitz (2003, 2010), Ollman (1976), Parsons (1971, chs. 5–7), and Sayers (2007b, 2011).

[38] I cannot, for obvious reasons, expand upon this here, but for some more of this view from the perspective of social organisation and struggle, see Raekstad and Gradin (2020). I'm currently working on another book reconstructing what are called Marx's materialist dialectics, theory of praxis, base and superstructure, and materialist conception of history, where this will be explored in greater depth.

wages and benefits, decreasing workplace domination, stopping workplace sexual harassment, and so on). Having done so, you find that your needs develop as well and you set your goals higher: more freedom and control over your working life, in your community, etc. Having seen that you can organise together and carry out complex tasks over time, and having tasted a degree of empowerment and emancipation, you become better able to, and more interested in, running the show yourself with your comrades in fully free, equal, and democratic ways. Achieving these goals, satisfying these new needs, will in turn require confronting and defeating one or more final bosses. Of course, this is not to deny or obscure the many and important differences of strategy and tactics advocated and employed by different socialists—far from it. Rather, it's to emphasise the ubiquity of the framework provided by Marx's theory of human development as a way of making sense of things as different as individuals playing games to classes overthrowing oppressive social systems.

Marx also thinks that humans tend to act in ways that maintain and increase their powers. Note that this is a tendency only, nothing like a universal or deterministic law of human nature. It doesn't mean that all human motives reduce simply to increasing their powers. Nor does it mean that people always act in ways that succeed in increasing their powers or in ways that would do so if the actions themselves succeed. All it means is that human motivations, broadly construed, tend to be structured such that humans tend, in general, to act in ways that increase their real possibilities to do and/or to be. Furthermore, the experience of increasing our powers tends to be enjoyable in itself. One particularly important subset of those powers is of course our social powers, whether helpful or harmful, from powers of organising ecologically sustainable modes of life in the free queer communes of the future, to the dominating and oppressive powers that are wielded by monarchs over subjects, masters over slaves, and capitalists over workers.

This has two important implications that we will return to in later chapters. First, it means that one vital aspect for making sense of struggles for social change is understanding the prospects for human development/further empowerment that inhere in the natural, social, and historical contexts of particular groups and individuals; what it is that prevents them from being able to take full advantage of those potentials; and what they need to do to change the latter. As we will see especially in Part III, Marx's critique of capitalism contributes substantially to doing just that. Second, it means that we should never expect people to give up their powers willingly and that we should expect people in positions of greater power[39] to struggle to maintain both the positions of greater power and the social relations that sustain them. Famously, no oppressed group ever won their emancipation from the good will of their oppressors. We will see in Chapter 7 that this is one reason why Marx thinks that, even though capitalists are also alienated and unfree under capitalism in ways they would not be under socialism, they will still reliably organise and struggle to maintain capitalism and prevent socialist transition.[40] Finally, these points will enable me to explore, in Chapter 9, how the two revolutionary contradictions of capitalism that Marx repeatedly emphasises throughout his later works—between powers and relations and production and between workers and capitalists—are rooted in his critique of capitalism as unfree and therefore holding back human development.

This shows us that Marx's conception of the interaction between powers and needs in and through lived and experienced activity forms a vital—if neglected—building block for his later work and ideas. We have seen that, for Marx, human beings are continually interacting with our human and non-human environments in ways that continuously shape and re-shape ourselves and what we're interacting with. We are continuously engaged in realising our powers to satisfy our needs in ways that develop our powers and needs in various ways—changing some, maintaining some, eliminating some, and/or creating new ones. The existence of such processes isn't inherently good or bad; it's simply a fact of life. However, these processes can take place in better or worse ways—in ways that empower and enrich us, increase what we can do, what we can become, what we can appreciate and enjoy, or in ways that diminish and constrain us. This in turn raises the question of how such a conception of human development can be used for real politics.

---

[39] This, in Marx's very broad conception of "power", includes not only broader forms of social power conferred e.g. by being a capitalist or high-level manager dominating their workers, or the political supremacy wielded by party apparatchiks, but also that conferred by greater wealth and privilege more broadly.

[40] Naturally, Marx does not hold this to be the case for each and every individual capitalist, as is pointed out e.g. in *The German Ideology*.

Human Development and Real Politics

Marx ultimately assesses things in terms of the ways and extent to which they further human development. On this view, a social institution is better than another if it advances human development more than its competing achievable alternative(s). Such a metric can be used in many different ways, thanks to its open-ended and pluralistic nature. One way it can be used is to directly justify things like new institutions or policies. Another way it can be used is more indirect: to specify some particularly relevant sets of conditions for human development, broadly construed, and evaluating things in terms of their (foreseeable) outcomes when it comes to satisfying these (derived) conditions. A conception of human development can be used not only to evaluate existing proposals (e.g. whether Participatory Economics or market socialism is a better alternative to capitalism), but also for identifying new and hitherto unnoticed issues (e.g. the importance of universal human emancipation through intersectional working-class self-emancipation as a goal).

It is important to realise that a metric of human development is a very different kind of thing from the normative principles and ideals common in much contemporary political theory. The rules one follows or attempts to follow in regulating one's own behaviour, the rules and norms which regulate different kinds of social interactions, institutions, and so on, the objects and states of affairs one desires and values, the goals and purposes one strives towards, the ideals one tries to realise or aspire to, are a different kind of thing from whether or not—and in which ways—one develops and flourishes, one's real prospects for doing so, and the various conditions that enable one to do so in different ways and to different extents.

Furthermore, if our normative focus is on human development broadly construed, various normative rules, precepts, and principles, while still important in all manner of different ways, inevitably take on a rather different—and more instrumental—hue. Goals, aspirations, rules, and norms, etc., can be seen as enabling, aiding, or hindering various forms of human development, and up for elimination or replacement when they no longer serve a useful purpose in that regard. Take, for example, theories specifying the appropriate and inappropriate modes of social interaction within a given social structure—say, the correct way to conduct market-capitalist exchange, or the best way of having a lord-serf relationship. If well-formulated and accurate, such theories might be argued to be of genuine moral import and potentially of significant value to agents organising themselves within, and morally reflecting upon, the lives they lead in the contexts within which they lead them. A principle specifying what constitutes a just transaction, for instance, may usefully "fit", or be appropriate to, capitalism as an economic system by usefully guiding and constraining agents, by aiding in the formulation and enforcement of laws and regulations, and so on, thereby helping societies with capitalist economies which adhere to this principle to function more smoothly, with fewer interpersonal and inter-group conflicts springing from e.g. different normative conceptions and expectations with regard to economic transactions. On the other hand, such principles may well be categorically worthless for the project of evaluating, criticising, and replacing capitalism itself, and would have to be violated in any foreseeable process of transition.[41]

Despite its openness and indeterminacy, there are many cases where straightforward assessments of greater or lesser human development are easy to make. It is, easy, for example, to see that, *ceteris paribus*, physically healthy people who are capable of acting courageously and compassionately, and of taking an active part in their own life and that of their friends, family, and wider community, possess a wider range of powers than people who are not physically healthy, capable of acting in these ways and, capable of actively participating in their community, and so on. Therefore, by our definition they are better-developed versions of themselves than they would have been if they had lacked these powers.[42] This

---

[41] These concerns are at the heart of Marx's critique of Proudhon, the Lassalleans, and other contemporaneous socialists who built their critique of capitalism and vision of socialism on theories of distributive justice, which you can find more about in the appendix.

[42] Note that this is only an appeal to intuitions about the principled feasibility of making comparative judgements of human development. It makes no claims about certain powers being (intuitively or otherwise) more valuable than others (although I think Marx, Sen, and myself would all agree that this is the case) or about only some powers being valuable and others not. This is why the *ceteris paribus* clause is important here: it excludes from the thought-experiment the logical possibility that those who are e.g. less capable of acting courageously have other (potentially more valuable) powers which those to whom they are being compared lack. This may of course be a problem in cases of *actual* comparisons, but this is a distinct empirical issue and must be treated as such. The empirical concern makes sense, but it is not clear, especially in light of the further simplifying mechanisms discussed below, that it poses any significant threat to the practical usefulness of this approach in general.

is not a list of what it would mean to be a fully developed human being, nor an appeal to intuitions about what such a list would look like. Rather, I am claiming that if all other things are equal it is intuitively obvious that a person who is more developed in terms of powers (e.g. being able to take part in one's community) and the things that clearly imply them (e.g. physical health is a functioning, and therefore trivially a power) can be considered to be overall better developed than they would be if they were less so. There is, then, no principled reason to suppose that comparative assessments of greater and lesser human development are impossible.

As a concrete example of how such comparative assessments of overall human development can function, consider Wilkinson and Pickett's argument that unequal distributions of wealth—due to the unequal social relations they both generate and result from, and these relations' detrimental impacts on satisfying humans' psycho-social needs—affect a vast range of morally salient social metrics, such as physical health, mental health, crime, poverty, and social mobility.[43] If this is correct, then more unequal social relations generate a large number of disadvantages throughout the whole population (and which are stronger among the most financially impoverished). On any plausible conception of human development it is clear that, *ceteris paribus*, a society which does better than another on a vast number of these metrics is one which better serves the development of the human beings that inhabit it. Even without further simplifying mechanisms, we can therefore see that an open-ended commitment to human development can guide at least some practical politics.[44]

Furthermore, using a theory of human development to assess competing alternatives can be made easier by identifying instances of *clustering of disadvantages* on the one hand and cases of *corrosive disadvantages* and *fertile functionings* on the other. *The clustering of disadvantages* refers to the fact that many kinds of disadvantage, underdevelopment, or lack of prospects for such, tend to come in clusters rather than in even distributions across a population. This allows us to identify and focus on the challenges faced by certain groups that are clearly overall worse off than others, regardless of potentially complicated

---

[43] Wilkinson and Pickett (2010).

[44] This kind of case is different from the cases of clustering and corrosive disadvantages discussed below, since social inequality is not an instance of one power or functioning impacting a set of other powers.

issues to do with indeterminacy, disagreement, ranking, and commensurability. By contrast, the existence of *fertile functionings* (where realising a power positively impacts many others) and *corrosive disadvantages* (where lacking a power negatively impacts many others), allows us to identify powers of special importance. We can then assess relevant competing alternatives by the extent to which they realise or prevent such particularly important powers.[45] This is essentially what Marx does.

Rather than applying a general theory of human development directly, Marx identifies a particularly important human power that he takes to be valuable in itself and for many other human powers. Powers that impact a range of others to a significant extent are of particular importance because (a) they impact a number of others and are therefore valuable as a means for these others and (b) regardless of how one ranks or weighs the other powers affected, regardless of how determinate or indeterminate the other powers are relative to one another, and regardless of whether or not there is disagreement about the value of some of these other powers, those powers which impact a range of others still come out as important and valuable in a wide range of cases. Such particularly important powers can be important constituents of other powers (e.g. maintaining physical survival is a constituent of any power of political involvement) or contribute causally to other powers (e.g. being literate causally affects one's power of political involvement). Once such instrumentally important powers have been selected, one can compare feasible alternatives (e.g. policies, legislation, institutions) in light of the extent to which they realise these instrumentally important powers.[46]

The particularly important power that Marx's critique of capitalism focuses on is our power of freedom as self-direction. His theories of alienation diagnose how capitalism prevents the exercise of this power and thereby restricts human development, while his proposed cures articulate what modern society must become in order to realise freedom and thus enhance human development. In this chapter, I have explained the complexity of Marx's theory of human development as the development of human powers, needs, and their interaction in lived human activity.

---

[45] For a good discussion of this from the capabilities-approach point-of-view, see Wolff and de-Shalit (2007, ch. 7.).

[46] Sen (1999, xii, cf. 38–53, 1993, 31–32); for its connection to Marx, see Raekstad (2018a).

In the next one, I will use this theory to reconstruct his conception of freedom and its value.

REFERENCES

SECONDARY

Adams, W. (1991). Aesthetics: Liberating the senses. In Carver (ed.), pp. 246–274.
Bookchin, M. (1974). *Post-scarcity anarchism*. Wildwood House.
Booth, W. J. (1992). Households, markets, and firms. In McCarthy (Ed.), pp. 243–271.
Callinicos, A. (2000). *Equality*. Polity.
Callinicos, A. (2006). *The Resources of Critique*. Polity.
Chitty, A. (1993). The early Marx on needs. *Radical Philosophy, 64*, 23–31.
Collier, A. (2009). Marx and conservatism. In A. Chitty & M. McIvor (Eds.), pp. 99–104.
Doyal, L., & Gough, I. (1991). *A theory of human need*. Palgrave Macmillan.
Geuss, R. (1981). *The idea of a critical theory: Habermas and the Frankfurt school*. Cambridge University Press.
Geuss, R. (2012). Economies: Good, bad, indifferent. *Inquiry, 55*(4), 331–360.
Hamilton, L. A. (2003). *The political philosophy of needs*. Cambridge University Press.
Hegel, G. W. F., Wood, A. W. (Ed.), & Nisbet, H. W. (trans.). (1991). *Elements of the philosophy of right*. Cambridge University Press.
Kropotkin, P. (1995). *The conquest of bread and other writings*. Cambridge University Press.
Lebowitz, M. (2003). *Beyond capital: Marx's political economy of the working class*. Palgrave Macmillan.
Lebowitz, M. (2010). *The socialist alternative: Real human development*. Monthly Review Press.
Leopold, D. (2007). *The Young Marx: German philosophy, modern politics, and human flourishing*. Cambridge University Press.
Marx, K., Fowkes, B. (trans.) & Mandel, E. (intro.). (1991). *Capital: A critique of political economy* (Vol. 3). Penguin.
Marx, K., Livingstone, R. (trans.), Benton, G. (trans.) & Colletti, L. (Intro.). (1992). *Karl Marx: Early writings*. Penguin.
Marx, K., & Nicolaus, M. (trans.). (1993). *Grundrisse: Foundations of a Critique of Political Economy*. Penguin.
Maslow, A. H. (1970). *Motivation and personality* (2nd ed.). Harper & Row Publishers.
Mészáros, I. (1972). *Marx's theory of alienation* (3rd ed.). Merlin Press.

Mészáros, I. (2011). *Social structure and forms of consciousness, volume II: The dialectic of structure and history*. Monthly Review Press.
Nussbaum, M. (1992a). Nature, function, and capability: Aristotle on political distribution. In McCarthy (Ed.), pp. 175–212.
Nussbaum, M. (1992b). Human functioning and social justice: In defense of Aristotelian essentialism. *Political Theory*, *20*(2), 202–246.
Nussbaum, M. (2003). Capabilities as fundamental entitlements: Sen on social justice. *Feminist Economics*, *9*(2–3), 33–59.
Nussbaum, M. (2011). *Creating capabilities: The human development approach*. Belknap.
Ollman, B. (1976). *Alienation: Marx's conception of man in capitalist society*. Cambridge University Press.
Ollman, B. (2003). *Dance of the dialectic: Steps in Marx's method*. University of Illinois Press.
Parsons, H. L. (1971). *Humanism and Marx's thought*. Charles C. Thomas Publisher.
Raekstad, P., & Gradin, S. (2020). *Prefigurative politics: Building tomorrow today*. Polity Press.
Raekstad, P. (2015). Two contemporary approaches to political theory. *International Critical Thought*, *5*(2), 226–240.
Raekstad, P. (2018a). Human development and alienation in the thought of Karl Marx. *European Journal of Political Theory*, *17*(3), 300–323.
Sayers, S. (2007a). Marxism and morality. *Philosophical Researches* (9), 8–12.
Sayers, S. (2007b). *Marxism and human nature*. Routledge.
Sayers, S. (2011). *Marx and alienation: Essays in Hegelian themes*. Palgrave Macmillan.
Sen, A. (1984a). Well-being, agency and freedom: The Dewey lectures 1984. *The Journal of Philosophy*, *82*(4), 169–221.
Sen, A. (1984b). *Resources, values and development*. Basil Blackwell.
Sen, A. (1987). *The standard of living (the Tanner lectures)*. Cambridge University Press.
Sen, A. (1992). *Inequality reexamined*. Clarendon Press.
Sen, A. (1999). *Development as freedom*. Oxford University Press.
Sen, A. (2010). *The idea of justice*. Penguin.
Soper, K. (1981). *On human needs: Open and closed theories in a Marxist perspective*. Harvester Press.
Springborg, P. (1981). *The problem of human needs and the critique of civilisation*. George Allen & Unwin.
van Ree, E. (2020). Productive forces, the passions and natural philosophy: Karl Marx, 1841–1846. *Journal of Political Ideologies*, *25*(3), 274–293.
Wilkinson, R., & Pickett, K. (2010). *The spirit level: Why equality is better for everyone*. Penguin.

Wright, E. O. (2010). *Envisioning real utopias*. Verso.
Young, G. (1978). Justice in capitalist production: Marx and bourgeois ideology. *Canadian Journal of Philosophy, 8*(3), 421–455.
Young, G. (1981). Doing Marx justice. *Canadian Journal of Philosophy, Supplementary Volume, 7*, 251–268.
Zibechi, R. (2012). *Territories in resistance: A cartography of Latin American social movements Oakland*. AK Press.

CHAPTER 3

Freedom

Marx has a positive concept of freedom as self-direction,[1] rooted in an account of humans' distinctive powers of consciousness and the importance of realising them for human development. To make sense of this, I will begin by sorting out what the idea of a human "nature" does and doesn't mean in (especially the later) Marx. With that in place, I move on to his account of humans' distinctive powers of consciousness and their connection to freedom. I explain Marx's concept of freedom as self-direction or self-activity, how it differs from the neo-Roman/republican concepts of freedom it's sometimes confused with, and why Marx thinks that freedom is important. Along the way, I will defend this concept of freedom against common misconceptions and argue that Marx's claims about its value remain plausible.

THE IDEA OF A HUMAN NATURE

There's a large and varied debate on Marx's thoughts about human nature, virtually no part of which is uncontroversial, which I won't venture deeply into here. What I will do here is offer some brief points

---

[1] This has long been the standard view, see *inter alia* Blackledge (2012), Sayers (2007, 2011), Swain (2019), and Tabak (2020).

about how Marx thinks about human species-being as related specifically to his concept of freedom and his critique of capitalism.

As we saw in the previous chapter, Marx is a thoroughly contextual thinker. Human beings have a wide variety of powers and needs, the nature and content of which is shaped by their natural, social, and historical contexts in a myriad of different ways. In the *Theses on Feuerbach*, Marx also explicitly rejects any kind of static and ahistorical conception of human essences that he identifies in thinkers like Feuerbach.[2] According to Marx, thinking about the nature of human beings in terms of some static, unchanging set of properties, features, and dispositions, unaffected and unchanged by the contexts they develop within, renders this "essence" something which "can be comprehended only as 'genus', as an internal, dumb generality which *naturally* unites the many individuals".[3] While Feuerbach wants to resolve the "religious essence into the *human* essence", Marx argues that "the human essence is no abstraction inherent in each single individual. In its reality it is the ensemble of the social relations".[4]

Of course, this does not mean that nothing is common among human beings. For example, we've seen that Marx affirms that human beings feel hunger under certain circumstances, and that human beings are social by nature—although what we desire when hungry and the particular forms that human sociality takes both vary contextually. Marx's above-quoted comments clearly rule out the idea of humans sharing some static and unchanging properties, unaffected by our lived interactions with our natural, social, and historical contexts. They do not, however, rule out the idea that human beings have, by virtue of the kinds of material, embodied animals that we are, certain inherent developmental potentials and tendencies that distinguish us from other animals.

We must distinguish between two relevant senses of the terms that Marx uses that variously get translated into "nature", "essence" and sometimes "being" in English.[5] One sense of something's "nature" is what we might call its current, contingent nature. This refers to what

---

[2] For more discussion of this, see Appendix.

[3] Marx (1992, p. 423/IV:3, p. 21).

[4] Marx (1992, p. 423/IV:3, p. 20–21).

[5] The terms Marx uses here are *Wesen* (especially in the early writings) and *Natur* (e.g. in the quote from *Capital* Volume I below). In the relevant texts, there seems to be no real difference in how they're used by Marx in the context of these discussions.

anything happens to be like at any one slice of time—its size, shape, speed, colour and shading, texture, reading abilities, preference for chocolate chip cookies, etc. Marx would think of this through his lens of powers and needs, such as our powers to read books or complete a computer game and our needs to drink good coffee. Any such collection will be highly contingent in nature; vary a great deal both within and between any natural, social, and historical contexts; and likely change a great deal over time in lots of different ways.

Another sense of "nature" refers to something much more limited, namely to whatever makes a thing the kind of thing that it is. Accordingly, in *Capital* Marx distinguishes between the nature shared by human beings by virtue of being the kinds of animals we are, or "human nature in general" and our contingent nature as shaped by our growth and socialisation in our particular contexts, or "human nature as historically modified in each epoch".[6] When, in the *Poverty of Philosophy*, Marx writes that "[a]ll history is nothing but a continuous transformation of human nature",[7] what he's saying is that what human history, and in particular historical change, consists in is the continuous transformation of our naturally, socially, and historically configured sets of powers and needs. This is, as we've seen, incompatible with the kind of static and ahistorical conception of an essential human nature that Marx attributes to Feuerbach. However, it's perfectly compatible with the idea that there is some such thing as an essential human nature—provided that it's of a different kind.

Indeed, it would be shocking if Marx didn't think there are any inborn differences between human beings and other animals. We've just seen that Marx writes about the historical modification and transformation of human nature. This logically presupposes that there must be a human nature to modify. Just like (as Marx famously points out to Proudhon) it's logically impossible to commit theft in the absence of pre-existing property, so too is it logically impossible to modify or transform a human nature that doesn't exist. The other side of this coin is that it's only

---

[6] Marx (1990, p. 759, footnote 51/II:6, p. 559, footnote 64). This distinction is essentially the same as one of the ways of explaining the Hegelian distinction between First Nature (e.g. the evolved potentials we've inherited from our biological evolution) and Second Nature (the natures we develop on the basis of our First Nature, rooted in our evolved powers of consciousness and the resulting forms of socially and historically created contexts we develop within and are shaped by).

[7] MECW 6, p. 192/I:6, p. 207.

possible to explain why human beings are shaped by historical conditions like class location on the basis of some idea of human nature. Why? Because only some conception of the potentials and dispositions inherent in human beings can explain how human beings are able to be affected by those historical conditions—and in ways that differ from the way that e.g. a rock, tree, or ant would be—and why those historical conditions will tend to have certain predictable effects on human beings, like slavery and other forms of unfreedom reliably harming us. Denying any particular nature to human beings would also commit Marx to ruling out any possible explanation for why humans can do a wide variety of things that other animals can't, why humans are capable of so much greater plasticity and variation across developmental contexts, and even why freedom matters to us at all.

Fortunately, Marx has a theory of human nature that enables him to say something about all of these things. On his view, what distinguishes human beings in general from other animals is our distinctive powers of consciousness.

Consciousness, Self-Direction, Freedom

Throughout his works, Marx consistently refers to distinctive human powers of consciousness. These powers are linked to other important concepts, like universality and freedom. They're also associated with humans' greater individual and collective developmental plasticity and with their greater individual and collective variation across different natural, social, and historical contexts. I cannot examine the complexities of these two points in detail here.[8] Instead, I will limit myself to addressing the most important question it raises for our purposes: how, on

---

[8] Some of the most interesting and challenging developments of this idea can be found in Mészáros (1972, 1995, 2011). For some of the best commentary discussing all of these aspects of Marx's notion of species-being see Fromm (2004), Geras (1983), Hudis (2013), Kain (1988, 1992), Kamenka (1969, 1972), Leopold (2007), Ollman (1976), Sayers (2007, 2011), and Wood (2004). All of these, in various ways, expand upon the different elements that I've only alluded to here, such as humans' powers of consciousness, of self-direction, their role and importance for human flourishing and happiness, the notion of universality at play here, humans' capacity for mutual recognition, humans' greater plasticity and contextual variation compared to animals, and the importance of human artistry and creativity in labouring activity.

the basis of the view of human powers and needs sketched in Chapter 2, does Marx conceptualise the human species-being or species-nature?[9]

For Marx, species are distinguished by their powers. More precisely, they're distinguished by what I have termed their internal powers. The internal powers the human species-being consists in are, on Marx's account, universal among human beings,[10] restricted to human beings, and distinctive of human beings as a species. A human being realises their species-being/nature in any given activity if and only if these species-specific internal powers are exercised in the performance of that activity. Concerns about human self-direction and participation in social/collective deliberation and decision-making go back as far as Marx's earliest philosophical and political writings.[11] A turning point is marked by the shift, in the *Economic and Philosophical Manuscripts of 1844*, to focus more specifically on human activity, especially on everyday labour. Here he writes that "free conscious activity constitutes the species-character of man" and that capitalism, because of the alienation it entails, "tears away from him his *species-life*".[12]

Marx describes the human species-being or nature in the following way:

> The animal is immediately one with its life activity. It is not distinct from that activity; it *is* that activity. Man makes his life activity itself an object of his will and consciousness. (...) Conscious life activity directly distinguishes man from animal life activity. Only because of that is he a species-being. (...) Only because of that is his activity free activity.[13]

He goes on to discuss further the distinction between human beings and animals:

---

[9] Note that these are two different English translations for the same German term in Marx: *Gattungswesen*.

[10] Barring pathology and exceptional circumstances, on which see below.

[11] See this and the following chapter, as well as Hudis (2013, p. 37–55).

[12] Marx (1992, p. 328–329/I:2, p. 240–241/369–370). Note that the original "him" refers to the preceding masculine German noun der Mensch (the human being) which makes the original sentence, unlike its English translation, semantically gender-neutral.

[13] Marx (1992, p. 328/I:2, p. 240/369).

It is true that animals also produce. They build nests and dwellings, like the bee, the beaver, the ant, etc. But they produce only their own immediate needs or those of their young; they produce one-sidedly, while man produces universally; they produce only when immediate physical need compels them to do so, while man produces even when he is free from physical need and truly produces only in freedom from such need...[14]

In other words, what sets human beings apart from other animals is their internal power of conscious self-directed activity, or self-direction/self-activity for short. Human beings are endowed with consciousness, and this immediately sets their activities apart from those of other animals. Consciousness enables human beings to set themselves apart from their activity because it enables them to critically reflect on, deliberate on, direct, and alter that activity as needed. It enables them to produce universally, as opposed merely for the benefits of their own and those close to them, and to produce even when free from immediate physical needs—i.e. when not experiencing the push of simple, instinctual impulses. Finally, these passages suggest (as I return to in Chapter 7), that a particularly important realm of freedom is that of productive activities, or labour, where humans use their consciousness to determine and realise their own ends or purposes through their interaction with each other and the rest of nature.

This is a view that stayed with Marx for the rest of his life. In Volume I of *Capital*, for instance, he writes that:

> We presuppose labour in a form in which it is an exclusively human characteristic. A spider conducts operations which resemble those of the weaver, and a bee would put many a human architect to shame by the construction of its honeycomb cells. But what distinguishes the worst architect from the best of bees is that the architect builds the cell in his mind before he constructs it in the wax. (...) Man not only effects a change of form in the materials of nature; he also realizes [*verwirklicht*] his own purposes in those materials. And this is a purpose he is conscious of, it determined the mode of his activity with the rigidity of a law, and he must subordinate his will to it. (...) This means close attention. The less he is attracted by the nature of the work and the way in which it has to be accomplished,

---

[14] Marx (1992, p. 329/I:2, p. 241/369).

and the less, therefore, he enjoys it as the free play of his own physical and mental powers, the closer his attention is forced to be.[15]

Conscious self-directed activity is still, as this passage makes clear, considered to be unique to, universal among, and distinctive of human beings. Furthermore, the end of the passage cited echoes key points about the damage wrought by alienation. The less one is attracted by the nature and activity of one's work, the less one enjoys it as the free or self-directed "play" of mental and physical powers, the greater the exertion required to perform it. However, this is *not* to say that work, absent alienation, will be simply the "free play" of mental and physical powers. On the contrary, Marx believes work will always require some sort of focus, attention to detail, persistence in the face of obstacles, etc.[16]

An idea of human nature in terms of powers of consciousness is, naturally, very different from the kind of static and ahistorical view that Marx criticises Feuerbach for having. Like all other human powers, they develop only through a process of growth and maturation on the part of an organism in continuous interaction with its wider environment. They exist and maintain themselves only in and through people's continuous processes of interaction with their natural, social, and historical contexts. This in turn means that how our powers of consciousness develop, and how they can be exercised and expressed, depend in crucial ways on how our internal potentials interact with those circumstances. Marx's idea is therefore not that all members of homo sapiens have full powers of consciousness—this would obviously be false. Rather, it's that, in general, and barring pathology and exceptional circumstances, the members of homo sapiens, will, as a result of their inborn potentials tend to develop certain powers of consciousness. The "universality" at work here is thus far from the stricter, more metaphysical senses of the word, and closer to the kinds of general claims made about species' inherent potentials and tendencies we find in most sensible claims about humans and other animal species. We easily and correctly say that humans can see colours, walk upright, and communicate through language, because we think that,

---

[15] Marx (1990, p. 284/II: 6, p. 192–293). Compare this to Marx's elaboration on the above-cited remarks in the *Economic and Philosophical Manuscripts of 1844*. Cf. also Marx (1991, p. 959/II:15, p. 795).

[16] See also Marx (1993, p. 712/II.1.2, p. 589): "Labour cannot become play, as Fourier would like...".

in general, and barring exceptional circumstances, the members of homo sapiens, will, as a result of their inborn potentials, tend to grow and develop these powers.[17] For Marx, the main difference between these other human powers and our powers of consciousness is that the latter is distinctive of our species. As we will see in Parts II and III, Marx's theories of alienation build on this by diagnosing how certain social conditions thwart the exercise of this human power in important ways.

We can now understand why consciousness is at the root of Marx's explanation for our greater developmental plasticity and behavioural variation compared to other animals. Humans' powers of consciousness make us (more) able to reflect upon the environments we're faced with, our actions, our purposes or goals, and the results of our actions. They also enable us to deliberately choose our own purposes, standards, and means for attaining them in light of our perceived needs and interests, as well as change our purposes, standards, and means in light of our perceived needs and interests. Of course, both the materials available to us and the internal powers that enable us to make use of them and the needs that drive us to do so are shaped by, and so vary across, our relevant natural, social, and historical contexts. In this way, humans' distinctive powers of consciousness are, for Marx, the reason why we are able to further develop our powers of production and alter our social relations in ways that better make use of these potentials—always in particular forms that are continuously maintained through and shaped by our interactions with our human and non-human environments. The idea that people's conceptions of self, society, and politics are shaped by their lived material conditions, is thus not only compatible with, but built upon Marx's conception of human nature.

If Marx were writing today he'd likely formulate this differently in light of recent advances in the human and other animal sciences. For one, he'd likely articulate a more complex view of animal behaviour, which includes an appreciation of the behavioural variation and plasticity that we now know that many non-human animals are capable of. In connection with this, he'd likely speak of consciousness less in binary terms as something an organism simply has or not, and more as something that

---

[17] This might sound very Aristotelian, minus Aristotle's sexism, ethnocentrism, and peculiar doctrine of natural slavery. While I think that Aristotle's influence on Marx is undeniable, there are some important differences between their views here and in general, for some of which see earlier on in this chapter and for others see the appendix.

comes in degrees. Ideas of language and recursion would likely then play a central role in explaining why, as far as we can tell at present, human beings have greater cognitive capacities than other animals we've encountered so far. It's not very fruitful to speculate about the exact forms these modifications would take, but it is worth noting that, in the end, they might well generate many of the same conclusions with respect to humans' greater powers of consciousness than other animals, along with a connected commitment to the value of consciously self-directing our activity.

Freedom as Self-Direction

For Marx, freedom consists in conscious self-direction. As we've just seen, "[c]onscious life activity [that] directly distinguishes man from animal life activity" and only "because of that is his activity free activity".[18] On this view, a person is free in an activity if and only if they self-direct that activity. This requires one to be able to determine one's own purposes, decide on the means to realise them, and control how the activity is carried out. An inherently materialist conception of freedom, it rejects any kind of metaphysical separation between thinking, willing, and the rest of the world. Human capacities for freedom are created and continuously reproduced by the material world and our knowledge of that world further empowers us to direct our interactions with it, increasing our freedom. On this view, the laws of nature don't oppose our freedom, they enable it.

Like all other powers, having and exercising the (full) power to self-direct one's activity requires the right combination of internal powers and external conditions. The previous section showed that, for Marx, human beings have the internal powers required to consciously self-direct their activity. In this section, we look at some of the external conditions that it requires. These conditions include the normal requirements for human growth and survival, as well as the right kinds of social relations and level of material production. Since human beings are social animals, many of our activities will be collective in nature. For Marx, this is simply a fact about human beings. If we accept this fact, a question presents itself: how can we find ways of structuring our collective activities such that they are

---

[18] Marx (1992, p. 328/I:2, p. 240/369).

self-directed by all who are part of them, rather than directed by someone or something else?

As the exercise of an internal power, freedom can be prevented in a variety of ways. One way it can be prevented is by being subjected to the will or arbitrary power of another person. Activities in which you are subjected to the will or arbitrary power of another—like patriarchy, slavery, or capitalist labour processes—subject you to the uncontrolled power and thus direction of another person, which prevents you from directing that activity yourself. Even if the power holders never exercise their power, the fact of its existence hinders you from being able to fully determine your own purposes and decide on your preferred means for realising them in important ways, thus thwarting your potential self-direction. Another way that self-direction can be prevented is by subjecting someone to certain socially generated, impersonal forms of power which they cannot control, like the impersonal powers of capitalist competitive markets. When such impersonal powers similarly prevent people from being able to fully determine their own purposes, decide on their preferred means in important ways, and/or control their activities, such forms of impersonal domination likewise prevent those subject to them from directing their activities themselves, rendering them unfree. Marx never explains what exactly the necessary and sufficient conditions for impersonal powers counting as dominating are. However, the case of impersonal domination he focuses on, capitalism's competitive markets, combines four very clear elements. They contain a socially generated form of power, this power is not controlled by those subject to them, it does not reduce to power wielded by identifiable individual power-holders, and it undermines self-direction, e.g. by preventing people from fully determining their own purposes. In Chapter 7, we will see how Marx argues that capitalism features both personal and impersonal forms of domination.

A third way in which people can be made unfree is through impositions of natural necessity, as when Marx, in Volume III of *Capital*, writes that:

> Freedom, in this sphere, can consist only in this, that socialized man, the associated producers, govern the human metabolism with nature in a rational way, bringing it under their collective control instead of being dominated by it as a blind power; accomplishing it with the least expenditure of energy and in conditions most worthy and appropriate for their human nature. But this always remains a realm of necessity. The true realm

of freedom, the development of human powers as an end in itself, begins beyond it, though it can only flourish with this realm of necessity as its basis. The reduction of the working day is the basic prerequisite.[19]

This passage is tremendously important. While it clearly states that collective self-management—in opposition to the blind power of competitive markets or the personal power of capitalists—is necessary for human freedom, it's also argued to be insufficient. Why? Because there may still remain a realm of natural necessity that thwarts self-direction. As we saw in the preceding chapter, by necessity Marx means the requirements for survival and healthy functioning, things that we need to secure to be able to live decent lives—including, but not limited to, our basic necessities for food, water, housing, clothes, and so on. If we have to work e.g. a certain number of hours per day to secure our necessities in order to avoid the unacceptable alternative of things like poverty, starvation, and even death, we are, in effect, being forced to carry out certain actions. Why? Because someone is forced or coerced to do something if and only if they have no reasonable alternatives to doing it, and because alternatives like poverty, starvation, death, and so on are not reasonable alternatives. The fact that our historically conditioned natural circumstances[20] force us to act in certain ways implies that certain purposes are forced upon us, as is a limited range of means for achieving them. This in turn reduces our ability to (fully) self-direct those labouring activities, rendering us less free than we otherwise would be. Not being socially constituted in the same sense as feudal or capitalist relations of production are, it's no form of domination and, depending on circumstances, there may be little point in bemoaning it. It is, however, an important feature of Marx's ideas that the development of the productive powers has not only enabled free socialist relations, but also effectively reduced the pressures and constraints of natural necessity, enabling an even greater realm of free production. This is an important way in which, for Marx, the development of the productive powers/forces has enabled greater emancipation than has hitherto been possible.[21]

---

[19] Marx (1991, p. 959/II:15, p. 795).

[20] See the discussion of how necessity is historically determined in the previous chapter.

[21] For more on this, see Mészáros (2011). It should be noted that the "powers/forces" here are two different translations for the same German term, Kräfte. The term Kraft is the same term as the term Marx uses for "powers" in his discussions of human development,

We can now see that Isaiah Berlin's famous accusation that Marx's positive concept of freedom allows people to force you to be free is incorrect.[22] Briefly put, Berlin's argument is that positive concepts of freedom like Marx's involve living and/or acting in the right way. If this is the case, it's possible that somebody else knows better than you how you can and should live and act in the correct, free ways, and it's therefore also possible for them to force you to live and act in the correct, free ways, thereby forcing you to be free.[23]

There may be concepts of freedom that such an argument might apply to, but Marx's is not among them. For Marx, if you are being forced to act or live in certain ways by someone or something else, then you are no longer determining your own purposes and means and you are thus rendered unfree. Berlin's argument can be salvaged by adding the premise that the right kind of institution (e.g. state, party, church, etc.) can rightly be said to constitute a "real you", in which case its actions and directions would count as yours, so its directing you would now count as a (now very different) kind of self-direction. There are two problems with this. First, the work here is done by an extremely implausible premise that few followers of freedom would accept, and its conclusion would follow regardless of which concept of freedom one has. On a negative concept of freedom as the absence of interference, for instance, if a state or party's actions count as your own, you'd only be interfered with by yourself, so here too, once we add this premise, you would be forced to be free for the very same reasons. In other words, what does the work here isn't any concept of freedom and its supposed risks, but rather a very peculiar and implausible idea about selfhood. It thus completely fails as a critique of Marx's positive concept of freedom.[24] At no point does Marx embrace anything like such a conception of the self. The second problem with this addition is that it's not one that Marx ever makes and that it has no basis whatsoever in any of his writings.[25] It therefore cannot be accepted as a

which is why I prefer to speak of "powers of production" and "productive powers" from here on.

[22] Berlin (2002), in particular the essay "Two Concepts of Liberty".

[23] See Geuss (2005, p. 69).

[24] As has been shown in Geuss (2005, p. 70).

[25] It might be argued that this idea is implied when Marx points out that people only develop and individuate themselves within society. While this may be part of where this misinterpretation comes from, it's certainly a mistake. Obviously, the fact that people grow

plausible interpretation. In short, Berlin's critique fails both as a critique of a positive concept of freedom and as a critique of Marx.

It should now also be clear that interpreting Marx's concept of freedom simply in terms of not being subject to the will or arbitrary power another is incorrect.[26] This way of thinking about freedom—typically called the neo-Roman or republican concept of freedom—defines freedom as "non-domination", where domination is, in turn, defined as being subject to the will or arbitrary power of another. The "other" in question must be either an identifiable individual—like a monarch, slave owner, or capitalist—or an institution unified enough that it's sufficiently like a person to be said to have a will—like a senate, government, or corporation. Inherited from Roman thinkers, this concept of freedom was common in Marx's day, but increasingly faced problems trying to deal with more diffuse and impersonal forms of power, like those inherent in norms of gender and sexuality and the impersonal forms of domination inherent in competitive market forces.[27] These powers are socially generated, prevent those subject to them from fully determining their own purposes and means, and are not controlled by those subject to them, and so, according to Marx, they are rightly experienced as oppressive and unfree. This is one reason why, as we will see in Chapter 7, Marx's diagnosis of capitalism repeatedly draws attention to the impersonal domination inherent in capitalist competitive markets and the necessity of replacing them with democratic planning.

Marx writes of freedom explicitly in terms of self-activity, as being the exercise of our powers for conscious self-direction. While this requires not being subject to the will or arbitrary power of others, it is more demanding. As we have seen, freedom as self-direction further requires not being subjected to certain impersonal social powers that we cannot control or even to certain kinds of force or coercion imposed by natural

---

up, are shaped by, and become the particular individuals they are only in and through interaction with others within some society does not entail that the society one grows up in equates or amounts to their selves, "true" or otherwise.

[26] Roberts (2017, 2018).

[27] Republican/neo-Roman concepts of freedom can, of course, account for how e.g. internalised norms and impersonal relations contribute to and reinforce relations of personal domination. What they cannot do without becoming positive theories is account for how e.g. impersonal relations make people unfree in ways that don't reduce to personal relations of domination.

necessity. These cannot adequately be captured by a concept of freedom as simply not being subject to the will or arbitrary power of (identifiable) other individuals,[28] because neither impersonal social powers nor natural necessity reduce to certain identifiable individuals having power over others. While impersonal social powers may force us to do things we neither want nor need, preventing us from effectively deciding on the means and purposes of our activities and controlling how we carry them out, these powers don't reduce to the power wielded by identifiable individuals. That is, after all, what makes them impersonal. While the constraints of natural necessity may likewise thwart our ability to self-direct our activities, these too don't reduce to identifiable individuals wielding power over others. Finally, while there is plenty of textual evidence for the idea that Marx has a positive rather than a neo-Roman/republican concept of freedom, I've found no positive evidence for preferring the latter to the former.

One way of trying to salvage the idea that Marx has a neo-Roman/republican concept of freedom is to claim that Marx has not one, but two or three different concepts of freedom in his works and that he uses only the neo-Roman/republican concept of freedom to criticise capitalism.[29] The main problem with this argument is that is has no textual basis and that it appears to be simply an ad hoc stipulation to explain away the fact that everything that Marx does write about freedom supports a positive interpretation.

Before moving on to a discussion of its value, it's worth emphasising that Marx's concept of freedom develops in the particular context of working-class organisation and struggle for self-emancipation. The ongoing development of his positive concept of freedom is thus part-and-parcel of his contribution to the working class's ongoing process of self-development and consciousness-raising, serving to better enable the diagnosis of the new (especially impersonal) forms of domination that capitalism involves and better theorise how to overcome them—on which

---

[28] Roberts (2017) attempts to cash our Marx's analysis of impersonal domination in terms of personal domination, but as I show in Chapter 7, Sect. (2), this doesn't quite fit Marx's texts or ideas, whereas my positive account does. To make this passage easier to read, I've opted to write of identifiable individuals in a broad way that includes both individual persons and individual institutions that are unified enough to be considered to have wills.

[29] Roberts (2018).

see Chapters 7 and 8. In this sense, his concept of freedom is arguably a tool for better making sense of our lived experiences under capitalism, better grasping the harmful forms of power that it entails, and in so doing help enable us to replace it.[30] This becomes even clearer when we move on to one of the greatest strengths of Marx's concept of freedom, namely his account of why it's valuable in the first place.

The Value of Freedom

To understand why Marx thinks that freedom is valuable, it's first of all important to have a basic idea of how it's thwarted under capitalism (which is more fully explored in Chapter 7). On my reading, Marx's theory of alienation[31] is at heart an analysis of how capitalism thwarts the exercise of humans' internal power of conscious self-direction. He distinguishes four kinds of alienation. Alienation from the product of labour consists in the fact that, under capitalism, workers reproduce and strengthen certain social structures that keep them in bondage. One of the implications of these social structures is that one's work and its content are determined by factors outside and seemingly independent of the workers themselves (alienation from labour). The fact that this occurs in productive activity means that workers in such societies are alienated from their internal power for conscious self-directed activity in a particularly damaging way (alienation from species-being). And humans under such conditions are alienated from other humans because the abovementioned forms of alienation entail, in a very specific way, the existence of another role which must be filled, namely the role of the capitalist, who comes to own the alienated products and labour as *loci* of power over workers, and from whom workers are, therefore, alienated (alienation from other human beings). If capitalism thwarts human freedom in these ways, how is that bad from the point of view of human development we have been discussing? Or, from the other side, what is the value of freedom for Marx?

For Marx, freedom is valuable both because it's a particularly important aspect of human development in itself and because it benefits the development of a wide range of other human powers. First, the exercise of

---

[30] For more on this sort of understanding of concepts, see Raekstad and Gradin (2020).

[31] Here I should point out that I agree with most commentators that Marx uses the terms *Entäusserung* and *Entfremdung* largely, if not completely, synonymously, although there is some scholarly disagreement on this issue which I cannot discuss here.

our internal powers for conscious self-directed activity is valued as in itself important for people to lead healthy and happy lives. As internal powers which can become actualised, full powers under the right circumstances, they are valued not merely as one aspect of human development—that is, as an aspect of the development of human powers—but as a particularly important mode of human development. Unlike the development of other human powers, by developing the powers distinctive of the human species Marx holds us to become fully human beings. What such a claim is supposed to amount to is not fully explained, but it clearly involves, at least *inter alia*, a particular importance or status being attached to the development of these powers when compared to the others he mentions. Conditions of alienation, in which the human species-being is not exercised, estrange humans from their own powers and bodies; activity under such conditions is an activity in which a person "does not confirm himself in his work, but denies himself, feels miserable and not happy, does not develop free mental and physical energy, but mortifies his flesh and ruins his mind"; and, Marx claims, workers feel neither as themselves nor at home when labouring under such conditions.[32] Under alienated conditions, the worker "feels that he is acting freely only in his animal functions – eating, drinking and procreating, or at most in his dwelling and adornment – while in his human functions he is nothing more than an animal".[33]

In short, precluding the exercise or realisation of the human species-being in human activity significantly devalues that activity and negatively impacts people's experience thereof, detrimentally affecting their lives and happiness. This is not, for Marx, an inevitable condition for humankind, and he therefore criticises past political economists for failing to distinguish between human labour in general (which need not be like this) and labour under capitalism (which is).[34] The former can be free, but only by abolishing the latter.

In addition to this, enjoying freedom as self-direction also positively impacts the development of many other human powers. For Marx, humans being empowered to self-direct their activities is a case of a *fertile*

---

[32] Marx (1992, p. 326/I:2, p. 238/367).

[33] Marx (1992, p. 327/I:2, p. 239/367).

[34] For example Marx (1993, pp. 610–615/II.1.2, pp. 498–502, and 1990, pp. 137–138, footnote 16/II.6, p. 80).

functioning, where the exercise or realisation of a power significantly affects a range of others in a positive way. Under the alienated conditions Marx diagnoses, "*life activity, productive life* itself appears to man only as a *means* for the satisfaction of a need, the need to preserve physical existence", making life activity a "mere means" for existence or survival.[35] We have already seen why this is the case. Conditions of alienation, in which humans' internal power to engage in conscious self-directed activity is prevented from being exercised, causes economic activity to lose its intrinsic enjoyment and motivation. Consequently, instead of satisfying intrinsic needs and enjoyments, work under capitalism becomes a mere means to satisfy needs outside of itself—to preserve one's life, wealth, and so on.

These effects of alienated, unfree labour in turn detrimentally impact the development of the human senses—both the familiar five and others. The five senses, as well as "the so-called spiritual senses, the practical senses (will, love, etc.) (…) all these come into being only through *their* objects [by which I take Marx to mean the providers of their requisite power-specific inputs], through *humanized* nature".[36] In other words, these various human powers develop and flourish only through an ongoing process of development in which human powers are exercised to satisfy human needs—i.e. they require cultivation. But the cultivation of the human senses—i.e. of these human powers—is corroded under circumstances of alienation: "*Sense* which is a prisoner of crude practical need has only a *restricted* sense". Marx expands on this as follows:

> For a man who is starving the human form of food does not exist, only its abstract form exists; it could just as well be present in its crudest form, and it would be hard to say how this way of eating differs from that of *animals*. The man who is burdened with worries and needs has no *sense* for the finest of plays; the dealer in minerals sees only the commercial value, and not the beauty and peculiar nature of the minerals; he lacks a mineralogical sense; thus the objectification of the human essence, in a theoretical as well as a practical respect, is necessary both in order to make man's *senses human* and to create an appropriate *human sense* for the whole of the wealth of humanity and of nature.[37]

---

[35] Marx (1992, p. 328/I:2, p. 240/369, emphases in the original).

[36] Marx (1992, p. 353/I:2, p. 270/394, emphases in the original).

[37] Marx (1992, pp. 353–354, I:2), ibid., emphases in the original.

What Marx is saying here is that when humans engage in activities which they cannot self-direct, these activities lose their intrinsic enjoyment and motivation. As a result, people engage in them only if and when they are necessary in order to satisfy some other, extrinsic, needs—e.g. to prevent starvation or attain wealth. Under such circumstances, the human senses—which include both the familiar five, as well as other receptive internal powers—develop only in a basic and simplistic manner, failing to develop as well as they otherwise would. Conditions of alienation prevent the development of an appropriate *human sense* in that they prevent the development of sensory internal powers in the unique ways that humans are capable of (or would otherwise be capable of).

If this psychological picture is accurate, then alienated conditions of labour are an instance of a *corrosive disadvantage*—where the absence of one power negatively impacts a range of others. In this case, alienated conditions prevent the internal power for engaging in conscious self-directed activity from becoming a full power and from being exercised, as a result of which the development of a range of other internal powers is negatively impacted. By contrast, being able to exercise the internal power of conscious self-direction positively impacts the development of numerous other human powers.

There is one obvious worry about this: is the importance Marx attributes to self-directed activity a plausible one? We can break this down into a cluster of smaller sub-questions. Is the importance that Marx attributes to self-directed activity for intrinsic enjoyment and motivation plausible? Is the importance that Marx attributes to self-directed activity really something that is universal among human beings, or merely the erroneous universalisation of a culturally specific and restricted value? Is the importance of self-directed activity restricted to human beings, and is it really essentially linked with human consciousness as Marx believes it is? All of these are at least in principle empirical questions in the sense that empirical investigation and its results can bear on their plausibility. The last question I leave aside as difficult to deal with properly here. However, modern psychology does provide us with some insights that enable us to say something about the former two questions—viz. the questions about self-directed activity's importance and about the universality of its importance among human beings.

I shall now argue that the experimental findings associated with *Self-Determination Theory*, henceforth SDT, provide some support for these two theses.[38] SDT begins from the same basic conception of human beings that Marx does: human beings are animals which are continuously engaged in reciprocal interaction with their environments, activating their powers in order to realise their needs, and in so doing giving rise to new collections of powers and needs. The environments within which these processes take place, for Marx as for SDT, can enable, preclude or prevent, aid and nurture, or hinder and forestall the developing organism's powers.[39] SDT posits three universal human psycho-social needs: competence, the feeling of mastery and being able to operate and act effectively in one's environment; relatedness, the need to interact with, connect with, and care for others; and autonomy, which I get into below.[40] The concept of "needs" utilised by SDT is not, obviously, the same as the one I am attributing to Marx. Instead, needs in SDT's sense are defined as "the innate psychological nutriments that are essential for ongoing psychological growth, integrity, and well-being".[41] What SDT here posits as "needs" are innate and universal. To the extent that they are realised in human activity they greatly promote human development and functioning and conversely to the extent that they are not realised in such activities. In other words, the realisation of e.g. autonomy is taken to positively impact the development of a wide range of human powers.

The importance of these ideas here is that some of their associated experimental findings provide support for the importance that Marx attributes to self-directed activity and for the claimed universality of this importance. To make sense of this, we need to know what exactly SDT means by a need for "autonomy". According to SDT:

> The need for autonomy describes the need of individuals to experience self-endorsement and ownership of their actions—to be self-regulating in the technical sense of that term. The opposite of autonomy is heteronomy,

---

[38] See also Rækstad (2012).

[39] For example Deci and Ryan (2002, p. 6), Ryan and Deci (2018, Part II) and Vansteenkiste and Ryan (2013, p. 264).

[40] This is a field that is very much still growing and developing. For an overview of the general idea of need satisfaction and thwarting in SDT, see Ryan and Deci (2018). For an overview of some current themes and debates, see Vansteenkiste et al. (2020).

[41] Deci and Ryan (2000, p. 229), emphasis in the original removed.

as when one acts out of internal or external pressures that are experienced as controlling....[42]

Thus, in SDT autonomy is defined in terms of experienced governance by the phenomenal self, i.e. as, in a certain sense, the *experience* or *feeling* of self-direction. Marx, by contrast, is concerned first and foremost with the *fact of*, or *actual*, self-direction. Nevertheless, the connection between self-direction and autonomy is intuitive and clear. Arguably, one important way of people achieving the experience of self-direction is by securing that their activity really is self-directed.[43]

We will now see how SDT supports both the thesis that self-directed activity is of the importance that Marx attributes to it and the thesis that the importance of self-direction is universal among human beings in general. Recall that, on Marx's account, thwarting the human species-being in an activity significantly devalues that activity and negatively impacts people's experience thereof. Furthermore, to Marx the exercise of our powers of self-direction impacts a range of other powers in a positive way.

Beginning with the importance of self-directed activity, SDT holds that what are called "controlling aspects" such as externally imposed imperatives, demands to fulfil a particular role, or requirements to perform a task in order either to attain an external reward or avoid negative repercussions tend to thwart people's experience of autonomy and thereby crush intrinsic motivation.[44] Intrinsic motivation here refers to the motivation of an activity being the enjoyment that the performance of that activity itself generates—for example playing a game of lacrosse purely for the enjoyment one finds in the process of playing it. By contrast, extrinsic motivation is where an activity is performed for reasons external to that activity—such as playing a game of lacrosse for the money needed to

---

[42] Ryan and Deci (2018, p. 86); see also Ryan and Deci (2006, p. 1562). The detail of their formulations sometimes vary subtly, but the core point about autonomy being defined in terms of certain experiences is crucial.

[43] Note that, despite some interesting historical connections, this should not be confused with, e.g. Kant's conception of autonomy as acting in accordance with the laws laid down by reason.

[44] See Ryan and Deci (2018, Ch. 6). This has even been confirmed on a neurological level, see Murayama et al. (2010). For an overview of the neuroscience of intrinsic motivation, see Di Domenico and Ryan (2017). For a brief overview of the undermining effects of rewards, see Ryan and Deci (2018, pp. 145–147).

put food on the table.[45,46] Furthermore, empirical studies indicate that securing autonomy in human activities consistently leads to improvements in the experience of happiness, esteem, and general health and well-being. By contrast, a lack of autonomy, and a greater degree of controlled motivation—like actions being motivated solely by attaining money, power, status, and so forth—over intrinsic motivation is associated with the opposite of the aforementioned, e.g. with lack of esteem, as well as with greater risks of physical and psychological ill-health and pathologies, including depression, problems with social functioning, and even lower productivity.[47] These findings thus provide some support for the nature of the importance Marx attributes to self-direction. They support Marx's general claim that self-direction is important for living healthier and happier lives, for nurturing intrinsic enjoyment and motivation, and for positively impacting the development of a range of valuable powers.

Let us move on to the question of the universality of the importance that Marx attributes to self-directed activity. An argument against Marx's position along these lines can easily be imagined: The importance that Marx attributes to self-directed activity merely reflects his own cultural biases, the value he attributes to it is simply absent in other human cultures and it is therefore plausible to suppose that the importance of self-directed activity is not, *pace* Marx's parochial presuppositions, universal among human beings. Now, since the importance that Marx attributes to self-directed activity is *not* dependent on the beliefs that people have about the value of self-direction or their attempts to attain it, it is in principle possible to test the universality of its importance empirically. The same can obviously be said for SDT's conception of autonomy. Just like we can test how human beings react by performing essentially the same tasks under more or less autonomous conditions, we can also run these tests in different human societies that either do or do not value autonomy and see whether or not the same effects are

---

[45] For SDT extrinsic motivation is a matter of degree and comes in a number of different forms. By definition, SDT holds that all intrinsically motivated action is experienced as autonomous, while extrinsic motivations differ in their degrees of autonomy (Ryan and Deci 2018, p. 14). We need not go into this here.

[46] See Ryan (1995) and Ryan and Deci (2018, Ch. 8).

[47] See e.g. Chen et al. (2015), Deci et al. (2001), Kuvaas (2009), and Vansteenkiste et al. (2007). For more general overviews, see Ryan and Deci (2018, Ch. 10) and Ryan and Deci (2020).

observed. Such studies have been carried out, and they support the claim that autonomy and its importance for human development is in fact universal among human beings across cultures—including ones in which autonomy is explicitly and widely valued and ones in which it is not.[48] This too provides some support for Marx's thesis that the importance of self-direction for human development is in fact universal among human beings.

In this chapter, we have seen how Marx develops a positive concept of freedom as self-directed activity or self-activity. Under conditions of unfreedom, he argues that the intrinsic motivation and enjoyment inherent in a given activity is thwarted, and the development of numerous and significant other human powers is corroded. Conversely, being able to exercise these powers, realising human freedom, is valuable both as a particularly important aspect of human development in itself and because it furthers the development of a wide variety of other valuable powers. With this understanding in place, we can now turn to consider how Marx uses a concept of human freedom to critique first the state and capitalism (Part II) in favour of democracy, and then more specifically capitalism (Part III) in favour of socialism.

References

Primary

Marx, K., & Nicolaus, M. (trans.). (1993). *Grundrisse: Foundations of a critique of political economy*. Penguin.

Marx, K., Fowkes, B. (trans.) & Mandel, E. (intro.). (1990). *Capital: A critique of political economy* (Vol. 1). Penguin.

Marx, K., Fowkes, B., (trans.) & Mandel, E. (intro.). 1991. *Capital: A critique of political economy* (Vol. 3). Penguin.

Marx, K., Livingstone, R. (trans.), Benton, G. (trans.) & Colletti, L. (Intro.). (1992). *Karl Marx: Early writings*. Penguin.

Secondary

Berlin, I. (2002). *Liberty: Incorporating four essays on liberty*. Oxford University Press.

---

[48] See e.g. Chen et al. (2015), Chirkov et al. (2003, 2005), Deci et al. (2001), Lynch et al. (2009), Rudy et al. (2007), Soenens et al. (2012), and Soenens and Beyers (2012).

Blackledge, P. (2012). *Marxism and ethics: Freedom, desire, and revolution*. State University of New York Press.

Chen, B., Vansteenkiste, M., Beyers, W., Boone, L., Deci, E. L., Van der Kaap-Deeder, J., Duriez, B., Lens, W., Matos, L., Mouratidis, A., Ryan, R. M., Sheldon, K. M., Soenens, B., Van Petegem, S., & Verstuyf, J. (2015). Basic psychological need satisfaction, need frustration, and need strength across four cultures. *Motivation and Emotion, 39*(2), 216–236.

Chirkov, V., Ryan, R. M., Kim, Y., & Kaplan, U. (2003). Differentiating autonomy from individualism and independence: A self-determination theory perspective on internalization of cultural orientations and well-being. *Journal of Personality and Social Psychology, 84*, 97–109.

Chirkov, V., Ryan, R. M., & Willness, C. (2005). Cultural context and psychological needs in Canada and Brazil: Testing a self-determination approach to the internalization of cultural practices, identity, and well-being. *Journal of Cross-Cultural Psychology, 36*, 423–443.

Deci, E. L., & Ryan, R. M. (2000). The "what" and "why" of goal pursuits: Human needs and the self-determination of behavior. *Psychological Inquiry, 11*(4), 227–268.

Deci, E. L., & Ryan, R. M. (2002). Overview of self-determination theory: An organismic dialectical perspective. In E. L. Deci & R. M. Ryan (Eds.), pp. 3–33.

Deci, E. L., & Vansteenkiste, M. 2004. Self-determination theory and basic need satisfaction: Understanding human development in positive psychology. *Ricerche di Psicologia, 27*(1), 23–40.

Deci, E. L., Ryan, R. M., Gagné, M., Leone, D. R., Usunov, J., & Kornazheva, B. (2001). Need satisfaction, motivation, and well-being in the work organizations of a former eastern bloc country: A cross-cultural study of self-determination. *Personality and Social Psychology Bulletin, 27*(8), 930–942.

Di Domenico, S. I., & Ryan, R. M. (2017). The emerging neuroscience of intrinsic motivation: A new frontier in self-determination research. *Frontiers in Human Neuroscience, 11*(145).

Fromm, E. (2004). *Marx's concept of man*. Continuum.

Geras, N. (1983). *Marx and human nature: Refutation of a legend*. Verso.

Geuss, R. (2005). *Outside ethics*. Princeton University Press.

Hudis, P. (2013). *Marx concept of the alternative to capitalism*. Haymarket Books.

Kain, P. J. (1988). *Marx and ethics*. Clarendon Press.

Kain, P. J. (1992). Aristotle, Kant, and the ethics of the young Marx. In McCarthy (Ed.), pp. 213–242.

Kamenka, E. (1969). *Marxism and ethics*. Macmillan.

Kamenka, E. (1972). *The ethical foundations of Marxism* (2nd ed.). Routledge & Kegan Paul.

Kuvaas, B. (2009). A test of hypotheses derived from self-determination theory among public sector employees. *Employee Relations, 31*(1), 39–56.

Leopold, D. (2007). *The young Marx: German philosophy, modern politics, and human flourishing*. Cambridge University Press.

Lynch, M. F., La Guardia, J. G., & Ryan, R. M. (2009). On being yourself in different cultures: Ideal and actual self-concept, autonomy support, and well-being in China, Russia, and the United States. *The Journal of Positive Psychology, 4*(4), 290–304.

Mészáros, I. (1972). *Marx's theory of alienation* (3rd ed.). Merlin Press.

Mészáros, I. (1995). *Beyond capital: Towards a theory of transition*. Merlin Press.

Mészáros, I. (2011). *Social structure and forms of consciousness, volume II: The dialectic of structure and history*. Monthly Review Press.

Murayama, K., Matsumoto, M., Izuma, K., & Matsumoto, K. (2010). Neural basis of the undermining effect of monetary reward on intrinsic motivation. *Proceedings of the National Academy of Sciences of the United States of America, 107*, 20911–20916.

Ollman, B. (1976). *Alienation: Marx's conception of man in capitalist society*. Cambridge University Press.

Raekstad, P., & Gradin, S. (2020). *Prefigurative politics: Building tomorrow today*. Polity Press.

Roberts, W. C. (2017). *Marx's Inferno: the political theory of capital*. Princeton University Press.

Roberts, W. C. (2018). *Marx's social republic: Political not metaphysical* (13 p). (Unpublished Manuscript).

Rudy, D., Sheldon, K. M., Awong, T., & Tan, H. H. (2007). Autonomy, culture, and well-being: The benefits of inclusive autonomy. *Journal of Research in Personality, 41*, 983–1007.

Ryan, R. N. (1995). Psychological needs and the facilitation of integrative processes. *Journal of Personality, 63*(3), 397–427.

Ryan, R. N., & Deci, E. L. (2006). Self-regulation and the problem of human autonomy: Does psychology need choice, self-determination and will? *Journal of Personality, 74*(6), 1557–1586.

Ryan, R. M., & Deci, E. L. (2018). *Self-determination theory: Basic psychological needs in motivation, development, and wellness*. The Guilford Press.

Ryan, R. N., & Deci, E. L. (2020). Intrinsic and extrinsic motivation from a self-determination theory perspective: Definitions, theory, practices, and future directions. *Contemporary Educational Psychology, 61*(101860).

Rækstad. (2012). "Menneskelig utvikling og menneskelige behov"/"Human development and human needs" as part of the seminar on "growth, wealth and happiness—Are they connected?" (together with Roar Eilertsen and professor Ove Jakobsen). *The Welfare Conference 2012a*. Oslo.

Sayers, S. (2007). *Marxism and human nature*. Routledge.

Sayers, S. (2011). *Marx and alienation: Essays in Hegelian themes*. Palgrave Macmillan.
Soenens, B., Park, S.-B., Vansteenkiste, M., & Mouratidis, A. (2012). Perceived parental psychological control and adolescent depressive experiences: A cross-cultural study with Belgian and South-Korean adolescents. *Journal of Adolescence, 35*, 261–272.
Soenens, B., & Beyers, W. (2012). The cross-cultural significance of control and autonomy in parent-adolescent relationships. *Journal of Adolescence, 35*, 243–248.
Tabak, M. (2020). *Marx's philosophy of revolution and freedom: A critical reconstruction*. Self-published.
Vansteenkiste, M., Neurinck, B., Niemiec, C. P., Soenens, B., De Witte, H., & Van den Broeck, A. (2007). On the relations among work value orientations, psychological need satisfaction and job outcomes: A self-determination theory approach. *Journal of Occupational and Organizational Psychology, 80*, 251–277.
Vansteenkiste, M., & Ryan, R. M. (2013). On Psychological growth and vulnerability: Basic psychological need satisfaction and need frustration as a unifying principle. *Journal of Psychotherapy Integration, 23*(3), 263–280.
Vansteenkiste, M., Ryan, R. M., & Soenens, B. (2020). Basic psychological need theory: Advancements, critical themes, and future directions. *Motivation and Emotion, 44*(1), 1–31.
Wood, A. W. (2004). *Karl Marx* (2nd ed.). London: Routledge.

PART II

Alienation and Democracy

Having discussed their normative components, I turn now to the two critiques of capitalism that Marx develops in his two theories of alienation and their corresponding visions of a free future: democracy and socialism, respectively. I don't want to put any great weight on the word "theory" here. What I discuss in the following chapter as Marx's "first theory" of alienation, I call a theory for two reasons: it is part of an interesting critique of the basic institutions of contemporary society that can be found in Marx's early works and it is clearly distinct from the later, more detailed critique of capitalism that he develops from 1844 onwards, that the latter develops from in interesting ways, both methodologically and substantively. The chapters of Part II will show that the early Marx had a theory of alienation distinct from the one he developed in the 1844 manuscripts[1]; that this theory is not centred solely on a critique of the modern state, or Hegel's conception thereof[2]; that this theory centred on the suppressing of human species-powers principally by their being subjected to external power and domination, rather than in any significant way consisting in some sort of "split" between citizen and private person distinctive of the modern civil society/state complex[3]; and that this in

---

[1] *Contra* Colletti (1992), Lukács (1974), and Plamenatz (1975).
[2] *Contra* Berki (1990), Breckman (1999), McGovern (1988), and Mészáros (1972). Against this view, and for mine, see Draper (1977).
[3] *Contra* Avineri (1968), Duquette (1989), Hudis (2013), McGovern (1988), and Tucker (1970, 1972).

turn means that this early account of alienation applies much wider than merely to capitalist civil society and the state, but also e.g. to feudalism.[4] The fact that Marx's theory of alienation applies not just to the modern state, but also to capitalist civil society, sets even the very early Marx apart from a great deal of liberal and more moderate republican ideas.

There are both substantive and methodological reasons for dealing with Marx's early critique here. For one, the development of Marx's later theory of alienation and socialism in 1844 and beyond cannot be understood in the absence of his earlier political theories. His later theories developed from his earlier thoughts, retaining their core commitments. For another, Marx's approach to, or method of, political theory changes in important ways over the period during which Marx develops from a radical democrat to a socialist, but, critically, both approaches are instances of Marx developing a realist political theory on the basis of the normative commitments canvassed in Part I. Despite its importance, the relation between these two critiques of capitalist society has not received sufficient attention and is not well-understood.

Consequently, Part II has three goals in relation to Part III. Firstly, together they demonstrate how Marx developed a radical realist political theory based on a commitment to human development in two distinct ways. Secondly, they show that and how a theory of this kind rightly changes in response to further descriptive knowledge. The basic structure of many of Marx's normative commitments, his views on human nature and society, and so on, remain very similar from his first critique to the second. Marx's deeper investigations into the nature of capitalism and its alienation, through his study of political economy, leads him to develop his vision further into a form of socialism. At the same time, and this is my third point, we can see that his conception of democracy remains central to his vision of a future society both genealogically and ideologically. His notion of democracy retains ideological centrality because the vision he outlines in some of his earliest writings remains an essential component of his later vision of socialism. It retains genealogical centrality because it is this vision that, along with its underlying normative components, is the key to understanding the development of Marx as a socialist thinker.

---

[4] Although these points have not all been noted and fully explicated together, some authors do come close, esp. McLellan (1970, 1971).

In the early democratic writings, Marx's realist critique is "realisation-oriented", in that it consists in comparing competing achievable alternatives in terms of their social realisations. Thus, Chapter 4 offers an account of Marx's first theory of alienation as a diagnosis of the unfreedom of the capitalist economy and of the modern state, while Chapter 5 turns to his corresponding vision of a free alternative, democracy. Note that democracy, in Marx's sense, is not simply a form of the state or polity. Rather, it is a form of social organisation which encompasses both polity and economy, and which entails doing away with a separate state apparatus altogether. As an alternative to capitalism and the modern state, Marx argues that democracy is able to realise freedom, thus better enabling human development and flourishing.

Finally, in Chapter 6, I discuss Marx's critical search for an agent capable of bringing about his institutional alternative, without which his proposed democracy would not be achievable. What does it mean for something to be "achievable" in this context?[5] First of all, such an alternative has to be possible, by which I mean that it is able to survive and maintain itself over time in light of certain basic facts about human nature, planetary conditions, and so on. It must also be "viable", by which I mean that the proposal in question is both possible and would generate roughly the consequences its proponents claim, and that it does not generate negative effects which would overwhelmingly outweigh these positive ones. Finally, an alternative must be "achievable", meaning that it fulfils the following necessary and jointly sufficient conditions: (i) that it is viable; (ii) that there is a factor, process, or agent A; (iii) in context or kind of context c; (iv) such that, in c, A can bring about the alternative in question. The early critique of capitalism and the state that Marx develops in his first theory of alienation is realisation-oriented in that it focuses on the comparative assessment of competing achievable (in the sense of (i)-(iv)) alternatives. Thus, the modern state is critiqued in favour of socialism on the grounds that the latter is a superior achievable alternative.[6]

---

[5] This builds on Wright (2010, esp. pp. 20–9).

[6] These requirements reveal intuitively appealing points-of-entry for criticism. A theory of this kind can be criticised for being impossible, e.g. because it is not compatible with basic facts about human nature. It can be criticised for being possible but not viable, insofar as the alternative proposed will either not bring about the desired effects its proponents claim that it will, or that it will bring about negative side-effects which would overwhelmingly outweigh any effective benefits in other areas. And it can be criticised for

Marx's recommended vision must be not only possible, but also achievable under the conditions of contemporary capitalist societies. This is why his search for a viable form of revolutionary agency, to be discussed in Chapter 6, becomes so crucial. It is also why, having discovered the revolutionary agent in capitalism, his investigations of the nature and effects of capitalism shifts so greatly with his adoption of the "Standpoint of the Proletariat".[7]

---

being unachievable, despite perhaps being both possible and viable, in the sense that there is no agent in our current context which can bring about the alternative in question. For democracy to be an achievable alternative it must not only be possible in light of basic planetary conditions, human nature, and other basic facts about the world we inhabit and plausibly manage to do what its proponents claim without too many negative side-effects. There must also be a political agent (or combination thereof) that can introduce democracy in or from the context within which it's being proposed.

[7] Cf. Part III of "Reification and the Consciousness of the Proletariat" in Lukács (1974), and Löwy (2005). Note that Lukacs, unlike Löwy, seems to miss the fact and timing of this vital shift in Marx's thinking.

CHAPTER 4

The First Theory of Alienation

The earliest uses of one of Marx's two main terms for alienation (Entfremdung), occur not in dedicated discussions of capitalism, but, more broadly and rather sparsely—and with virtually no explication. This being said, it seems to be focused on forms of socially generated powers seemingly external to and independent of those who create them, which then come back to dominate and oppress their creators. It also invokes connections with freedom and subordination; empowerment and disempowerment; thoughts on the causes and ways of overcoming religious delusions; as well as with powers unique to, universal among, and distinctive of human beings as a species. In this chapter, I unpack these ideas by looking at Marx's views on the development of capitalist society out of feudalism, his argument that both feudalism and capitalism are alienating, and his diagnosis of how both the capitalist state and the economy are alienated and unfree.

Let's begin with Marx's claim that feudal society of the Middle Ages constituted a perfection of Entfremdung. Marx writes that the feudal "political constitution was the constitution of private property, but only because the constitution of property was political".[1] In other words, the basic nature of feudal society, according to Marx, is a result of the nature

---

[1] Marx (1992, p. 90/I:2, p. 33).

of a particular form of private property. Private property here denotes first and foremost the kinds of property that confer significant social power, like property in land, cattle, workshops, factories, and other means of production, rather than mere personal property in things like clothes and toothbrushes. In the case of feudalism, this especially means private property in land. But if the nature of feudal society was the result of the feudal form of private property, this was, Marx claims, only so because the control over such property was, by its very nature in this form of society, a political thing.

In other words, there was no separation between polity and economy under feudalism, between the political state and civil society, a point to which Marx returns throughout the early notes. Thus, in feudalism according to Marx, the forms of economic control over productive resources were at the same time directly forms of political and legal power. He elaborates on this point as follows:

> In the Middle Ages there were serfs, feudal property, trade guilds, scholastic corporations, etc. That is to say, in the Middle Ages property, trade, society and man were *political*; the material content of the state was defined by its form; every sphere of private property had a political character, or was a political sphere, in other words politics was characteristic of the different spheres of private life. (...) In the Middle Ages the life of the people was identical with the life of the state [i.e. political life]. Man was the real principle of the state, but man was *not free*. Hence there was a *democracy of unfreedom*, a perfected system of alienation. The abstract reflected antithesis of this is to be found only in the modern world. The Middle Ages were an age of *real* dualism; the modern world is the age of *abstract* dualism.[2]

This quotation will require some unpacking. To begin, the term "state" (der Staat) here refers to political life, but, I contend, not to political life in the sense of concerns to do with the polity per se, but in terms

---

[2] Ibid, square brackets in Colletti. Translation of "Entfremdung" has been modified from "estrangement" to "alienation", since I believe that Marx uses the two terms interchangeably and basically synonymously – a fact which is worth conveying for my purposes throughout this book. This assumption is naturally a contested one, but is the subject of broad (though not complete) consensus in the literature. I do not here have the space to defend this assumption; instead, I will modify the translations for the term as required and note in the relevant footnotes which German term has been translated from which original English translation.

of the general public concern. I believe that Marx's use of the term "der Staat" here is his translation of "res publica", which means the "public thing", or public concerns or affairs. This is a reading that sits well both with the letter to Ruge in 1842, where Marx discusses his work on a critique of Hegel and complains that *res publica* is "quite untranslatable into German".[3] It is further supported by Marx's use of the term throughout his journalism of 1842–1843 where it is used in the sense I have outlined.[4] Correspondingly, Marx contrasts, *inter alia*, the law of a state for its citizens to the law of one party or faction against another,[5] and distinguishes between a "state" and things like the "state organ" (Staatsorgan),[6] "government" (Regierung),[7] or "state administration" (Staatsverwaltung).[8] Lastly, reading "state" as a translation of *res publica* denoting public concerns or affairs is confirmed by Marx's explicit definition of "the state" as the matter of general concern: "the *state* is the 'matter of general concern', and in reality by 'matters of general concern' we mean the state".[9]

Clarifying this definition of "the state" allows us to see what Marx means when he writes that the material content of "the state" was defined by its form, and that every sphere of private life had a political character. All of this simply means that the social relations and institutions that make up the social structure of feudal society were defined by the legal forms that recognised, defined, and maintained them. Consequently, every sphere of a person's life was formally and politically recognised as the kind of thing that it was. Social roles like serfs, freemen, noblemen, guild apprentices, guild masters, and so on, were all subject to formal,

---

[3] MECW 1, p. 383/III:1, p. 22. The point Marx is making here is notoriously unclear, but is likely a political one, possibly expressing exasperation with German thinkers, in particular Hegel, the value of republican ideas and institutions, or perhaps even that censorship made it impossible to translate *res publica* into the German Republik (see Hunt 1974, p. 31).

[4] For particularly good examples of this not referred to below, see I:1, p. 153, 156, and 276–7.

[5] I:1, p. 108.

[6] Ibid.

[7] Ibid, p. 164, and p. 285.

[8] I:1, p. 124. For some discussion of this particular point, see Chitty (2006).

[9] Marx (1992, p. 187/I:2, p. 127).

though often distinct, kinds of legal recognition and enforcement. Moreover, different aspects of a person's life were not only recognised by systems of law, but by different systems of law: as a member of a free city one fell under the city's laws and legal codes; as subjects of a monarch one fell under the monarch's laws and tribunals; as members of a religion one fell under religious laws and courts; as guild members under the guild's rules and bylaws, etc.

Each major aspect of a person's life, in being recognised and defined in these ways, had therefore a political character. There was no distinct political constitution separate from these other social relations and institutions.

The later parts of the above-cited passage will become clearer once we look at more of Marx's discussion:

> In the original models of monarchy, democracy and aristocracy there was at first no political constitution as distinct from the real, material state and the other aspects of the life of the people. The political state did not yet appear as the *form* of the material state. Either the *res publica* was the real private concern of the citizens, their real content [as among the Greeks] (…) Or else the political state was nothing but the private caprice of a single individual so that, as in Asiatic despotism, the political state was as much a slave as the material state. The modern state differs from such states with a substantive unity between people and state (…) in (…) that the constitution itself develops a *particular* reality alongside the real life of the people and that the political state has become the *constitution* of the rest of the state.[10]

What Marx is saying here is that in Antiquity, the Middle Ages, and so on, the human being was the principle of the state in the sense that people's day-to-day material lives were identical with their political lives. Either the state was the public concern of the people, or it was the concern merely of a minority (either a group or an individual) and those who did not participate were not, in Marx's terminology, members of the state (=the public concern) at all. In either case, those who participated actively in social decision-making controlled social life (relatively) transparently.

---

[10] Marx (1992, p. 90–1/ I:2, p. 33–4).

What would it mean to be a proper part of the state in this sense of public concern? Firstly, we note, "[d]eliberation and decision are the means by which the state becomes *effective* as a real concern".[11] If someone is a part of the state, then:

> it is obvious that their very *social existence* already constitutes their *real participation* in it. (...) To be a conscious part of a thing means to take part of it and to take part in it consciously. Without this consciousness the member of the state would be an animal.[12]

In short, to be a member of a state in Marx's sense means that one is a conscious participant in society's deliberation and decision-making. This conscious participation in social life is also connected with the distinction between humans and animals. Without being able to exercise or realise our species-specific powers of conscious participation and deliberation in social decision-making we are rendered less than fully human, insofar as we are not able to exercise the powers universal among, distinctive of, and unique to our species.

This constitutes the core of Marx's conception of alienation: socially generated powers—of monarchs, feudal overlords, capitalists, and others—that come to dominate and oppress (at least some of) those who produce and reproduce them, thus thwarting the latter's freedom.

Accordingly, the Middle Ages constituted a perfection of alienation in the sense that it perfected a system of exclusion of (almost all of) the people from any exercise of their human powers of conscious self-direction in societal affairs. Without venturing into detail about Marx's conception of freedom at this point, we can say that feudalism constitutes a *"democracy of unfreedom"* due to the fact that, in such a society, in principle every person is subject to the power of another—only, perhaps, excluding the supreme monarchs (although one might argue that even the king or queen is, in principle, subject to the will of a deity). This subjection to externally imposed power, in turn, entails that subjects are denied their self-direction and thus unfree.[13] What, then, of the capitalist state and civil society?

---

[11] Marx (1992, p. 187/I:2, p. 127).

[12] Ibid both. Emphases in the original.

[13] This comes across, albeit indirectly, in the *Rheinische Zeitung* articles on the freedom of the press, I:1, p. 121–69. Freedom is further identified as the essence of man in I:1,

As we saw above, the modern world develops the separation between a polity outside of, and at least formally distinct from, material economic life. This process of abstraction of the polity from civil society or the economy, begun under absolute monarchy and then perfected by the French Revolution, has transformed the estates (Stände), the previous locus of social organisation, into social classes devoid of juridical and political recognition and enforcement. This has "accomplished the separation of political life and civil society".[14]

Expanding on this, Marx writes that modern civil society, i.e. the capitalist economy[15]:

> is distinguished from that which preceded it by the fact that civil society does not sustain the individual as a member of a community, as a communal being [*Gemeinwesen*]. On the contrary, whether an individual remains in a class or not depends partly on his work, partly on chance. The *class* itself is now no more than a *superficial* determination of the individual, for it is neither implicit in his work, nor does it present itself to him as an objective community, organized according to established laws and standing in a fixed relationship to him. It is rather the case that he has no real relation to his substantive activity, to his *real* class. (...) (The civil society of the present is the principle of *individualism* carried to its logical conclusion. Individual existence is the ultimate goal; activity, work content, etc. are *only* means).[16]

---

p. 143. For a beautiful connection between freedom, democracy, modern Christianity, and mere animal existence, see III:1, p. 48–53.

[14] Marx (1992, p. 146/I:2, p. 89).

[15] It must be borne in mind that the term "civil society" (bürgerliche Gesellschaft) among German thinkers such as Marx and Hegel is significantly different from the ways in which that English term is used today. Today "civil society" is commonly used to refer to organisations and movements outside of both the proper capitalist economy and the state structure, such as athletic associations, NGOs, popular movements, etc. "Bürgerliche Gesellschaft", however, was employed by 19th Century German thinkers as a translation of the term "civil society" employed, in particular, by Scottish Enlightenment thinkers such as Adam Smith, Adam Ferguson, etc., where the term referred either to the (variable) economic base of a society (hence Ferguson's "Essay on the History of Civil Society"), or, more narrowly, to the economic base of specifically commercial – i.e. capitalist – society, whilst also continuing an earlier usage of "civil society" as opposed to "natural society". Marx makes the connection between civil society and the economy, as the object of study of political economy, in his *Preface to* A Contribution to the Critique of Political Economy.

[16] Marx (1992, p. 147/I:2, p. 90).

What Marx seems to be saying here is that the advent of capitalism breaks up various traditional forms of community—whether alienating or not—and separates out an economic sphere characterised by a kind of isolation and atomism. Earlier divisions between such concrete communities are abolished in law and broken up in reality. This, in turn, leaves an economy where one's labour, position, and so on are, at least to a much greater extent, merely the effect of a combination of individual endeavour and fortune of circumstances and events. Since socio-economic existence, and the social divisions a modern economy entails, are no longer directly acknowledged, shaped, and regulated by law and the other aspects of the formal political system, they lose their political character and thus their aforementioned "*real* dualism".

This is not at all to say that economic life is, or must be, unregulated per se in such a society. All it means is that a person's position within a web of social relations, and the subsequent ways in which that person may or may not be able to interact with other members, live their lives when outside of e.g. a workplace, and how they might move around from one position to another (e.g. from an employed worker to an independent craftsman to a small manufacturer) are not themselves necessarily explicitly recognised, defined, and enforced by legal/political means. There are no doubt exceptions to the claim Marx is making here, but the existence of exceptional cases should not blind us to the broad accuracy of his assertions.

Now, let us return to the issue of the split between the political state/polity and civil society (i.e. the economy), and the atomism of the latter. Recall that, according to Marx, one's material life, is an essentially social or collective thing, defined by the social relations and structures within and through which it is lived. Insofar as one's material or day-to-day life in large part is one's working life, this atomisation of an economic sphere entails that people's economic life becomes, to them, merely a matter of satisfying one's own individual needs. One's concrete activity, work, content, etc. thus becomes only the means for securing purely individual ends or purposes. As Marx writes, the "atomism into which civil society is plunged by its *political* actions" is a necessary consequence of the fact that the "community" or "communistic entity" within "which the individual exists, civil society, is separated from the state".[17]

---

[17] Marx (1992, p. 145/I:2, p. 90).

By the same token, a capitalist society separates out a polity distinct from, and in opposition to, the economy. In contrast to the atomised and anti-social rat-race a person finds themselves in *qua* member of a capitalist economy (a.k.a. bourgeois civil society), in this abstracted political sphere "he is the imaginary member of a fictitious sovereignty, he is divested of his real individual life and filled with an unreal universality".[18] This appearance is, of course, illusory, and this, in turn, generates Christianity in its modern form:

> In the so-called Christian state it is *alienation* [*Entfremdung*] which carries weight, and not *man himself*. The only man who carries weight, the *king*, is specifically distinct from other men...[19]

We see here why it is that people are alienated in a modern state or polity: human beings themselves carry no weight within it, they do not participate in any meaningful way when it comes to its deliberation and decision-making on public affairs or concerns. Instead, only the monarch has such powers,[20] and that person is explicitly distinct from all others. For Marx, this has profound implications for the forms of consciousness that people develop in capitalist society, in particular our political and religious ideas.

Right after discussing the alienated nature of capitalism, Marx writes that:

> The members of the political state are religious because of the dualism between individual life and species-life, between the life of civil society and political life. They are religious inasmuch as man considers political life, which is far removed from his actual individuality, to be his true life and inasmuch as religion is here the spirit of civil society and the expression of the separation and distance of man from man.[21]

---

[18] Marx (1992, p. 220/ I:2, p. 149). Brackets in the original.

[19] Marx (1992, p. 225/I:2, pp. 151–152). Translation of "Entfremdung" modified from "estrangement" to "alienation".

[20] Note that I here use the words "powers" and "forces" interchangeably when discussing what Marx refers to as "Kräfte"; I use two different English words here solely for stylistic reasons.

[21] Marx (1992, p. 225/I:2, pp. 151-2). Translation of "Entfremdung" modified from "estrangement" to "alienation".

Here, Marx is claiming that both of these kinds of consciousness—both the modern political one and that of the modern Christian religion—are merely illusory constructions. However, these illusions are in no way random; nor are they mere compensations or false attempts at alleviating general human fears and ignorance, or a reflected perfection of an ahistorical human nature—as for Feuerbach and many other Young Hegelians. Rather, they are constructions reflecting, and actively responding to, the specific social conditions of the modern world with its atomised economy and really abstracted/separated polity. For Marx, it is only in a democracy, where the communal spirit of e.g. religion is realised, that people will no longer be alienated. As a result, the need for such fictitious sovereign communities will disappear, and so too will these systematic delusions themselves.

Whereas the system of feudal estates "separates man from his universal essence" and thereby "transforms him into an animal that is identical with its own immediate determinate nature"—thus constituting a merely "*animal history* of mankind, its zoology"—modern society makes the "opposite mistake", it "isolates the *objective* essence of man, treating it as something purely *external* and material. It does not treat the content of man as his true reality".[22] The "content" in question here concerns the social or material content of human beings, namely their participation in a nexus of social/communal relations and institutions within and through which their lives are lived. Whilst feudal society subjugates and dominates all its subjects, modern society, i.e. a capitalist economy and the modern state, abstracts (i.e. separates) the latter from the former.

Further, in its modes of consciousness modern society treats production and reproduction as something merely external and material. More precisely, in modern societies the systems of thought and belief that develop about humanity, human life, etc. do so from the points of view of the Christian religion and/or of the political sphere. As a result of this, they tend to conceptualise production (e.g. of basic goods and services) and reproduction (e.g. the making, maintaining, and rearing of children; cooking, cleaning, and maintaining an otherwise liveable home; and so on) as merely something external to the nature of human life and society, as nothing more than a necessary precondition of little further consequence. Since, however, this is what constitutes the lived, concrete nature

---

[22] Marx (1992 p. 148/I:2, p. 90). My brackets.

of humanity, inasmuch as it is what constitutes its day-to-day life, the modern age, due to the fact that everyday economic life is viewed solely as something external and merely material, fails to treat this objective nature of humans as their true reality.

The contradiction here is not one merely between modern forms of consciousness and the realities of economic life. Instead, it's a contradiction between these forms of consciousness *and* a *merely political*—in the sense of focusing solely on the modern, abstracted polity—political practice on the one hand, and the realities of the economic existence in modern civil society on the other. It is in this sense that the modern age is the age of "*abstract* dualism" mentioned above: The modern age is the age of a dualism of the political and the economic spheres where one is abstracted from the other.

This, in turn, causes a split and contradiction within the members of such societies:

> The perfected political state is by its nature the *species-life* of man in *opposition* to his material life. All the presuppositions of this egoistic life continue to exist *outside* the sphere of the state in *civil* society… Where the political state has attained its full degree of development man leads a double life, a life in heaven and a life on earth, not only in his mind, in his consciousness, but in *reality*. He lives in the *political community*, where he regards himself as a *communal being*, and in *civil society*, where he is active as a *private individual*, regards other men as means, debases himself to a means and becomes a plaything of alien powers.[23]

Notwithstanding the political and religious delusions Marx has already outlined, capitalism and its abstracted polity are alienating in that, first of all, they destroy any kind of conscious community or collective organisation of economic life. Secondly, in the economic sphere one not only debases oneself to a mere means, comes to see others, and collective association in general, as mere means for advancing one's own interests, and so forth, one also, crucially, becomes a "plaything of alien powers".[24] Why is this so according to the early Marx?

---

[23] Marx (1992, p. 220/I:2, pp. 148–149).
[24] Ibid. both.

People in capitalist societies are unable to exercise or express their internal species-powers for conscious self-direction, and more specifically in deliberation and decision-making on their social existence. This is because any collective entities that people might do so through are politically eliminated from the (capitalist) economic sphere, and because this sphere furthermore subjects persons to the whims and impositions of social powers that they cannot control. Since this realm, and the alien powers it imposes, are also outside the scope of political decision-making, due to the latter's restriction to matters of polity, no merely political republic (a.k.a. no merely political state), and therefore no merely political solution, can overcome alienation.

By contrast, alienation can be overcome only by making the economy subject to the conscious, collective deliberation and decision-making of (all of) the people. Only this would remove the atomisation of civil society, render it the object of the public concern, and eliminate its alien powers and imperatives. This, in turn, entails eliminating the abstraction of the political state from its economic foundations.

Already as a radical democrat, then, Marx is beginning to diagnose how people subjected to capitalist social relations become playthings of alien powers and reject the capitalist separation between economic and political spheres. This distinguishes him from many liberals and republicans, past and present, who do neither. Note that this is not a question of subjecting the economy to the rule of a separate government, or a question of government action not being constricted by property rights. Rather, it's a question of removing the separation between economic and political spheres altogether. This in turn drives Marx to develop a vision of democracy that's significantly more radical than is typically recognised.

In this chapter, we have seen that Marx argues that both the capitalist economy and the modern state are alienating, by virtue of the fact that people are subjected to socially generated powers which prevent them from consciously participating in, and directing, their public concerns or affairs. In so doing, I have shown that the early Marx did in fact have a theory of alienation distinct from the one he developed in the 1844 manuscripts; that this theory is not centred solely on a critique of the modern state or Hegel's conception thereof; that this theory centred on the suppressing of human species-powers principally by their being subjected to external power and domination, rather than in any significant way consisting in some sort of "split" between citizen and private person distinctive of the modern civil society/state complex; and that this, in turn, means that this early account of alienation applies much wider than merely to capitalist civil society and the state, but also e.g. to feudalism. Having an understanding of the critical diagnosis of modern society that the early Marx develops, I now proceed to the cure he proposes: democracy.

REFERENCES

SECONDARY

Chitty, A. (2006). The basis of the state in the Marx of 1842. In Moggach (Ed.), pp. 220–241.

Marx, K., Livingstone, R. (trans.), Benton, G. (trans.) & Colletti, L. (Intro.). (1992). *Karl Marx: Early writings*. Penguin.

CHAPTER 5

Democracy

For the early Marx, the solution to the alienation and unfreedom of capitalism and the modern state is democracy. To show why, I will first briefly explain some of the ideological background for Marx's radical ideas, before turning to his conception of democracy and his discussion of its most important requirements—like freedom of the press and overcoming the split between polity and economy. We will then see how Marx proposes democracy to replace both the modern state and capitalism. In so doing, the early democratic Marx develops a notion of democracy that's much more emancipatory and ambitious than many republicans of his day and prefigures his socialism to come.

Marx's positive political programme as a radical democrat seems to have been well-established before he developed his first theory of alienation. The latter really develops in his 1843 notebooks on Hegel[1] and is then more fully elaborated in *On the Jewish Question*. However, there is solid evidence in Marx's notes, earliest letters, his doctoral dissertation, his early journalism, and from the radical company he kept while at university, that he fits a mould of ideas often associated with the more radical enlightenment and republican thinkers all the way through to the Young

---

[1] "Entfremdung" does make sporadic appearances in earlier writings, like his doctoral dissertation. However, these appearances seem to fall short of the developed theories of alienation found from 1843 onwards.

Hegelians he associated with. These include commitments to substance monism and atheism; to a secular set of values; to ideas of democracy and/or republics; to freedom and equality before the law[2]; to freedoms of speech, press, association, and conviction; and to the complete secularisation of government and the law. Many of these ideas were well-established among the Young Hegelians that Marx associated with during and after his studies, who sought to draw on the best insights of the philosopher Georg Wilhelm Friedrich Hegel, and continue the historical process of emancipation they thought was under way by negating current restrictions on freedom. Consider Ludwig Feuerbach, most famous for his critiques of Christianity. While often presented as basically apolitical, he was in fact politically involved in clandestine student organisations, democratic republicanism, interested in feminism, and even joined the German Social Democratic Party two years before his death, thus fitting this mould as well as the more obviously political figures such as Ruge and Bauer.[3] While the Young Hegelians' early emphasis was on religious delusions and oppression, Marx, for reasons we saw in the preceding chapter, came to focus much more on social and economic struggles. Documenting this is beyond the scope of this chapter—and has been done elsewhere— but it is worth noting that Marx had a clear and strong set of political commitments before he worked out his two critiques of capitalism.

Nevertheless, the early Marx presents democracy as the solution to alienation—just as socialism is from 1844 onwards—and it's in this context that it will be examined here. Marx holds that, in contrast to all other political forms, in "a democracy the constitution, the law, i.e. the political state, is itself only a self-determination of the people and a determinate content of the people".[4] Its "*formal*" principle is therefore identical with its "*substantive*" principle.[5] In other words, the institution that claims to rule for and on behalf of the community of individuals really does so. How? By virtue of the fact that its actions reflect the expressed wishes of the people who are subject to it as an appropriate and transparent consequence of the conscious participation of those people

---

[2] While Marx agrees with equality before the law, it's worth noting that he explicitly rejects equality as a useful political value, e.g. in *Critique of the Gotha Programme*.

[3] See Leopold (2007, pp. 204–205).

[4] Marx (1992, p. 89/I:2, p. 32).

[5] Marx (1992, p. 88/I:2, p. 31).

in its deliberation and decision-making. This conception of democracy is humanist in the sense that it both conceives of human beings[6] as, and makes it the case that human beings are, the one and only subject of the political process; thus "democracy proceeds from man and conceives of the state [= the public concern] as objectified man".[7]

This conception of democracy is closely related to that of other radical democrats like Spinoza,[8] and consists of the participation of all in the deliberation and decision-making on the affairs of the state in the sense of the public concern—i.e. in the subjection of all social activity to the collective rule of its participants. Furthermore, this vision of democracy expresses a return to "the organic community typified by the city-states of Antiquity [, as such Marx] (…) distinguishes *between* 'democracy' and the 'political republic'".[9]

What Marx calls the social or "communistic essence" of society is thereby re-appropriated by all of the people. The various social forces created by, and inherent in, human society are no longer wielded by alien powers external and opposed to that of the vast majority of the population. Instead, these social powers are taken over by the body of the people, subjected to their rule, and thereby transformed into powers under their own command.

---

[6] Note that the term Marx uses in these kinds of statements, der Mensch (literally the human being, almost always translated as "man"), is gender-neutral, unlike its English or French counterparts.

[7] Marx (1992, p. 87/I:2, p. 31), cf. McLellan (1970, p. 150).

[8] Marx's notes on Spinoza's works in IV:1, p. 233–276 should be mentioned here, along with the fact that Marx was, throughout his life, an avowed fan of many radical enlightenment writers such as Diderot. The way he discusses democracy is very close to the one that can be found in his notes on Spinoza's *Tractatus*, see IV:1, p. 240–241 (785). Linking Marx to Spinoza has a long pedigree including Engels, Plekhanov, Althusser, and Negri, who tend to emphasise the importance of Spinoza's materialism. Linking Marx's ideas to more specifically to Spinoza's ideas on democracy is also far from rare, see e.g. Abensour (2004), Balibar (2008), Igoin (1977), Kouvelakis (2003), and Matheron (1977). The connection between Marx and Spinoza himself should not, however, be overstated, as Marx clearly criticises Spinoza's philosophy in *The Holy Family* and *The German Ideology* as a kind of metaphysics he believes to be rendered irrelevant by later forms of materialism. It goes without saying that his concept of freedom is also stamped by Spinozist influence.

[9] Colletti (1992, p. 41), though I reject his indication of any significant Rousseauan influence. See also Katz (1994).

We must note, however, that Marx's conception of democracy is largely one of what I shall call institutional substance rather than of institutional form. By institutional form I mean the concrete rules or procedures according to which an institution is organised. In contrast, by institutional substance I mean the content that a given institutional form produces, realises, or achieves. Institutional substances, in this sense, are multiply realisable. A genuinely direct democracy, for instance, may be realised through the instantiation of a number of distinct institutional forms or procedures, such as simple majority voting, supermajority voting, or strict consensus decision-making. On the other hand, any given institutional form may fail to realise in one context the institutional substance that it realises in another one. For example, while ancient Athens and (hypothetical) ancient Coruscant may have largely identical institutional forms—same constitution, rules, laws, decision-making procedures, etc.— the latter may have substantially different institutional substance owing to e.g. an extreme inequality of wealth giving rise to buying and selling of votes, thereby subverting the potential for genuine direct democracy which is actualised in Athens. In the sense of institutional political forms, Athens and (hypothetical) Coruscant may, indeed, be largely identical; but the addition of one further factor makes it the case that the substance of their respective polities differs significantly.

A distinction between institutional form and institutional substance is always a contextual one. If we are interested in e.g. whether a group is democratic, it makes sense to consider democracy as the institutional substance and different decision-making procedures as the institutional forms which may or may not—and may or may not to various degrees— realise this institutional substance. But we may, by contrast, be interested in a different question concerning the same group; for instance, whether the group's decision-making procedure works by consensus or not—or, if it does operate by consensus, then which forms or procedures bring this about. In one case, the consensus decision-making procedure might take place in the absence of any explicit formal rules and without any specialised functions. In another case, it might involve official functions like facilitators, timekeepers, and vibe watchers; it might involve a rigorous four-step (or more) process; it might or might not utilise a range of hand signals; and so on. The distinction between the institutional substances on the one hand, and the institutional forms which may or may not realise them on the other, is thus contextually determined: it is determined by the things we are interested in investigating (democracy; consensus decision-making), and the questions we wish to ask about them.

When, rarely, Marx sets out an institutional vision, it's almost always[10] one of institutional substance rather than of institutional form. Above all, this is because the question he is interested in is what a fundamentally new and better kind of society would have to be like. More proximately, when it comes to his early theory of alienation and democracy, he is concerned with what kind of basic social organisation—however realised—can be expected to eliminate alienation. He thus specifies what human society needs to be like in order to be considered a democracy (or, later, socialism) and fulfil its institutional promise, but he does not provide a specification of the more specific institutional forms through which this is to be instituted. His vision of democracy in terms of institutional substance at this stage includes, strictly speaking, only the vision of subjecting every major aspect of social life to participatory democratic control.

Having said this about the primary focus on institutional substance, Marx's notes do offer some reflections on the necessary and possible institutional forms it may have. First of all, as I will come back to below, Marx's vision of democracy continues the Young Hegelian and radical enlightenment strand of secularisation not just of political institutions, but of thought and life *tout court*. From his discussion of the United States and engagement with Bauer in *On the Jewish Question*, it is clear that he supports the secularisation of all major social institutions, while going further to assert that humanity must be freed from religious delusions in general. This is a project which can only be brought about by removing the social bases which give rise to it, which Marx believes can only occur in a democracy.

Secondly, although Marx is aware of the potential problems involved in representation or delegation,[11] he does not view it as inherently suspect:

> The question is not whether civil society should exercise legislative power through deputies or through all people as individuals. What is crucial is the extension and greatest possible *universalization* of the *vote*, i.e. of both *active* and *passive* suffrage…

---

[10] Leopold (2007) discusses some rare exceptions.
[11] For example I:2, p. 133. Compare this with I:1, p. 285.

[T]he vote is the *immediate, direct, not merely representative but actually existing* relation of civil society to the political state. (…) Only when civil society has achieved *unrestricted* active and passive *suffrage* has it *really* raised itself to the point of abstraction from itself, to the *political* existence which constitutes its true, universal, essential existence.[12]

In other words, what is essential for Marx is *not* a question of direct or representative democratic forms, but the extension of voting rights as a means to the substantial extension of really democratic participation.[13]

This brings me to the third point, namely that both here and in his discussion of democracy what is at stake is the full political participation of all adult persons. At no point are exceptions made along lines of class, race, religion, gender, nationality, or anything else—though his lack of writing on many of these issues, e.g. women's suffrage, makes his exact views at this time hard to pin down. This separates Marx from many liberals and more moderate republicans, who often explicitly excluded e.g. the working classes (including slaves and servants), women, people of colour, and so on from participation in their idealised republics.

Fourthly, Marx thinks of democracy not just in terms of participatory decision-making, but also in deliberative terms. Certain particular freedoms—especially freedom of the press—are considered absolutely vital for any free and democratic society. This is demonstrated strongly in the early *Rheinische Zeitung* articles on the freedom of the press.[14] Here Marx criticises all legal restrictions on press freedom as being merely veiled assertions of one faction against another; harshly rejects the arguments put forward by its proponents in the Prussia of his day; and forcefully asserts the broad theses that censorship laws pervert the press as an institution, has disastrous consequences for a society's spirit, and is fundamentally incompatible with a society's freedom, independence, and political maturity. He writes, for example, that "in order to combat *freedom of the press,* the thesis of the *permanent immaturity* of the human race has to be

---

[12] Marx (1992, p. 191/I:2, p. 130). I will show below how this extension of political suffrage will, Marx believes, result in the introduction of true democracy.

[13] In the passage cited Marx is, of course, discussing the perfection of the political state and not of a democratic society—though he believes the former will bring about the latter.

[14] I:1, p. 121–169. See also some of the discussions on the ban of the *Leipziger Allgemeinen Zeitung* in I:1, p. 291–293, and 328–333, as well as, in a slightly different context, I:1, p. 313–318. See also Hardt (2000).

defended" and that if "the immaturity of the human race is the mystical ground for opposing freedom of the press, then the censorship at any rate is a highly reasonable means against the maturity of the human race".[15] Importantly, these ideas are spelled out in terms that refer back to his commitment to human development. Marx thus writes that:

> What undergoes development is imperfect. Development ends only with death. Hence it would be truly consistent to kill man in order to free him from this state of imperfection. That at least is what the speaker concludes in order to kill freedom of the press.[16]

On the positive side, Marx claims that freedom of the press is a positive good *qua* its embodiment of the idea of freedom; that a free press has a value distinct from, and independent of, that of its particular products; that it is essential for securing criticism of, and rational and collective deliberation on, political actors and actions; and that it is vital for overcoming mystification in social and political life. Furthermore, he criticises the *Preussische Staats-Zeitung* specifically for, *inter alia*, its conception of its audience as merely passive receptacles to be mastered by the commandments of great works and national media. In so doing, Marx claims, the newspaper reveals the medieval foundations hiding behind its modern rhetoric[17]—a statement which sits well with his conception of feudalism as perfected domination, subjugation, and alienation discussed above.

Fifth, unlike modern republics, democracy for Marx does not involve an essential contradiction between private and particular interests on the one hand and general ones on the other, because no separate economic sphere is excluded from communal rule.[18] Since there is no separate economic sphere, Marx's vision of democracy is distinct from a merely political democratic republic, which upholds such a split. Accordingly, Marx criticises the debates between monarchies and republics for still remaining a "conflict within the framework of the abstract state" (Marx 1992, p. 89/I:2, p. 32). In so doing, Marx could not be clearer that his vision of democracy goes beyond simply transforming political states

---

[15] MECW 1: 153/I:1, p. 141.
[16] Ibid. both.
[17] I:1, p. 123–124.
[18] See e.g. Marx (1992, p. 145–147/I:2, pp. 90–91; p. 220/I:2, pp. 148–149).

into democratic republics. However, he does think that the political state, once "perfected" by the introduction of universal suffrage, will nevertheless serve to bring about full democracy. Thus "the perfection of this abstraction is also its transcendence".[19] He expands on this as follows:

> By really establishing its *political* existence as its authentic existence, civil society ensures that its civil existence, in so far as it is distinct from its political existence, is *inessential*. And with the demise of the one, the other, its opposite, collapses also. Therefore, *electoral reform* in the *abstract political state* is the equivalent to a demand for its *dissolution [Auflösung]* and this in turn implies the *dissolution of civil society*.[20]

What Marx seems to be saying here is that by allowing all the members of a society to participate in the political process—i.e. by allowing all members of the economy also to become real, participating parts of the political state—the existence of these two spheres, *qua* distinct social spheres, is dissolved. This can mean one of two things. Either it can mean that simply extending political participation to all persons implies, in a logical sense, that the two spheres are no longer distinct because they now have all the same real members. Or it can mean that the extension of political participation will suffice to bring it about that the economy becomes subjected to democratic control, as a result of which the separation between state and civil society is dissolved by the fact that they now both become, where they previously were not, subjected to democratic control. The former reading holds that the extension of universal suffrage logically entails the elimination of any civil society/state separation, whilst the latter reading holds that universal suffrage will suffice to bring it about that this separation is overcome by the democratic polity taking over control over the economy and subjecting it to democratic rule.

In the former interpretation, the extension of voting rights is viewed as *constituting* democracy; in the latter interpretation, it is seen as something which will *bring about* democracy. I believe the latter reading is to be preferred for the following reasons:

---

[19] Marx (1992, p. 191/I:2, p. 130).
[20] Marx (1992, p. 191/I:2, p. 130–131).

1. Marx's distinction between a perfected, but still *merely* political republic and democracy proper is hard to sustain on the first reading, where democracy seems to consist in nothing more than the extension of membership in the merely political republic. Obviously, this is not the case on the latter reading.
2. Marx sees democracy as eliminating the split persons are subject to under present conditions between being a "private person" and being a "citizen". The role of a "citizen" involves being, and thinking of oneself as, a member of a species and a community, as a person committed to others' and general interests as well as one's own, conceiving as other as ends in themselves as well, and so forth. The role of being a "private person", however, involves being, and thinking of oneself as, a person who lives as an atomised individual, who has only egoistic particular interests, who sees other persons and social existence in general as mere means for achieving one's own selfish ends, etc.[21] On the first (logical) reading it is very hard to see how persons do not in fact live two kinds of lives—one in the economy, one in the polity—with all of the different and potentially conflicting norms, motivations, imperatives, practices, and so on that Marx critically diagnoses. Bringing all of society under full democratic control, however, seems perfectly able to do so insofar as there is now only one set of institutions through which social deliberation and decision-making occurs. This is what the second reading entails, as a result of which it should be preferred.
3. Finally, Marx's concern with alienation at this stage includes, as I have shown, the alien powers imposed by the separate sphere of civil society. Only the subjection of this sphere to full democratic control will suffice to overcome this. In the second reading it is clear how this would happen: universal suffrage will bring about the subjection of the economy to democratic authority. On the first reading, this is not the case, since merely extending suffrage does not, by itself, subject the economy and its alien powers to any kind of democratic control. Consequently, the second reading, which affirms that the economic sphere must and will be subjected to democratic power, must be preferred to the first reading, which does not.[22]

---

[21] Marx (1992, p. 220/I:2, p. 148–149).

[22] It is likely that Marx is strongly influenced by his reading of ancient history here, particularly the history of ancient Athens. We might doubt whether the pathway he

We are now in a position to see how democracy will overcome capitalist alienation and dissolve its associated religious and political delusions. A democracy overcomes alienation simply by being a democracy. Alienation, in this early theory, consists in human beings being subjected to the social powers they create and which have become powers seemingly external to and independent of their creators—whether in the hands of a king, the nobility, or the impersonal forces of a capitalist economy. These powers then come back to dominate the people that created them, thwarting the exercise and expression of their human species-powers of conscious deliberation and decision-making in public affairs, thus rendering them unfree. Since democracy consists in subjecting every major aspect of social life to the conscious, collective deliberation and decision-making of all of its participants, there are no such external, uncontrolled social powers or forces to which people are subjected. As such, a democracy is a form of human society which allows the human species-powers to be exercised and expressed, as a result of which it is unalienated and free.

The creation of a properly democratic society thus entails the overcoming of alienation. Marx sums this up as follows:

> Only when real, individual man resumes the abstract citizen into himself and as an individual man has become a *species-being* in his empirical life, his individual work and his individual relationships, only when man has recognized and organized his *forces propres* as *social forces* so that social force is no longer separated from him in the form of *political* force, only then will human emancipation be completed.[23]

The overcoming of alienation entails, for Marx, the supersession of religion, and the overcoming of the kind of alienation of modern civil society and the state entails the supersession of modern Christianity by way realizing its "spirit" in the real, secular world:

---

proposes is really a plausible one for contemporary societies. In doing so, however, we must bear in mind both that Marx's highly optimistic expectations to universal suffrage seemed plausible to him in light of the history he was drawing on. Lastly, we should point out that something like this path to revolution—i.e. full social reconstruction beginning with the implementation of universal suffrage within the modern state—is revised after, and in response to, the experiences of the Paris Commune in 1871, as he very explicitly discusses both in *The Civil War in France* and in the *1872 Preface to the* Communist Manifesto.

[23] Marx (1992, p. 234/I:2, p. 162–163).

> The religious spirit can be realized only in so far as that stage in the development of the human spirit of which it is the religious expression emerges and constitutes itself in its *secular* form. This happens in the democratic state. Not Christianity but the human foundation of Christianity is the foundation of this state…
>
> The sovereignty of man – but of man as an alien being distinct from actual man – is the fantasy, the dream, the postulate of Christianity, whereas in democracy it is a present and material reality, a secular maxim.[24]

Here I take Marx to mean that a democracy brings about the "sovereignty of man" in the secular, i.e. real and material, world by eliminating the domination and subjugation of human beings by socially generated powers which they cannot control. Being the masters of their own social existence, the members of a democracy are no longer impelled to believe in unfounded illusions to give them a false feeling of sovereignty. Furthermore, as we have already seen, a democracy institutes the collective self-rule of all of its participants, thereby bringing about the real brotherhood of humanity, in contrast to the atomised existence one experiences in a capitalist economy. With the replacement of this atomised form of material life, and the corresponding elimination of the polity/economy split, the local conditions which give rise to Christianity in its modern form disappear as well. This will, Marx believes, result in the falling away of religion in general, and modern Christianity in particular, from personal and public life, since the conditions that give rise to them will have been removed.

In this chapter, we have seen that the early Marx proposes democracy to cure the alienation of modern society and why this vision is much more radical than is commonly understood, involving *inter alia* democratising the economy and even doing away with the modern polity/economy split altogether. Implementing this cure requires an agent capable of, and interested in, replacing capitalist society with a democracy. The next chapter shows how this brought Marx to the proletariat as a revolutionary subject and with it the greatest turning point of his political thought.

---

[24] Marx (1992, p. 225–226/I:2, p. 151–152).

References

Primary

Marx, K., Livingstone, R. (trans.), Benton, G. (trans.) & Colletti, L. (Intro.). (1992). *Karl Marx: Early writings*. Penguin.

Secondary

Abensour, M. (2004). *La Démocratie contre l'État: Marx et le moment machiavélien* (2nd ed.). Éditions du Félin.
Balibar, E. (2008). *Spinoza and politics*. Verso.
Colletti, L. (1992). Introduction to Marx 1992, pp. 7–56.
Collier, A. (2009). Marx and conservatism. In A. Chitty & M. McIvor (Eds.), pp. 99–104.
Hardt, H. (2000). Communication is freedom: Karl Marx on press freedom and censorship. *Javnost—The Public, 7*(4), 85–100.
Igoin, A. (1977). De l'ellipse de la théorie politique de Spinoza chez le jeune Marx. *Cahiers Spinoza, 1*, 213–228.
Katz, C. (1994). The socialist polis: Antiquity and socialism in Marx's thought. *The Review of Politics, 56*(2), 237–260.
Kouvelakis, S. (2003). *Philosophy and revolution: From Kant to Marx*. Verso.
Leopold, D. (2007). *The young Marx: German philosophy, modern politics, and human flourishing*. Cambridge University Press.
McLellan, D. (1970). *Marx before Marxism*. Penguin.
Matheron, A. (1977). Le *Traité théologico-politique* lu par le jeune Marx. *Cahiers Spinoza, 1*, 159–212.

CHAPTER 6

From Realisation-Oriented to Agent-Centred Political Theory

Two related shifts in Marx's work occur in the latter half of 1843 and the beginning of 1844, both of which turn on the proletariat. Both are also the outcome of a longer developmental process Marx went through during the years 1842–1844 and must be understood in that context. That process begins with Marx's early journalistic discovery of the importance of underlying social and economic relations to political and legal conflicts. It moves on through historical analyses, critiques of Hegel and others to the formulation of his first theory of alienation along with its proposed cure in democracy. It takes a decisive step, in *A Contribution to the Critique of Hegel's Philosophy of Right: Introduction*, with his identification of the proletariat as the revolutionary class. This leads Marx further into political economy, socialist literature, and becoming acquainted with working-class organisations. The first shift that occurs is one of theoretical focus. Marx's political theory goes from being principally focused on a diagnosis and critique of modern society to becoming a diagnosis and critique of capitalist society from the perspective of the proletarian class. Consequently, he shifts from one kind of realist approach to another, from a realisation-oriented to an agent-centred one.[1] Accordingly, his perspective shifts to focus much more on the real forces for change that capitalism generates. The second is a shift of theoretical content. Marx's diagnosis of capitalist unfreedom is much further developed in a new theory of alienation, as does his conception of a free society to cure it in his vision of socialism.

This chapter will summarise this sequence of events insofar as they are important for the development of Marx's political theory, culminating in the new perspective from which Marx develops his second theory of alienation. The chapters in Part III will then show how Marx uses this approach to develop his more dedicated, socialist critique of capitalism.

In his famous *Preface to* A Contribution to the Critique of Political Economy Marx mentions the embarrassment he experienced when, as the editor of the *Rheinische Zeitung* from 1842 to early 1843, he was faced with the Rhenish Landtag's discussions of the laws against the theft of wood and on the division of landed property, the condition of the Moselle peasantry, and the debates on free trade and protective tariffs.[2] He writes that:

> In the year 1842-3, as editor of the *Rheinische Zeitung*, I first found myself in the embarrassing position of having to discuss what is known as material interests. The deliberations of the Rhenish Landtag on forest thefts and the division of landed property; the official polemic started by Herr von Schaper, then Oberpräsident of the Rhine Province, against the *Rheinische Zeitung* about the condition of the Moselle peasantry, and finally the debates on free trade and protective tariffs caused me in the first instance to turn my attention to economic questions. (…) The first work which I undertook to dispel the doubts assailing me was a critical re-examination of the Hegelian philosophy of law; the introduction to this work being published in the *Deutsch-Französische Jahrbücher* issued in Paris in 1844. My inquiry led me to the conclusion that neither legal relations nor political forms could be comprehended whether by themselves or on the basis of a so-called general development of the human mind, but that on the contrary they originate in the material conditions of life, the totality of which Hegel, following the example of English and

---

[1] Shortly after coming up with this term, I discovered that it has already been employed to denote realist approaches to political theory in Geuss (2010, p. 46). By contrast, my usage of the term denotes one specific class of possible realist approaches.

[2] See. I:1, pp. 199–236, and 296–327.

French thinkers of the eighteenth century, embraces within the term 'civil society'; that the anatomy of this civil society, however, has to be sought in political economy. The study of this, which I began in Paris, I continued in Brussels, where I moved owing to an expulsion order issued by M. Guizot. The general conclusion at which I arrived and which, once reached, became the guiding principle of my studies can be summarized as follows. In the social production of their existence, men inevitably enter into definite relations, which are independent of their will, namely relations of production appropriate to a given stage in the development of their material forces of production. The totality of these relations of production constitutes the economic structure of society, the real foundation, on which arises a legal and political superstructure and to which correspond definite forms of social consciousness...[3]

This is a claim which Engels, in his letter R. Fischer dated the 15 April 1893, corroborates in even stronger terms, writing that he heard Marx say that it was specifically the debates on the laws against theft of wood which shifted his focus from purely political questions to economic ones, thereby ultimately turning him towards socialism. This spurred Marx, as he himself points out, to a critical examination of Hegel in his 1843 notes. As Part II has shown, the diagnosis of capitalism and the state that Marx develops there is partly economic, in that it briefly discusses the alien powers that capitalism imposes on people and its exclusion from conscious control, in addition to his critique of the modern state as alienating. Marx also offers an envisioned cure, democracy, which he believes can overcome this alienation.

However, if such a cure is to be instituted, democracy must not just be possible and viable; it must also be an achievable alternative in modern societies. Recall that this means: (i) that it is viable; (ii) that there is a factor, process or agent A; (iii) in context or kind of context c; (iv) such that, in c, A can bring about the alternative in question. Marx already believes that: (i') democracy is a viable institutional alternative to capitalist civil society and the state. His commitment to introducing democracy to cure the ills of contemporary society therefore naturally leads Marx to a concern with (ii)–(iv). He reflects that:

---

[3] Marx (1992, p. 425/II:2, p. 100).

> Clearly the weapon of criticism cannot replace the criticism of weapons, and material force must be overthrown by material force. But theory also becomes a material force once it has gripped the masses...
> The point is that revolutions need a *passive* element, a *material* basis. Theory is realized in a people only in so far as it is a realization of the people's needs. (...) It is not enough that thought should strive to realize itself; reality must itself strive towards thought.[4]

The first sentences express, I think, the following line of thought: Philosophical criticism is no substitute for concrete action when it comes to bringing about social change. Social change must be brought about by a "material force", i.e. by some causally efficacious factor, process, or agent. Criticism, or critical political theory, can, however, become such a causally efficacious "material force" only if it can succeed in sufficiently influencing the actions of a large enough body of people, causing them to act in the ways needed to bring about revolutionary social change. Such a body of people is the "material basis" of a critical political theory.

Marx moves on to claim that a critical political theory must become the realisation of people's needs. Recall that our discussion in Chapter 2 established that in Marx "needs" means drives or strivings. This applies here too. As such, the claim that a theory is only realised in a people when it becomes the realisation of their needs means that a theory is realised only if and when it contains and expresses the real needs—i.e. the real drives or strivings—of the people it addresses. If a theory can succeed in expressing the real needs of the people, then it can make reality itself strive towards thought, in the sense that a real material force strives towards the goal or direction expressed in the theory. Put differently, such a political theory must succeed in directing a body of people so that they bring about (at least some of) what the theory advocates or seeks to promote.

The link between these two components is intuitive. Revolutions require material force to bring about a change from one kind of basic social structure to another. A political theory can become such a material force only if it has an adequate group of people acting in accordance with it—which Marx here calls the theory's passive or material element. For a theory to be able to do this, it must somehow articulate, express, and appeal to the drives or strivings which the people it is intended to influence already are subject to. If the theory is able to do so, people's drives

---

[4] Marx (1992, pp. 251–252/I:2, pp. 177–178).

or strivings can be altered, modified, or re-directed in a way that accords with the goal or direction contained within the theory. This would mean that the theory has become a material force. If it can manage to do this, the theory satisfies not only (i), but also (ii)–(iv), providing an achievable alternative to what it rejects. By doing so, "[c]riticism has plucked the imaginary flowers on the chain not in order that man shall continue to bear that chain without fantasy or consolation but so that he shall throw off the chain and pluck the living flower".[5]

Marx's search for a revolutionary agent predates these more explicit reflections. Already in his earlier notes on Hegel, he discusses the estate of direct labour consisting of propertyless workers, an estate which lacks any position or privilege in society and which has some special kind of importance for the other estates. In a letter to Ruge in May 1843,[6] Marx rejects the former's pessimism about social change on the grounds that modern society—i.e. the capitalist economy and the state—is generating a layer of suffering, oppressed, but thinking human beings, the existence of which is incompatible with the continuation of modern society. This layer and its revolutionary potential are, furthermore, seen in terms of class struggle with roots in the economic sphere.

However, the first articulation of the working class as a revolutionary agent, along with the word "proletariat" denoting this class, comes later. It makes its appearance after the passages discussed above in *A Contribution to the Critique of Hegel's Philosophy of Right: Introduction*—composed and written from mid-October to December 1843. Here the proletariat is singled out as revolutionary class due, in part, to its "radical chains". It is a class generated in modern civil society; it lacks titles, privileges, or substantial standing or influence in modern society; it is impoverished; and it can only emancipate itself by at the same time emancipating all of society. This is because the requirements of the proletariat's emancipation—overthrowing the capitalist economy and the state in favour of democracy—imply the emancipation not only of the members of this class, but the emancipation of all the other members of society as well. Marx goes on to write that:

---

[5] Marx (1992, p. 244/I:2, p. 177).

[6] III:1, pp. 48–53, esp. pp. 52–53.

> The only liberation of Germany which is *practically* possible is liberation from the point of view of *that* theory which declares man to be the supreme being for man. (…) The *emancipation of the German* is the *emancipation of man*. The *head* of this emancipation is *philosophy*, its *heart* the *proletariat*. Philosophy cannot realize itself without the transcendence [*Aufhebung*] of the proletariat, and the proletariat cannot transcend itself without the realization [*Verwirklichung*] of philosophy.[7]

This largely reiterates elements we discussed above, but with one crucial amendment: the revolutionary agent is identified as the proletariat. Realising the recommendations of "philosophy" (or critique, or a critical political theory, etc.) requires abolishing the proletariat as the class most subject to suffering and alienation in the contemporary world. This abolition requires that the recommendations of philosophy—namely democracy—replace the capitalist economy and the state. The proletariat is defined in terms of the real movement of social struggle, of which it is (the most important) part. This movement itself contains within it, implicitly, the direction it tends towards, namely the "dissolution" of modern civil society/capitalism and the state in favour of a democracy. Consequently, the proletariat, as the class striving for democratic revolution, is defined as the "dissolution of [modern] society as a particular class".[8]

Having pinpointed an agent for his political theory, Marx has argued: (ii') that there is a class, namely the proletariat; (iii') in and generated by modern society; (iv') such that, in modern society, the proletarian class really can bring about democracy. This means that his realisation-oriented political theory satisfies not only (i), but (ii)–(iv) as well, presenting democracy as an achievable alternative to capitalism. I will later discuss Marx's thoughts on how the political theorist should relate their work to this agent and its ongoing struggles.

For now, I want only to indicate how his discovery of the proletariat as the revolutionary agent changes the direction of Marx's research. Before I do so, however, a brief biographical recapitulation is in order. The journey that began with Marx's journalistic "embarrassment" in 1842 led him to take a much closer look at modern society, consisting as it does of modern civil society and the state. He went on to formulate a severe diagnosis of

---

[7] Marx (1992, p. 257/I:2, p. 183).
[8] Marx (1992, p. 256/I:2, p. 182).

its ills in his first theory of alienation, envisioned an alternative to replace it—democracy—and finally discovered the agent to bring this vision into being, the proletariat. This line of inquiry led him to investigate the conditions of the modern capitalist economy as such. Renewing his investigations, Marx now wants to understand how the capitalist economy and the alien powers it imposes function in detail, how this economy generates different and conflicting classes and class interests, the effects the capitalist economy has on the proletariat, and what would be required for the proletarian struggle to be victorious. All of this led Marx to his study of political economy and to his making contact with the socialist movement of his day. This time, however, Marx's theoretical focus has shifted. His early theory of alienation is formulated as a general critical political theory of society, democracy proposed as its cure, and only thereafter does his search begin for an agent to introduce it. Now he instead begins from a conception of the nature of capitalism and the social forces it generates, and proceeds to develop a diagnosis and cure on that basis.

Marx now develops what I call an "agent-centred" approach to political theorising, by which I mean that it fulfils the following necessary and jointly sufficient criteria:

1. An agent-centred political theory starts from a descriptive account of a particular context or a kind of context c.
2. From this descriptive account, it draws a conception of the social forces that c generates, be they factors, processes, or agents of whatever kind.
3. The available factors, processes, or agents available in c *constrain* such political theory in the sense that only types of alternatives which really can be brought about by one or more of the available factors, processes, or agents are open for political theorising, whether these alternatives are ones of policy, legislation, economic and political institutions, or whatever. More precisely, alternatives must be:
    (a) viable, in the sense of both being possible in the sense of being able to survive and maintain themselves over time in light of certain basic facts about human nature, planetary conditions, and so on, and being able, at least in principle, to generate the consequences its proponents claim without generating negative effects which outweigh these positive ones;

(b) there must be at least one factor, process, or agent, or combination thereof, F;
(c) in context or kind of context c;
(d) such that, in or from c, F really can bring about the alternative in question.

4. Within the bounds of these constraints, such a political theory develops a conception of at least two or more alternatives within or from c, at least one of which is recommended over at least one of the others in terms of the social realisations it generates, or can reasonably be expected to generate.
5. The available factors, processes or agents available in c also *positively determine* the form and content of the advocacy of the political theorist in that such advocacy must:

(a) seek to address itself (successfully) to an agent, A;
(b) in a suitable manner, i.e. by some suitable means;
(c) such that A will act appropriately (and/or not inappropriately), in light of the other factors, processes, and agents F, in or from c, to bring about the alternative in question.

In short, agent-centred political theory invites us to begin from an understanding of a kind of politics and its context—e.g. capitalist society. This should include not just the institutions, norms, values, and so on that it contains, but also the social forces that are generated by and part of it—e.g. the developmental tendencies of capitalist free markets, of capitalist and working classes and class struggle, etc. An understanding of a form of politics and the social forces that are part of it allows us to imagine various ways in which it will develop, e.g. if the working class wins the class struggle against capitalism. A political theorist can then develop theories that help to guide their preferred agents, within the relevant context, in ways that help empower those agents to bring about the preferred forms of development—e.g. the self-emancipatory struggle of the working classes culminating in a socialist revolution. Evidently, this approach remains staunchly realist, insofar as it starts from a conception of what real politics is like and seeks to improve the actions of some of the agents involved therein. Indeed, while Marx's agent-centred approach ends up being rather different than what he has been doing previously, it's worth pointing out that bringing about the right social realisations remains central. It thus makes sense to see the shift to agent-centred political theory as developing a more sophisticated form of realisation-oriented realism, rather than something entirely separate from it.

The proletariat, on Marx's view, is a *revolutionary subject*, in my sense, in that it is *both* the principal factor, process, or agent proposed to bring about socialism *and* the agent Marx's theory needs to appeal to for this to succeed. The principal factors, processes, or agents he thinks will bring about his desired alternative is therefore the same as the agent he seeks to influence. In other agent-centred thinkers, the two can come apart. For instance, Adam Smith sees the capitalist economy as the factor or process that will bring about the greater freedom and improved living conditions for workers, while appealing to the agency of beneficent legislators to put the right laws and policies in place to allow this to occur.[9]

An agent-centred approach differs from a merely realisation-oriented one in a number of respects. Perhaps the most important of these is that an agent-centred approach insists, as per (1) and (2), on the greater importance of first attaining an adequate understanding of the context the theorist is located and acting within. This understanding, in turn, yields the knowledge the theorist requires concerning the means available for any possible political action in the relevant context and of the restrictions they are under. Only after such an understanding has been attained does the agent-centred theorist move on to examine which alternatives are available for political theorising. Having examined these alternatives, and recommended one or more alternatives over one or more others, an agent-centred theorist moves on to the question of how best to bring this or these about. Of the relevant social forces a society generates, the theorist must address themselves to at least one viable agent that can act appropriately in the manner required to bring about the theorist's preferred alternative. This forms the basis for some of Marx and Engels' critiques of other socialists. For example, in the *Communist Manifesto*, Marx and Engels criticise the utopian socialists for failing to ground their approach in an accurate understanding of capitalism and its class struggle. Because they don't recognise that proletarian class struggle is necessary to bring about socialism, they try appealing to a wealthy and powerful agent that cannot be relied upon to do so, namely the capitalist class, and in so

[9] Raekstad (2020 and forthcoming).

doing (by trying to avoid class struggle and successfully appeal to capitalists) end up undermining the only social agency (working class struggle) that can.

In this chapter, we have seen how Marx's search for an agent of social change leads him to identify the proletariat as a revolutionary subject, and how that changes his approach to political theory from a realisation-oriented one to an agent-centred one. Before moving on, I will stop to note the most important effects that this shift had on Marx's work, namely the further development of Marx's critical theory of capitalism. Once re-examined from this new methodological perspective, along with his newly added insights from political economy and the socialist movement of his day,[10] Marx's diagnosis of capitalism develops into a new and much more extensive theory of alienation. Alongside this, he also develops a new conception of the cure it requires, namely socialism. Building on this more developed critique of capitalism, Marx further shifts his views on how political theorists ought to relate themselves to, and interact with, the social forces and agents of their society. The chapters in Part III will thus reconstruct this new theory of alienation along with its proposed cure in socialism, as well as his views on how theorists should act and relate themselves to the agents they seek to address.

References

Primary

Engels, F., & Henderson, W. O. (Ed. and Intro.). (1967). *Engels: Selected writings*. Penguin.

Marx, K., Livingstone, R. (trans.), Benton, G. (trans.) & Colletti, L. (Intro.). (1992). *Karl Marx: Early writings*. Penguin.

Secondary

Geuss, R. (2010). *Politics and the imagination*. Princeton University Press.

---

[10] In this regard, Marx notes mentions the importance of English, French, and German socialist works, singling out Moses Hess's writings, those of Wilhelm Weitling, and Friedrich Engels' *Outlines of a Critique of Political Economy* (in Engels, 1967, pp. 148–176) among the latter as especially influential, see Marx (1992, pp. 280–282/I:2, pp. 325–326). Hess' Über das Geldwesen is particularly interesting for its connections with Marx's work of the period 1844–5.

Raekstad, P. (2020). Adam Smith: Radical neo-roman and moderate realist. *Archiv für Geschichte der Philosophie, 103*(1), 70–92.

Raekstad, P. (Forthcoming). The model of the legislator: Political theory, policy, and realist utopianism. *Contemporary Political Theory.*

PART III

Alienation: The Unfreedom of Capitalism

With his agent-centred approach to political theorising in place, Marx develops a much more detailed diagnosis of capitalism in his new theory of alienation, along with a new conception of its cure: socialism. This goes on to re-shape his practice as a political theorist.

The chapters of Part III show a number of things. First, they show how Marx develops and utilises an agent-centred, and thus another kind of realist, critique of capitalism. Second, they argue that this critique remains defensible in light of some of the findings in the human sciences—especially against the objections levelled by Max Weber and Friedrich Hayek. Naturally, I do not attempt to show that Marx's critique of capitalism is correct on all points or defend it against all possible objections that might be offered against it. That bar is much higher and lies beyond the scope of this work.

Third, these chapters complete my demonstration that Marx's normative commitments to human development and freedom carry over into his later critique of capitalism. Here we will see how Marx uses his positive theory of freedom to develop a diagnosis of how capitalism involves relations of both personal and impersonal forms of domination. He formulates a vision of socialism tailored to eliminating them by not only democratising workplaces, but also abolishing the hierarchical division of labour, replacing competitive markets with democratic planning, and distributing according to need. This continues to challenge contemporary debates about the requirements of free economic institutions.

In light of these goals, the chapter breakdown of Part III is as follows. In Chapter 7, I lay out my interpretation of Marx's diagnosis of capitalism in what I call his second theory of alienation. At the core of this theory of alienation is an analysis of how capitalist relations of production thwart human freedom in the sense of self-directed activity. I thus argue that alienation is not, at heart, about a particular kind of feeling or experience, loss of meaning, *anomie*, and so forth; call this the subjectivist reading.[1] Rather, on the objectivist reading I favour, alienation diagnoses a state of affairs in which people socially generate certain powers which come to dominate them. More specifically, his later theory of alienation explains how, under capitalism, people generate forms of personal domination (of workers by capitalists and managers) and impersonal domination (by capitalist social relations themselves, over all who are subject to them). Marx distinguishes between four kinds of alienation: alienation from product; alienation from productive activity; alienation from species-being; and alienation from others. The discussion below will go through each of them in turn, paying specific attention to the connections between them—connections which are often overlooked or downplayed. Just like the first theory of alienation discussed in Chapter 4, the second theory of alienation is fundamentally an analysis of how the structures and relations of modern society thwart human freedom.

With Marx's diagnosis in place, Chapter 8 moves on to his notion of its cure: socialism. Since the diagnosis of modern society has changed with Marx's increased understanding of political economy, so too must his conception of its remedy. I show that Marx's commitment to radical democracy is retained in his vision of socialism; what changes is the addition of further, specifically economic, components in response to the challenges pointed to in his new theory of alienation. Thus, a future socialist society must be a full participatory democracy—including freedoms of speech, press, association, etc. Furthermore, socialism must also feature a democratically planned economy; abolish capitalism's hierarchical division of labour; and give to each according to their needs, while allowing them to contribute according to ability.

---

[1] This should not be confused with (other) discussion of "subjective" versus "objective". It's thus not about e.g. subjective versus objective conditions for revolution or whether conscious awareness or ideas are involved in it (since obviously ideas are necessary for social relations with generalised commodity exchange, like capitalism), or about whether it is in some sense "real" or merely imagined.

Finally, Chapter 9 will reconstruct Marx's evolving understanding of the role of the theorist within his scheme of an agent-centred political theory. The role of the theorist, on Marx's view, is not only to provide a diagnosis and cure for capitalism; it is also to present these to the revolutionary subject that his theory pinpoints in such a way that it, *qua* social force, becomes better able to bring about the real movement from the condition diagnosed to the cure envisioned. Part of this will involve showing how Marx's critique of capitalism is not only compatible with, but a core component of, his later views on the revolutionary contradictions of capitalism, and is thus entirely consistent with his views on what is often called dialectical and historical materialism. The chapter also explains why Marx begins to de-emphasise the more normative sides of theorising capitalism and why we have reason to pay more attention to them. With all these components in place, we will be able to have a complete understanding of how Marx develops a radical realist critique of capitalism which remains compelling and defensible today.

CHAPTER 7

Alienation and Unfreedom

Marx's second theory of alienation is an analysis of how capitalism thwarts freedom. The basic view I present in this chapter goes as follows: Alienation from the product of labour consists in the fact that, under capitalism, workers and capitalists reproduce and strengthen (by accumulation) certain social structures that keep them in bondage to the impersonal powers of capitalist social relations. One of the implications of these social structures is that workers' work and its content, its purposes, means, and execution, are determined by factors outside and seemingly independent of workers themselves, i.e. by social powers that they cannot control (alienation from labour). This means that workers in such societies are further alienated from their species-specific powers of consciousness in a particularly strong and significant way (alienation from species-being). Finally, workers under such conditions are alienated from (certain) other people, because the above-mentioned forms of alienation entail the existence of capitalists, who own the alienated products as *loci* of power over workers, thus wielding socially generated power over workers which workers cannot control. As a result, workers are dominated by and alienated from them (alienation from others). After some general comments about my interpretation of Marx's theory of alienation, I discuss each of these aspects in turn, showing that and how they're connected to each other. In so doing, we will see how Marx diagnoses both the personal and impersonal forms of domination and unfreedom inherent in capitalist social relations in ways that we would do well to pay more attention to.

The Nature of Alienation

Let's note a few things about this view from the outset. For one, it centres on a diagnosis of how humans under capitalism are prevented from self-directing their activities. In contrast to Marx's first theory of alienation, it focuses on capitalism specifically. However, this is not to say that much of the analysis cannot also be brought to bear on other forms of society. The broad idea of alienation as socially generated powers that return to dominate and control their creators applies, in principle, to all forms of social domination, like the power wielded by feudal lords or state bureaucrats over their subjects. Marx recognises this, e.g. when in 1844 he writes of "feudal landed property" as "land which has been alienated from man and now confronts him in the shape of a handful of great lords"[1] and that in "feudal landownership we already find the domination of the earth as of an alien power over men".[2] Notwithstanding this, the theory of alienation that Marx dedicates himself to from 1844 onwards is designed to describe and criticise capitalism. As such, one cannot simply transpose parts of this second theory of alienation into a critique of other forms of society without due modifications, explaining the specific mechanics of, e.g. alienation in feudalism or central planning.

Another point worth noting is that, on this account, *none* of the four kinds of alienation I discuss focus on a person's *experience* or *feeling of being alienated* from anything. This does not mean that the affective or experiential aspects of alienation are uninteresting or insignificant. Far from it; people's experience of disempowerment and disconnection from their productive lives, co-workers, and wider society are natural concomitants to life under capitalism, which are moments of both interest and importance, some of which my discussion below will bring out. However, it does mean that I explicitly reject the *subjectivist strain* of psychologistic or affective readings which take Marx's (second) theory of alienation to

---

[1] Marx (1992, pp. 317–318/I:2, p. 359), translation modified.
[2] Marx (1992, p. 318/I:2, p. 359).

be fundamentally concerned with the experiences of disempowerment, disconnection, separation, *anomie*, loss of meaning, sadness, confusion, lack of experiences of self-realisation, problems of identity, etc., which life under capitalism may or may not generate.[3] Marx certainly does discuss some of these elements, but they are the *consequences* or *implications* of some part or aspect of the alienation he diagnoses, not its *constituents*. I thus place myself among the *objectivist strain* of commentators on Marx's (second) theory of alienation, who take it to be something which does not consist in beliefs, feelings, or attitudes. Instead, they take the (second) theory of alienation fundamentally to be a description of a condition or a state of affairs, which is what it is independently of the beliefs, feelings, or attitudes anyone may or may not have as a result of what it describes.[4] Moreover, I will argue that alienation from product, often misconstrued even among other objectivist readings, is a central piece of the puzzle.

A third point I would like to draw attention to is that my analysis shows that the different kinds of alienation Marx distinguishes are not only closely interlinked; they also build upon one another in intuitive and enlightening ways. I thus reject Kamenka's claim that "Marx's 'proof' that man's alienation from his species is *implied* by his alienation from the product of his labour (…) consists of nothing more solid than (…) metaphorical transitions".[5] On the contrary, I think Marx is entirely correct about his own view when he writes in the *Economic and Philosophical Manuscripts of 1844* that he aims, and is able coherently,[6] to grasp:

---

[3] Including, inter alia, Avineri (1968), Bronfenbrenner (1973), parts of Jaeggi (2005) and Schacht (1971), Swain (2012, 2019), and Wood (2004).

[4] Including, inter alia, Allen (2011), Arthur (1986), Holloway (1997, 2010), Gray (1986), Hudis (2013), Israel (1971), other parts of Jaeggi (2005), Schacht (1971), Leopold (2007), Lukács (1974), Mészáros (1972), Musto (2010), Ollman (1976), Padgett (2007), Postone (1996), Sayers (2011), Swain (2012, 2019), Tabak (2012), Walliman (1981), and Wolff (1992, 2003). Note that Swain (2012, 2019) appears in both camps, since his view is a hybrid of the two.

[5] Kamenka (1972, p. 77).

[6] By "coherent" here I mean not just negatively coherent in the sense of logical consistency, but also in the further positive sense which Kamenka denies, namely in the sense of there being comprehensible and plausible (in their own terms) links between the different kinds of alienation Marx distinguishes and discusses.

The essential connection between private property, greed, the separation of labour, capital and landed property, exchange and competition, value and the devaluation *[Entwerthung]* of man, monopoly and competition, etc. – the connection between this entire system of alienation *[Entfremdung] and the money* system.[7]

With these basics in order, we can now turn to the oft-neglected, but crucial, first kind of alienation Marx discusses in his second theory: alienation from product.

Alienation from Product

Alienation from the product of labour consists in the fact that, in capitalist production, workers and capitalists reproduce and strengthen (by accumulation) the capitalist social relations that impersonally dominate them. To see why, let us begin where Marx does, with the claim of impoverishment: "The worker becomes poorer the more wealth he produces, the more his production increases in power and extent".[8] We must wait till the end of this section to see precisely what Marx means by this—just as in Marx's original we have to wait until the end of the discussion of the first kind of alienation. My explanation begins by recognising an immeasurably important feature of labour, namely that:

> Labour not only produces commodities; it also produces itself and the workers as a *commodity* and it does so in the same proportion in which it produces commodities in general.[9]

In other words, the labour process produces not only goods and services; it also produces and reproduces the network of social relations within and through which it takes place. Capitalist labour processes don't just make goods and services—though that's one thing they do. They also continuously produce and reproduce the capitalist social relations that these labour processes are part of.

---

[7] Marx (1992, p. 323/I:2, pp. 235/364), translation of Entfremdung modified from "estrangement" to "alienation", The erroneous "Entwertung" in Colletti's square brackets replaced by Marx's original "Entwerthung".

[8] Marx (1992, p. 323/I:2, pp. 325/364).

[9] Marx (1992, p. 324/I:2, pp. 235/364).

Under capitalism, the social relations that workers reproduce in and through production come to dominate them, rendering them unfree. Marx writes that "the object labour produces (...) stands opposed to it as *something alien*, as a *power independent* of the producer".[10] The realisation of labour in its production of an object "appears as (...) *loss of and bondage to the object*, and appropriation as *estrangement*, as *alienation [Entäusserung]*".[11] The object becomes "alien to him, and begins to confront him as an autonomous power; that the life which he has bestowed on the object confronts him as hostile and alien".[12] The more the worker produces under such conditions, Marx claims, "the more he falls *under the domination of his product, of capital*".[13] In summarising the discussion of this later on, Marx writes that this is alienation of practical human activity under the aspect of "the relationship of the worker to the *product of labour*, as an alien object that has power over him".[14]

Let's break this down, beginning with the worker's loss of object. Wage labour under capitalism produces and reproduces both various goods and services and the capitalist social relations within and through which this production occurs. This includes producing and reproducing the labour involved as a specific kind of commodity, namely as wage labour. Wage labour, under capitalism, occurs in such a way that the wage labourers own and control neither the materials they work on nor the objects they produce. Consequently, the object produced is something external to the labourers.

To understand how this lost object comes to confront labourers as an alien and hostile power, we must begin by noting two ways in which all labour is dependent on the external world. First of all, all work or labour requires materials on which to work, "in which it is active and from which and by means of which it produces".[15] Secondly, all work or labour also requires, for obvious reasons, "the means of physical subsistence of the

---

[10] Marx (1992, p. 324/I:2, pp. 236/364–365).

[11] Marx (1992, p. 324/I:2, pp. 235/365). Translation of Entfremdung to "estrangement" retained for aesthetic reasons.

[12] Marx (1992, p. 324/I:2, pp. 235/365).

[13] Marx (1992, p. 324/I:2, pp. 236/365, my emphases).

[14] Marx (1992, p. 327/I:2, pp. 238/368).

[15] Marx (1992, p. 325/I:2, pp. 237/365).

worker".[16] Without materials to work on, labour which requires materials cannot take place. Without the means of subsistence for labourers, there can be no (human) work or labour over time. Marx goes on to write that:

> In these two respects, then, the worker becomes a slave of his object; first in that he receives an *object of labour*, i.e. he receives work, and secondly in that he receives *means of subsistence*. Firstly, then, so that he can exist as a *worker*, and secondly as a *physical subject*. The culmination of this slavery is that it is only as a *worker* that he can maintain himself as a *physical subject* and only as a *physical subject* that he is a worker.[17]

The meaning of the first two sentences is sufficiently understood from what has just been said above. The last one is the crucial and new one. Under capitalism, workers produce products which they do not own, both means of production and consumable commodities; and these are owned by capitalists. To survive, workers need access to consumable commodities, and to gain access to consumable commodities they need the means by which to gain such access. Under capitalism, workers are collectively excluded from productive property/means of production, as a result of which the only way they can attain the means by which they can gain access to consumable commodities is by receiving a wage for working on the productive property of capitalists. Marx returns to this throughout his later political economy, including in Volume I of *Capital*, which talks of the workers being "free" in the double sense that "he can dispose of his labour-power as his own commodity, and that, on the other hand, he has no other commodity for sale, i.e. he is rid of them, he is free of all the objects needed for the realization [*Verwirklichung*] of his labour-power".[18]

By taking part in such a working relation, workers further produce and reproduce capitalist relations of production, along with the products which become their bearers; i.e. they produce commodities and capital. Both of these are owned by capitalists, not by the workers themselves. In so doing, workers also reproduce themselves in one particular role within those relations, namely in the role of workers. Workers can thus maintain themselves physically only as workers in the sense that the only way

---

[16] Marx (1992, p. 325/I:2, pp. 237/366).
[17] Marx (1992, p. 325/I:2, pp. 237/366).
[18] Marx (1990, p. 272–3/II:6, p. 185).

they can survive at a decent level is by reproducing capitalist relations of production and themselves as workers within that relation—otherwise sinking into poverty and destitution.[19] In this way, it is only by being workers—i.e. working for some capitalist—that workers can maintain themselves as physical subjects.[20]

The effects of this are apparent in the levels of inequality continually seen under capitalism, where it is plain that the gains in terms of productive powers are astounding, without the vast majority of the population necessarily benefiting from them much:

> *Political economy conceals the alienation in the nature of labour by ignoring the **direct relationship between the worker (labour) and production**. It is true that labour produces marvels for the rich, but it produces privation for the worker. It produces palaces, but hovels for the worker. It produces beauty, but deformity for the worker. It replaces labour by machines, but it casts some workers back into barbarous forms of labour and turns others into mere machines. It produces intelligence, but it produces idiocy and cretinism for the worker.*[21]

Workers are thus forced, by capitalist property relations, into working for some (but no one particular) capitalist. This coercion is just as real as threats of physical punishment—threats of poverty, destitution, and starvation, along with the often-accompanying feelings of shame, guilt, and isolation. We say that someone is forced or coerced to do something if and only if they have no reasonable alternatives to doing it. Clearly, being rendered homeless, malnourished, and/or otherwise impoverished is no reasonable alternative. So, while the force of material compulsion to subject ourselves to the domination of capitalist overlords is very real

---

[19] For more on this, see I:2, pp. 189–207 and 327–51. Note that this argument, as it appears in Marx, originally speaks of survival *at all*, i.e. of minimal physical subsistence. However, as his more considered passages in published works such as Volume I of *Capital* bear witness to, and in the interests of more charitable interpretation in light of certain minimum welfare provisions currently available in welfare states (though less and less so), we are justified in modifying the premise to securing a minimally decent level of subsistence, in part determined by contextual moral and historical factors (as Marx calls them).

[20] The final clause of the last cited sentence is very tricky, and less important in this context. Consequently, I leave it aside for the time being.

[21] Marx (1992, pp. 325–326/I:2, pp. 237/366), translation of "Entfremdung" modified from "estrangement" to "alienation".

indeed, it is also distinct from the simpler, violently physical, and perhaps more easily perceivable forms of coercion which prevail under, e.g. slavery.

This kind of capitalist coercion is made possible only by the fact that a class of capitalists control the products of the labour process—both means of production and consumable commodities. If workers were not excluded from the consumable commodities they produce, they would not need to receive wages from someone or something else in order to gain access to those commodities. If capitalists did not monopolise society's productive property, workers would have no need to work for capitalists. They could simply set up their own small farms and businesses, a network of cooperatives, a collection of communes, or any number of other configurations to meet their needs themselves.[22]

Failing to notice this has led to some hilarious misadventures on the part of individual capitalists:

> A Mr Peel (…) took with him from England to the Swan River district of Western Australia means of subsistence and of production to the amount of £50,000. This Mr Peel even had the foresight to bring besides, 300 persons of the working class, men, women and children. Once he arrived at his destination, 'Mr Peel was left without a servant to make his bed or fetch him water from the river.' Unhappy Mr. Peel, who provided for everything except the export of English relations of production to Swan River![23]

Mr. Peel had not neglected any purely physical items necessary for successful capitalist production—consumable commodities, means of production, and workers to utilise them. The source of Mr. Peel's error, according to Marx, lies in the fact that once these items are moved out of the context of capitalist social relations they cease to function as they do under the capitalism of his native England. In Western Australia, the would-be workers were faced with alternative consumable commodities and/or means of production which they could access. In other words, they were no longer excluded, as a class, from productive property. They were thus no longer under any material compulsion to work. In the

---

[22] See, e.g., Kropotkin (2013).

[23] Marx (1990, p. 932–3/II:6, p. 685). While the first French edition and the Penguin translation have "3,000" persons, both the German original and Marx's source, E. G. Wakefield's *England and America. A comparison of the social and political state of both nations*, have the number at "300", so I've corrected the quote accordingly.

absence of such force, these workers were able to choose to use their labour-power to enrich themselves rather than Mr Peel, the capitalist.

To many liberals, the exclusion of workers from the means of production and forcing them to work for capitalists seems natural and inevitable. In reality, these conditions are the product of violent state intervention and enforcement at the behest of the ruling classes both within and (through imperialism and colonialism) outside of the imperial core. Marx writes:

> Of course, the pretensions of capital in its embryonic state, in its state of becoming, when it cannot yet use the sheer force of economic relations to secure its right to absorb a sufficient quantity of surplus-labour, but must be aided by the power of the state – its pretensions in this situation appear to be very modest in comparison with the concessions it has to make, complainingly and willingly in its adult condition. Centuries are required before the 'free' worker, owing to the greater development of the capitalist mode of production, makes a voluntary agreement, i.e. is compelled by social conditions to sell the whole of his active life, his very capacity for labour, in return for the price of his customary means of subsistence, to sell his birthright for a mess of pottage.[24]

Expanding on this, the later chapters of Volume I of *Capital* discuss various forms of state primitive accumulation, with Marx writing that these methods "all employ the power of the state, the concentrated and organized force of society", to hasten the shift to capitalism and shorten the transition. In this regard, he concludes, "[f]orce is the midwife of every old society which is pregnant with a new one. It is itself an economic power".[25]

What Mr. Peel failed to realise, and what so many (other) colonisers recognised, is that capital is a social relation. Products of labour, the "means of production and subsistence", Marx points out, "while they remain the property of the immediate producer, are not capital"; they only become capital when they become "means of exploitation of, and therefore domination over, the worker".[26] Products become the means for

---

[24] Marx (1990, p. 382/II:6, p. 274). For more thorough accounts, see Kropotkin (1997, 2013) and Polanyi (2001).

[25] Marx (1990, pp. 915–916/II:6, p. 674).

[26] Marx (1990, p. 933/II:6, p. 685).

such things only when they are the bearers of certain social relations between persons and they become the bearers of such relations only if and when there is a class of people which is systematically excluded from them. The same point is made in *Theories of Surplus Value*, where Marx writes that "[c]apital is productive of value only as a relation, in so far as it is a coercive force on wage labour, compelling it to perform surplus-labour" and that it "only produces value as the power of labour's own material conditions over labour when these are alienated from labour".[27] In other words, the production of value in the capitalist mode of production presupposes workers' exclusion from the product of labour—in particular the means of production and necessary consumable commodities—because this is what forces workers to work for capitalists.

Moving the discussion to *Capital* brings me to an important point: the fact that what Marx in the *Economic and Philosophical Manuscripts of 1844* calls alienation from product is retained, minus the terminology, at the heart of Marx's diagnosis of capitalism throughout all of his subsequent works. Indeed, it's in the later writings on political economy that Marx most precisely articulates not only how capitalism forces workers into dominating labour relations, but also how the impersonal powers inherent in capitalist social relations themselves dominate those who are subject to them. In *The German Ideology*, Marx and Engels point out that "[i]n history up to the present it is certainly likewise an empirical fact that separate individuals have (…) become more and more enslaved under a power alien to them", which has "become more and more enormous and, in the last instance, turns out to be the *world market*".[28] Among many other places, Marx returns to point out that people under capitalism are dominated by impersonal social relations in Volume 1 of *Capital*, where he distinguishes between "the power of landed property, based on personal relations of domination and servitude" on the one hand, and, on the other hand, the "power of money [under capitalism], which is impersonal", going on to quote the French proverb "*L'argent n'a pas de maître*"/"money has no master".[29]

---

[27] Marx (1969, p. 93/II:3.2, p. 384).
[28] MECW 5, p. 51/I:5, pp. 41–42.
[29] Marx (1990, p. 247, footnote 1/II:6, p. 165).

While as we will see below, workers are certainly dominated by capitalists,[30] they are also dominated by capitalist social relations as such. Marx is clear that "capital is not a thing, it is a definite social relation of production pertaining to a particular historical social formation".[31] He is also clear that capitalist social relations dominate capitalists as well, writing that "the capitalist is just as enslaved by the relationships of capitalism as is his opposite pole, the worker, albeit in a quite different manner".[32] Even in *Capital* Volume I, this is explicitly conceptualised in terms of *inter alia* workers being subjected to the power of their products, where Marx writes of capitalism as "a mode of production in which the worker exists to satisfy the need of the existing values for valorization" instead of one where such "wealth is there to satisfy the worker's own need for development", and argues that just "as man is governed, in religion, by the products of his own brain, so, in capitalist production, he is governed by the products of his own hand".[33]

Here Marx is repeatedly drawing attention to the distinctive impersonal domination of capitalism. Under capitalism, "the relation of producers to the means of production, and of appropriators to the means of appropriation, as well as their relation to each other, is mediated, indeed constituted, by the market", more specifically by the kinds of competitive markets we see under capitalism.[34] These markets aren't merely devices of exchange or allocation. Rather, they regulate social production in general in ways that subject everyone involved to its own purposes, in particular the imperative of profit maximisation and whatever means are necessary to achieve it.

The powers inherent in these competitive markets are dominating and alienating. Like all social powers, they emerge out of the interaction of individual human beings. Just as the power of monarchs and slave owners emerge from the continuous interactions of people reproducing the right kinds of social relations (and persist only as long as those relations do), so too the powers of competitive markets emerge out of the interactions of people under capitalism. But unlike, e.g. the power of feudal lords,

---

[30] For Marx's discussion of this, see the following section.
[31] Marx (1991, p. 953/II:15, p. 789).
[32] Marx (1990, p. 990/II:4.1, p. 65).
[33] Marx (1990, p. 772/II:6, pp. 567–568).
[34] Wood (2002, p. 85).

the dominating power of capitalist social relations is distinctly impersonal, because it is not wielded or controlled by identifiable persons or sufficiently unified institutions (like states or churches). Nevertheless, Marx explicitly invokes the language of domination and subjugation to express how these powers make those subject to them alienated and unfree.

Importantly, Marx's concept of impersonal domination doesn't reduce to relations of personal domination, e.g. to the arbitrary power of multitudes of consumers in the marketplace, whose preferences cannot be contested.[35] This is for three main reasons. First, this sort of idea doesn't fit anything that Marx seems to have written. If Marx wanted to argue that consumers dominate workers (and capitalists) in these ways, he could easily have expressed this in terms of familiar concepts of personal domination, rather than repeatedly insisting on the distinctively impersonal forms of domination exercised by capitalist social relations themselves. Second, it misconstrues what the dominator is here according to Marx, who consistently pinpoints not consumers, but the social relations of capitalism, as what dominates workers and capitalists in these cases. Thirdly, this interpretation neglects some of Marx's most interesting and important developments as a theorist: his positive concept of freedom as self-direction and its power to diagnose the impersonal forms of domination and unfreedom people are subject to under capitalism. If we instead try to spell out such diffuse, impersonal forms of domination and do them justice, then it's not clear how that can be made to fit into the box of domination as not being subject to the will or arbitrary power of another, precisely because there's no individual person or sufficiently unified institution that can rightly be said to be the dominator here.[36]

This is an important way in which Marx builds on earlier analyses of capitalist unfreedom. Marx agrees with the labour republicans of the early 1800s[37] that capitalists dominate workers in the workplace and that, as we saw above, capitalist property relations force workers to subject themselves to the rule of some capitalist.[38] (The latter is today labelled "structural domination" and should not be confused with what Marx and

[35] Roberts (2017, pp. 99–101).

[36] As far as I know, this dilemma was first pointed out in Raekstad (2017) and has been widely made by this point.

[37] Gourevitch (2015).

[38] See Gourevitch (2015, pp. 106–116).

I call impersonal domination.) Marx adds to this an analysis of how the social relations of capitalism themselves dominate not only workers, but both capitalists and workers impersonally. As we will see in the following sections and in the discussion of the division of labour in Chapter 8, capitalist social relations include relations of personal domination of workers by capitalists and managers. Why, then, is the addition of impersonal domination important?

The impersonal domination of capitalism's competitive markets is essential for understanding the dynamics of capitalism and the conditions for freeing us from them. First, it entails that proposals for economic emancipation through democratising workplaces, like those of the labour republicans and many contemporary market socialists, are insufficient,[39] because they retain the impersonal domination of competitive markets. If Marx is right, workers in these societies would remain impersonally dominated and thus unfree. Second, it's important for making sense of some of the most important dynamics in capitalist societies. It's competitive markets that drive capitalists to do things like increase workers' oppression, forcing down wages and conditions, or causing the ecological devastation that is undermining the very conditions for human life on this planet—regardless of what they might otherwise want or prefer. Why? According to Marx, capitalism's competitive markets force capitalists to do anything they can to maximise profits—effectively imposing certain purposes and means upon them. If they don't, they'll risk getting out-competed and either going bankrupt or being bought up by their less scrupulous, and more successful, competitors. While Marx long focused on how this harms workers as human beings, his later writings came also to emphasise its harms to the environment. Thus he explicitly points out how "[c]apitalist production (…) only develops the techniques and the degree of combination of the social process of production by simultaneously undermining the original sources of all wealth - the soil and the worker".[40] These are two reasons why, as we'll see in Chapter 8, Marx thinks that a free future society must replace competitive markets with a democratic form of planning.

---

[39] González-Ricoy (2014), Gourevitch (2015), Schweickart (1996), and White (2011).

[40] Marx (1990, p. 638/II:6, p. 477). For this, see Saito (2017), who further points out that this can be considered an additional contradiction of capitalism.

In sum, the first kind of alienation, alienation from product, consists in the fact that, under capitalism, workers are alienated from the products of their labour because these are the bearers of certain social relations. These relations constitute a coercive power which imposes certain ends and means on those subject to them and which those subject to them cannot control, with tendencies and imperatives independent of, and potentially opposed to, anything the sum of individuals living within may or may not desire or wish for. As such, these relations constitute an alien power over and above the sum of individuals subject to them. Under capitalism, it is part and parcel of the nature of the relations workers' products are the bearers of that they are not owned or under the control of the workers themselves, but under the control of the capitalists under whom they are produced. This means that the only way workers can gain access to consumable commodities is by exchanging money (or some other suitable commodity) for them, and this is only possible for them to attain by working for a capital, i.e. for a capitalist. In so doing, workers enter into a labour process in which they produce products bearing capitalist social relations, thereby reproducing the capitalist social relations that dominate them and reproducing themselves as workers.

Furthermore, we have seen that capital accepts such a deal—i.e. hires a worker—only on the condition that the labour-power it hires is sufficient for successful accumulation[41] such that the capital can grow continuously and in competition with others. The growth in material wealth which capital is thus constantly bringing about goes, so far as possible from the capitalist's side, into increasing the magnitude of capital and the material wealth accruing to the capitalist. Insofar as this is the case, workers not only maintain the capitalist relations of production which dominate them, they further strengthen these relations insofar as they are, by accumulation, continually increasing the amount, concentration, and centralisation of capital. This capital, and its continual increase, constitutes an alien power outside of and independent of them, which in turn comes to dominate their working lives more narrowly, as well as the economy as a whole, and through that people's wider social existence.

Now Marx asks:

---

[41] I fully intend to stay away from the complexities of Marx's economic theories, including issues regarding the labour theory of value, surplus labour, profits, etc.

How could the product of the worker's activity confront him as something alien if it were not for the fact that in the act of production he was alienating himself from himself? So if the product of labour is alienation, production itself must be active alienation, the alienation of activity, the activity of alienation. The alienation of the object of labour merely summarizes the alienation, the alienation in the activity of labour itself.[42]

This passage is tricky, but I think it expresses the following line of thought. It only makes sense that one is alienated from the products of labour if one is also alienated in the act of producing them. In other words, it only makes sense that one ends up not having power over the objects one produces if it is also the case that one lacks power over the process that produces them. If one really controlled the act of production *in toto*, how could this *not* include also ending up with control over its resulting products (barring exceptional things like theft and military conquest)? If the thing we produce is something which we not only do not have power over, but also ends up exerting power over us—*qua* the social relations it is the bearer of—then the activity of production must be an activity over which we come not to have power (alienation of activity), and it must be an activity which, on a social scale, comes to generate such disempowerment (the activity of alienation). The alienation of the product we create merely "summarizes" the alienation of the labour process in that it is the produced product, the coming-together at the end, of a process of reproducing and strengthening capitalist relations of production, of which those products are the bearers. It's perhaps worth noting, in passing, that this too is a point Marx repeats, explicitly using the language of alienation and giving oneself up to an alien power, in later works on political economy.[43] This is the logical connection between alienation from the products of labour and alienation from the labour process. Let us now move on to the latter.

---

[42] Marx (1992, p. 326/I:2, pp. 238/367). Translation of "Entfremdung" and "entfremden" modified from "estrangement" and "estranged" to "alienation" and "alienated".

[43] See, e.g., Marx (1993, p. 307/II:1.1, p. 226) and Marx (1993, p. 488/II.1.2, p. 392).

Alienation from the Labour Process

According to Marx, there are three main aspects of alienation from the labour process: (i) the work becomes something external to the workers, something not part of their essential being; (ii) it becomes forced or involuntary labour in some sense; and (iii) the workers' activity belongs to another. I will elucidate each of these in turn before coming back to the relationship between alienation from products and alienation from the labour process.

Firstly:

> the fact that labour is *external* to the worker, i.e. does not belong to his essential being; that he therefore does not confirm himself in his work, but denies himself, feels miserable and not happy, does not develop free mental and physical energy, but mortifies his flesh and ruins his mind. Hence the worker feels himself only when he is not working; when he is working he does not feel himself. He is at home when he is not working, and not at home when he is working.[44]

Recall Marx's conception of human development and of the human species-being consisting of an internal power for conscious self-direction. When workers are forced to labour under social relations where their activity is directed not by themselves, but by powers and imperatives they cannot control and that are seemingly external to them, that labour becomes something external to workers. Since it belongs to workers' essential being—as human beings—that they have an internal power for conscious self-direction, and since its exercise is thwarted when humans' activities become subject to these kinds of powers, labour under such conditions does not belong to workers' essential (human) being or nature.

Secondly:

> [The worker's] labour is therefore not voluntary but forced, it is *forced labour*. It is therefore not the satisfaction of a need but a mere *means* to satisfy needs outside itself. Its alien character is clearly demonstrated by the fact that as soon as no physical or other compulsion exists it is shunned like the plague. External labour, labour in which man alienates himself, is a labour of self-sacrifice, of mortification.[45]

---

[44] Marx (1992, p. 326/I:2, pp. 238/367).
[45] Marx (1992, p. 326/I:2, pp. 238/367).

Since alienated labour prevents the exercise of our powers for conscious self-direction, it becomes undesirable. Nevertheless, it is something workers are materially coerced into doing, rendering it involuntary or forced labour. Such labour is not the satisfaction of a need: the labour itself does not satisfy any particular drive on the part of the worker. Instead, the labour becomes merely a means to satisfy needs outside of itself—needs for basic survival and financial security, for example. The alien character of this labour, the sense in which the labour is something workers are forced to do because of their social subjection to external powers and imperatives, is verified, Marx claims, by the fact that as soon as such compulsion disappears, the work itself is avoided as much as possible.

Third and finally:

> the external character of labour for the worker is demonstrated by the fact that it belongs not to him but to another, and that in it he belongs not to himself but to another. Just as in religion the spontaneous activity of the human imagination, the human brain and the human heart detaches itself from the individual and reappears as the alien activity of a god or of a devil, so the activity of the worker is not his self-activity. It belongs to another, it is a loss of self.[46]

Work under capitalism is sold like any other commodity; and in that sense, and for that reason, it can be described as belonging to another for as long as it lasts. Human practical activity, in an alienated economy, is not workers' own self-activity in and through which they employ their powers to fulfil their needs intrinsic to the process, and in turn develop and increase their individual and collective powers. Instead, it is a process through which workers do not satisfy any intrinsic needs— only extrinsic ones—and through which they generate certain powers over which they have no control, which impose a variety of external purposes and imperatives and thus come to dominate and control them.

Insofar as these powers are nothing more than workers' own powers, and insofar as they are outside of workers' control and subjects them to its purposes and imperatives, workers' activity under capitalism is not their

---

[46] Marx (1992, pp. 326–327/I:2, pp. 238–239/367). Translation of "Selbstthätigkeit" modified from "own spontaneous activity" to "self-activity" since it is (a) more accurate, (b) clearer with respect to my purposes and avoids potential misreadings of inserted new words which Marx doesn't use. Furthermore, Colletti's translation replaces this key concept in the original German with a few different and less accurate English phrases, with the effect that this key concept of Marx's tends to disappear in his translations.

self-activity, it is a loss of self, a loss of their own powers. Consequently, the relationship of the worker "to the *act of production* within *labour*" is not just a relationship between a worker and "his own activity as something which is alien and does not belong to him"; it is also "power as impotence, procreation as emasculation, the worker's *own* physical and mental energy, his personal life (...) directed against himself, which is independent of him and does not belong to him".[47]

Throughout his later works, Marx continues to emphasise the alienated and unfree labour processes inherent in capitalism. For example, in the *Grundrisse*, he talks of how capitalist production, the "working-out of the human content (...), this universal objectification as total alienation, and the tearing-down of all limited, one-sided aims as sacrifice of the human end-in-itself to an entirely external end".[48] In his *Results of the Immediate Process of Production*, he writes about how the "supremacy and subordination in the *process of production* supplant an earlier state of *independence,* to be found, for example, in all self-sustaining peasants".[49] Finally, in Volume I of *Capital*, Marx writes of how, under capitalism, the "work of directing, superintending and adjusting becomes one of the functions of capital" and that "[a]s a specific function of capital, the directing function acquires its own special characteristics".[50] As a result, for workers under capitalism it's "the act of the capital that brings them together and maintains them in that situation" and so the "interconnection between their various labours confronts them, in the realm of ideas, as a plan drawn up by the capitalist, and, in practice, as his authority, as the powerful will of a being outside them, who subjects their activity to his purpose".[51] He thus describes the capitalist division of labour as one that "implies the undisputed authority of the capitalist over men, who are merely the members of a total mechanism which belongs to him".[52] In other words, Marx's later works repeat all three components of alienation from the labour process: (i) the work becomes something external to the workers, something not part of their essential being; (ii) it becomes

---

[47] Marx (1992, p. 327/I:2, pp. 239/368).
[48] Marx (1993, p. 488/II.1.2, p. 392).
[49] Marx (1990, p. 1028/II:4.1, p. 99).
[50] Marx (1990, p. 449/ II: 6, p. 327).
[51] Marx (1990, p. 450/II: 6, p. 328).
[52] Ibid., 476–7/II: 6, p. 350–1.

forced or involuntary labour in some sense; and (iii) the workers' activity belongs to another.

Not only does Marx retain this analysis in his later works; he deepens it to explore the relations of domination and unfreedom that characterise capitalist labour processes and develops a striking analysis of capitalism's hierarchical division of labour. In *The German Ideology*, Marx and Engels had clearly derided the separation between mental and manual labour, and the relations of domination and authority that it's part and parcel of. But it's only in later works of political economy that Marx begins to explore this in a more fine-grained way that arguably prefigures later Marxist and anarchist discussions of the forms of power and privilege operating not just between owners and workers, but between a small elite of highly powerful and privileged managers and workers as well.

In Volume I of *Capital*, he writes that:

> If capitalist direction is thus twofold in content, owing to the twofold nature of the process of production which has to be directed - on the one hand a social labour process for the creation of a product, and on the other hand capital's process of valorization - in form it is purely despotic. As co-operation extends its scale, this despotism develops the forms that are peculiar to it. Just as at first the capitalist is relieved from actual labour as soon as his capital has reached that minimum amount with which capitalist production, properly speaking, first begins, so now he hands over the work of direct and constant supervision of the individual workers and groups of workers to a special kind of wage-labourer. An industrial army of workers under the command of a capitalist requires, like a real army, officers (managers) and N.C.O.s (foremen, overseers), who command during the labour process in the name of capital. The work of supervision becomes their established and exclusive function. When comparing the mode of production of isolated peasants or independent artisans with the plantation economy which rests on slavery, political economists count this labour of superintendence as part of the *faux frais de production*. But when considering the capitalist mode of production they on the contrary identify the function of direction which arises out of the nature of the communal labour process with the function of direction which is made necessary by the capitalist and therefore antagonistic character of that process. It is not because he is a leader of industry that a man is a capitalist; on the contrary, he is a leader of industry because he is a capitalist.[53]

---

[53] Marx (1990, p. 450/II: 6, pp. 328–329).

To begin, the capitalist labour process is "purely despotic" in nature because it's a process that initially is under the power of a single person, the capitalist, who directs and controls the labour of all workers who are part of it, thus making them unfree. As the forms of capitalist labour processes further extend and develop—e.g. from smaller-scale manufacturing into factory production—capitalists develop more specific social-relational forms or structures that are tailored to maintaining, reinforcing, and reproducing workers' unfreedom. The power to direct and control the labour process is delegated to an elite of managers, who take on a part of the capitalist's power and in return achieve a degree of control over their own and others' labour and the means of production, as well as more broadly greater power, wealth, and privilege, without themselves owning the means of production. This layer is often called the "Coordinator Class" among later Marxist and anarchist thinkers,[54] and it's striking that Marx is so early in identifying some of the dynamics that give rise to this more fine-grained economic differentiation in capitalism even before the expansions in management seen during the following century.[55]

We should note three things about this analysis. First, as we see at the end of the quote, such oppressive managerial relations are inherent and necessary *only to certain kinds of unfree labour processes*, specifically those where workers' activities must be controlled in rather detailed ways.

---

[54] For discussions of this concept, see Walker (1979) and Wright (1980). This concept should not be confused with the much broader and less coherent idea of a "Professional-Managerial Class", which, unlike the Coordinator Class, is not precisely defined in terms of a particular set of relations with respect to the means of production.

[55] It's perhaps worth pointing out that Marx is often, wrongly, accused of thinking that there are only two classes under capitalism. This has no basis in fact. For one, throughout his later works discussing history and politics—like the *Communist Manifesto*, *The 18th Brumaire of Napoleon Bonaparte*, and the *Civil War in France*—there's a much larger number of classes identified in capitalism alone, and though he does think that, at the time, society is getting polarised into two main camps, he also clearly says that there are several classes in each camp, not that there are, or ever will be, only two. For obvious reasons, this also means that the idea that Marx takes a view of class so narrow-minded as being based only in property ownership, rather than in social-relational positions, is ruled out. On the other hand, the fact that Volume I of *Capital* only focuses on two main classes is the obvious result of it zooming in only on certain very particular parts of the social relations of capitalism. It does not follow from that that real-existing capitalist societies only have two classes (and as is clear from Marx's other writings, he doesn't think this), for the same reasons that zooming in on a few laws of physics explaining how gravity works (in abstraction from, e.g. friction, air resistance, lift, and so on) doesn't mean that, or that those physicists think that, birds can't fly.

Accordingly, they are not taken to be inherent to the requirements of large-scale social organisation or to the complexities of industrial organisation or any idea of a technologically advanced society.[56] Second, the reason why Marx thinks that many capitalist political economists make the mistake of thinking that oppressive capitalist management practices are necessary to production in general is, as the end of the passage points out, that they conflate the requirements of organising collective labour utilising certain means of production *in general*, with organising collective labour *under capitalist relations of production* more specifically. Third, he thinks that these ways of managing the labour processes are inherently hierarchical, dominating, and unfree, because they involve capitalists and managers having socially generated power to direct and control the labour process, without the workers subject to it being able to control that power. This is one of the important reasons why Marx's vision of socialism demands an end to the hierarchical division of labour, which I explore in the next chapter.

Following Marx, we should not understand alienation from product and alienation from the process of production as wholly separate things. We must especially resist the temptation of thinking about alienation from product merely as experiencing or perceiving the physical items we make, and about alienation from the labour process merely as being or feeling disempowered in our labouring activities. We must instead think of them the way Marx tells us to: as two fundamental aspects of one and the same thing, namely as two aspects of alienation from practical human activity, in this case the activity of labour.[57] On this more dialectical view, alienation from products and alienation from the labour process are simply

---

[56] In 1872, Engels writes a text called *On Authority* that is sometimes argued to conflict with this. I can't get into the details of the text or its arguments here, especially because the wording of *On Authority* requires careful attention to detail and is often misleading to those who don't know the exact debates within the socialist movement it's responding to. Engels' text is primarily about large-scale organisation requiring binding decisions and the importance of delegation, which many later organisations and movements set up by anarchists and syndicalist did feature. Engels can be interpreted in a number of different ways here, including as making a general point about certain anarchists' doubts about how the First International should be structured or as straw-manning a more general rejection of top-down modes of organisation that Marx, anarchists, and many left Marxists share. Either way, we have seen that Marx's views on this are clear from his writings.

[57] Marx (1992, p. 327/I:2, pp. 239/368).

two aspects of our productive economic activities under capitalism. Alienation from product is the very real subjection and domination which our products—i.e. as both consumable commodities and as capital—exert over us through the social relations they are the bearers of. Alienation from the labour process likewise consists in the very real subjection and domination exerted over us, this time not from the point of view of the objects (including their dominating social-relational properties), but from the point of view of the labour processes through which these objects are produced and reproduced. In this conception, it makes perfect sense to say that the (alienation from) product is a "résumé" of (alienation from) the labour process. The former are the finished bearers of the social relations which the latter produces and reproduces, and they are both essential aspects of alienated practical activity, i.e. of human economic activity under the rule of capital.

This section has said nothing about why any of this is supposed to be a bad thing for Marx; that was discussed in Part I. Above all, the harms that are pinpointed here are not first and foremost to do with the paltry distribution of society's wealth to the working class—although this is mentioned with unmistakeable opprobrium. Unlike any particular distribution of wealth, the normatively problematic aspect of capitalism that these two components of Marx's diagnosis discuss is an intrinsic feature of capitalism as an economic system: the way in which it, by its very nature, imposes an evitable system of personal and impersonal domination. In so doing, it thwarts our freedom, with all the negative concomitants this entails for our experiences of our economic lives and for our development of a variety of other powers. Thus, the components of Marx's theory of alienation we have surveyed up until now show how capitalism thwarts freedom and thereby human development.

One of the criticisms that might be offered against this position is the following. At least in many Western countries it seems to be the case that many people in fact are motivated to work for other reasons than merely the monetary reward they get for doing so. The reasons for this may vary: a sense of duty to one's co-workers or workplace; a feeling of self-worth one gets from successfully carrying out a job; some measure of enjoyment in the actual work itself, and so on. In light of this, it might be argued, the picture Marx paints of the alienated wage labourer might once have been correct but is now out-dated. It is possible to go further than this and to claim that with the growth of technology we can expect work to become more and more fulfilling and rewarding for workers, and that

Marx's picture either is or soon will be surpassed thanks to the benefits of technological progress. This latter argument has no significant empirical support, and actual studies of these new and supposed wonderfully creative sectors, such as information technology, debunk it.[58] The former view, however, has some support and deserves attention.

The first point we should make in Marx's defence is that the objection springs only from a very limited data-set restricted to a small portion of the working class in the contemporary capitalist world-system, and, moreover, a particularly privileged part of the world's working class in an exceptionally privileged geographical, social, and historical location. To generalise from such a small segment of the working class and their lives to the rest of it is as unrepresentative as deriving strong conclusions about universal human nature from the study of only urban middle-class American college students—a well-known source of errors in psychological research.[59] There is, as far as I know, no research suggesting that anything similar is found among the vast sectors of the world's less uniquely privileged working class and there are no encouraging signs to suggest that their situation is likely to become more like that of the more privileged ones any time soon.

The second thing I would like to point out is that even workers in uniquely privileged sectors and locations are likely to suffer from the adverse effects that conditions of alienation imply, with its numerous negative implications for intrinsic enjoyment, motivation, and general prospects for human development. Although Marx's descriptions are damning, there is no reason not to think that the damage wrought by conditions of alienation cannot come in degrees. Workers in uniquely privileged situations might then suffer less than others like the ones Marx was describing; in fact, they might even suffer so much less that they really are able to find some measure of intrinsic enjoyment and motivation in their work. None of this entails, however, that the conditions of alienation these workers suffer do not significantly thwart their freedom, that this is significantly detrimental to the intrinsic enjoyment and motivation they might otherwise find in their work, and/or that this significantly damages the prospects for human development workers might otherwise enjoy were they not alienated.

---

[58] See Huws (2003, 2014).
[59] See esp. Henrich et al. (2010).

Another point one might raise against Marx's account is that with the advent of the modern welfare state the old material coercion that once forced people to work for capitalists has disappeared—either in part or in whole. Since modern welfare states enable people to survive and reproduce, at some minimal level, without working, it simply is no longer the case that workers have no other choice to satisfy their most basic needs by going to work for capital. It is hard to see how such an objection is not either deeply mistaken about Marx's account or either overly optimistic or pessimistic (depending on the attitude one takes towards it) about the nature and generosity of modern welfare states. On the one hand, material coercion in Marx should probably not be read as limited merely to threats of things like thirsting or starving to death. Arguably, beggars could survive even in Marx's day without a job; at least some of the old and sick could as well from minimal support systems available in families or local communities (including church aid of various kinds); and so forth. A decent standard of living is the sort of thing which varies considerably with natural, social, and historical contexts, a fact of which Marx was well aware. Modern welfare states do provide their citizens with a certain minimum; the fact that this is so in the more privileged countries of the world is in large part thanks to the successes of social movements of the last centuries. Historically speaking, however, they have been highly limited responses to such movements. Furthermore, they tend to be rolled back and coercively re-shaped in order to eliminate, as far as possible, any negative impacts it might have in terms of reducing the material coercion to labour under capital.[60] Briefly put, modern welfare states do provide significant benefits for workers, but they are far from sufficiently generous, all things considered, to reliably secure workers from coercion to labour over time.

Furthermore, it is far from clear that the level of benefits that modern welfare states provide in fact succeeds in eliminating the material coercion workers experience to work under the yoke of capital. Even the most privileged welfare states in the Nordic countries fail to provide their poor with what is considered to be an acceptably high standard of living for themselves and their children, considering the requirements for decent life in those countries, and this is well-known among those affected. There is no reason to suspect that these kinds of conditions will be better in any

---

[60] Piven and Cloward (1993) and Wahl (2011).

other part of the world. The objection, then, fails. It is not the case that modern welfare states are sufficiently generous to remove the material coercion to work for capital (or, in mixed economies, the state) both because it is not clear that the benefits they provide are sufficiently high, stable, and free from restrictions and coercion to work and because it is not clear that the benefits provided are high enough in light of the naturally, socially, and historically mediated requirements for a decent life in the societies in question. With that objection behind us, let us move on to some of the further two kinds of alienation that Marx discusses.

ALIENATION FROM SPECIES-BEING

Much ink has been spilled trying to come to grips with Marx's understanding of alienation from species-being,[61] most of which, as mentioned above, must be left aside here. In my view, the main critical thrust of Marx's second theory of alienation lies in the diagnosis presented in the first two kinds of alienation, which is where I have had to focus. In Part I, I explained what the internal power that Marx's notion of species-being or nature consists in and its location and role within Marx's commitment to human development. Here, I will briefly expand upon this and explain how capitalism's alienation from product and from the process of production results in workers (also) being alienated from their species-being.

According to Marx, the first two kinds of alienation result in people under capitalism becoming alienated from themselves in their active function, as well as from their species, because people become alienated from their species-life, which capitalism turns into a mere means for individual life in its alienated form.[62] Recall that, for Marx, the human species-being or nature consists in an internal power of conscious self-direction, and that this internal power is realised or exercised if and only if it is employed to direct human activity. Only in so doing do human beings become free. Marx writes that:

---

[61] See Fromm (2004), Geras (1983), Hudis (2013), Kain (1988, 1992), Kamenka (1969, 1972), Leopold (2007), Mészáros (1972), Ollman (1976), Sayers (2007, 2011), and Wood (2004). See also section (C) of Appendix 1.

[62] Marx (1992, p. 328/I:2, p. 369/240).

Man makes his life activity itself an object of his will and consciousness. (...) [Man] is a conscious being, i.e. his own life is an object for him, only because he is a species-being. Only because of that is his activity free activity. Alienated labour reverses the relationship so that man, just because he is a conscious being, makes his life activity, his *being* [*Wesen*], a mere means for his *existence*.[63]

To understand the significance of this, we must remember that, for Marx, it is above all in working on the natural world through production that human beings succeed or fail at realising or exercising their species-powers:

> Such production is his active species-life. Through it nature appears as *his* work and his reality. The object of labour is therefore the *objectification of the species-life of man*... In tearing away the object of his production from man, alienated labour therefore tears away from him his *species-life*, his true species-objectivity...[64]

Marx's point here is that it's above all in production that humans live their collective species-lives. It's in our characteristic (conscious) forms of productive activity that we distinguish ourselves from the rest of nature and come to realise ourselves within that nature. In other words, production is what constitutes human species-life in general. I thus agree with Sean Sayers that, for Marx (at least from 1844 onwards) "work is the fundamental and central activity in human life"[65] and a "fundamental part of the human process of self-development"[66] and with Mehmet Tabak that "objective activity (production, labor, etc.) is the essential human characteristic responsible for the concretization of human essence in and through nature".[67]

Now, recall what workers are alienated from when they are alienated from their objects: they are alienated not from physical things as such, but

---

[63] Marx (1992, p. 328/I:2, pp. 369/240–241), translation of "entfremdete" modified from "estranged" to "alienated".

[64] Marx (1992, p. 329/I:2, pp. 370/241), translation of "entfremdete" modified from "estranged" to "alienated".

[65] Sayers (2011, p. 14).

[66] Ibid., p. 21.

[67] Tabak (2012, p. 4).

from the social relations which the objects they produce are the bearers of. As we've seen in the discussion of the first two kinds of alienation above, Marx argues that alienation from productive activity is entailed, in a very specific sense, by the alienation from products seen under capitalism. On Marx's view, this productive activity is the "fundamental and central activity in human life",[68] which he calls the "*objectification of the species-life of man*".[69] If alienation from product entails the alienation from productive activity, and if productive activity can truly be said to amount to humans' species-life in general, then alienation from product can also be said to entail the alienation from human species-life in general.

This explains how, on Marx's view, alienation results in the "tearing away" of humans' species-life, but in what sense does alienation make human life activity—their being—into a mere means for their existence? As we have seen above, Marx argues that alienated labour thwarts the intrinsic enjoyment that workers' productive activity might otherwise contain. Because of this, people engage in productive activity only for purely extrinsic ends, such as maintaining one's physical existence. If alienated production thus inevitably results in one's productive activity becoming a mere means for extrinsic ends, and if production can be said to amount to one's species-life in general, then it follows that alienated production can be said to inevitably result in making human species-life and activity in general a mere means for securing one's extrinsic ends, such as one's continued existence.

The argument I have just sketched provides a valuable reply to a possible counter-argument to Marx's critique of capitalism. It might be argued that even though conditions of alienation in a capitalist economy do thwart certain human powers for conscious self-directed activity, there are—at least in some very privileged countries—many opportunities to exercise such powers in other realms of human life and endeavour. We can use such powers in the formation, execution, and revision of our plans of life; we can use such powers in the enjoyment of our leisure time; we can use, perhaps, some of them in political activities; we can exercise them in areas of civil society such as directly democratic propaganda organisations; and so on.

---

[68] Sayers (2011, p. 14).
[69] Marx (1992, p. 329/I:2, pp. 370/241).

The retort that Marx's analysis of alienation from species-being allows him to make here is that the problem of alienation is *not* only that certain highly important human species-powers are thwarted in capitalist production. It is also that thwarting these powers in human productive activity amounts to thwarting these important human powers in general, making alienation from production particularly detrimental both in terms of the realisation or exercise of the powers they thwart and in terms of their effects for impeding human development more broadly. This point makes a lot of sense when we recall that humans' species-powers are exercised through *activity*, along with the plausible and widely accepted premise that the internal aspects of the process of human development are shaped first and foremost by people's everyday activities and their demands.[70] When we exclude sleeping, productive activity is perhaps the kind of activity that working human beings spend more of their lives doing than any other. It thus makes sense to attribute to it the unique importance which, e.g. Adam Smith does when he writes that "the understandings of the greater part of men are necessarily formed by their ordinary employments".[71] There are other reasons we might want to assign productive interchange with nature a particularly important place as well. Productive interchange of some sort is universal across human societies. It is a precondition for the reproduction of any sort of human society over time. It has been with us for as long as our species has existed. We might therefore suppose that we are in some way particularly well-suited for it and that our species-specific powers have a special role in this regard. And we might think that activities of production provide especially salient opportunities for the exercise, actualisation, and development of various human

---

[70] It was widely accepted at least among the Scottish Enlightenment thinkers such as Adam Smith, see for instance Berry (1997, Ch. 4).

[71] Smith (1976, pp. 781–782). Note that by "understandings" here Smith does not mean merely our cognitive grasp of things, but the development of our wider cognitive and moral virtues. For more on this, see Raekstad (2016, 2020a). In the latter, I made this case as part of a reconstruction of Adam Smith's shift from focusing on freedom and independence in the polity to freedom and independence in the workplace, which he does in ways that I argue prefigure later labour republican ideas (on which see Gourevitch, 2015). Note that by 1844 Marx was well-acquainted with both sets of ideas. Finally, I want to point out that one of the limitations of this view, which Marx inherits, is its relative neglect of the relations and processes structing much of the lived activities of so many women at the time, and still, involved in unpaid reproductive labour, an oversight that later generations of Marxist feminists have rightly worked to remedy. I cannot explore this further, but for an excellent place to start see Bhattacharya (2017).

powers, and those of our species-being in particular. Finally, we should also note that workers are not very likely to be able to take advantage of many of the abstract possibilities for unalienated activity, as a result of the fact that they are too exhausted and drained from the long time they spend during unfree, alienated, as well as otherwise exhausting mental and manual labour. As a result, even if the abstract possibility is there, the length and severity of the effects of alienated production would still prevent it from constituting a real possibility for them.

For any single one or combination of these reasons it makes sense to think that, if our powers of self-direction are thwarted in productive activity, the realisation or exercise of them is being thwarted in a particularly significant way. It thus also makes sense to say that under conditions of alienation from product and from productive activity, people can be said to be alienated from their species-essence or species-being in general. Consequently, the damage alienation does both in terms of the realisation or exercise of humans' species-powers, and in terms of the wider effects this has on impeding human development, cannot be adequately alternatively expressed or compensated for in other domains or activities.

ALIENATION FROM OTHERS

Finally, Marx believes that to the extent that human beings under capitalism are alienated from their (social) products, productive activity, and species-being, they are also alienated from other humans, if only because the above are forms by which people are alienated from one another. He writes that "[a]n immediate consequence of man's alienation from the product of his labour, his life activity, his species-being, is the *alienation of man from man*".[72] What does Marx mean by this? In which sense does the already-examined alienation from product, activity, and species-being bring about or entail the alienation of some human beings from others?

Briefly put, it consists in this: the production and reproduction of capitalist economic relations involves alienation from product as a necessary component, and alienation from productive economic activity as a necessary aspect or implication thereof. But these forms of alienation depend on more than merely workers and the peculiar forms of alienation they are under, such as the full panoply of capitalist economic relations. One

---

[72] Marx (1992, pp. 329–330/I:2, pp. 242/370), translation of "Entfremdung" modified from "estrangement" to "alienation".

of the necessary components of such a relation is the capitalist, since it is the capitalist who is the immediate possessor of the products of labour and under whom the capitalist labour process must take place. Consequently, workers' alienation from their products and productive activity requires a capitalist. Since capitalists are the owners and wielders of capital, and capital constitutes a locus of power which comes to dominate and control workers' lives, the capitalist accordingly comes to appear as the locus of such power. Put differently, since owning capital grants capitalists power over workers that workers cannot control, the capitalist rightly comes to be seen as an agent of domination. Since in reality these are powers produced and reproduced by workers themselves, and since the capitalists who possess and (to some extent) control these powers use them to impose their ends, means, and control over workers' productive activities, the conditions of alienation we have just sketched entail the existence of capitalists from whom workers are alienated. Let's look at what Marx says.

Having started with an analysis of the concept and economic fact of the worker's alienation from product and from activity, Marx asks the following question: if the "product of labour is alien to me and confronts me as an alien power, to whom does it then belong"?[73] Clearly it does not belong to the gods. We might say that buildings belong to them or that something was done in their service, but they never controlled any process of production. The alien product and labour must belong to a person, a human being, and since this cannot be the worker it must be someone else: "If the product of labour does not belong to the worker, and if it confronts him as an alien power, this is only possible because it belongs to *a man other than the worker*".[74] If the worker:

> regards the product of his labour, (...) as an *alien, hostile,* and powerful object which is independent of him, then his relationship to that object is such that another man – alien, hostile, powerful and independent of him – is its master. If he relates to his own activity as unfree activity, he relates to it as activity in the service, under the rule, coercion and yoke of another man.[75]

---

[73] Marx (1992, p. 330/I:2, pp. 242/371).
[74] Marx (1992, p. 330/I:2, pp. 243/371).
[75] Marx (1992, p. 331/I:2, pp. 243/371–372).

This is not merely a matter of the worker's perceptions; it's a necessary aspect of capitalist relations of production, and thus a necessary condition for the ongoing alienation from products and from productive activity that such relations entail.

In sum, alienation from product and from productive activity requires capitalists who are the owners of the products and the more proximate controllers of the productive activity that workers are alienated from. Insofar as capitalists within such relations come to control workers' activity, they dominate workers and make them unfree. In this way workers come to be alienated from the other human beings that are capitalists.

Marx writes that:

[T]hrough alienated labour man not only produces his relationship to the object and to the act of production as to alien and hostile powers; he also produces the relationship in which other men stand to his production and product, and the relationship in which he stands to these other men. Just as he creates his own production as a loss of reality, a punishment, and his own product as a loss, a product which does not belong to him, so he creates the domination of the non-producer over production and its product...[76]

(...)

Thus through *estranged, alienated labour* the worker creates the relationship of another man, who is alien to labour and stands outside it, to that labour. The relation of the worker to labour creates the relation of the capitalist (...) to that labour. *Private property* [of the means of production in its capitalist form] is therefore the product, result and necessary consequence of *alienated labour*, of the external relation of the worker to nature and to himself.

Private property thus derives from an analysis of the concept of *alienated labour*...[77]

The process of production that produces products from which workers are alienated also reproduces the relation of workers with capitalists who control their labour and its products. By analysing the nature of

---

[76] Marx (1992, p. 331/I:2, pp. 243–244/372). Translation of "entfremdete Arbeit" modified from "estranged" to "alienated" labour.

[77] Marx (1992, pp. 331–332/I:2, pp. 244/372). Translation of "Entfremdung" as "Estrangement" kept for purely for aesthetic reasons.

the process of production under capitalism, Marx has, as he proudly proclaims, derived private property, by which he here means the private property of the capitalist in the means of production. Alienated labour therefore presupposes capital, and vice versa; they are both necessary components of the process of reproduction of the very same capitalist social relations.[78] In the sense that properly understanding one of them requires that we also understand the other—since they are mutually implicated in a structured process that they are both necessary components of—the one can be said to derive from an analysis of the other, and vice versa. Saying that both the capitalist process of production and capitalist private property in the means of production are components of the same ongoing set of social relations and that either can, in this specific sense, be derived from the other is not, however, to say that they are of equal importance or significance, either to Marx's project or in general. As his subsequent work shows, Marx thinks that the understanding of capitalism must above all be sought in its process of production.

Alienation from others is vital to Marx's account of the driving forces of socialist revolution. In the *Holy Family*, Marx and Engels write that:

> The propertied class and the class of the proletariat present the same human self-estrangement. But the former class feels at ease and strengthened in this self-estrangement, it recognises estrangement as its own power and has in it the semblance of a human existence. The latter feels annihilated in estrangement; it sees in it its own powerlessness and the reality of an inhuman existence...
>
> Within this antithesis the private property-owner is therefore the conservative side, the proletarian the destructive side. From the former arises the action of preserving the antithesis, from the latter the action of annihilating it...
>
> When the proletariat is victorious, it by no means becomes the absolute side of society, for it is victorious only by abolishing itself and its opposite. Then the proletariat disappears as well as the opposite which determines it, private property.[79]

---

[78] This process of argument is evidently a deeply Hegelian one that he also essentially follows both in the introduction to the *Grundrisse* and in the construction of *Capital*. I shall not discuss it further here since it would take us far off topic.

[79] MECW 4, p. 36/MEGA$_1$ I:3, p. 206.

As we can see, Marx thinks that while workers and capitalists are both subject to the alienation of capitalist social relations, their resulting social situation and experiences are very different. Workers are disempowered, unfree, and experience their lives and activities as such, and as a result they will seek to overthrow these oppressive social relations with free ones. By contrast, capitalists feel empowered and in control by virtue of their relational positions of greater power, wealth, and privilege vis-à-vis workers. Consequently, they will seek to preserve these relations of alienation and unfreedom against the actions of workers. Just like it's fruitless to appeal to the moral sense of our oppressors, Marx thinks it is fruitless to appeal to those in positions of great power, wealth, and privilege to grant us emancipation.[80] If capitalists succeed, capitalism remains. If workers succeed, capitalism is overthrown, and since overthrowing capitalism entails abolishing capitalist social relations, the positions defined by these relations, like worker and capitalist, will be abolished as well. As we will see in Chapter 9, this plays an important role in Marx's later thoughts on the revolutionary contradictions of capitalism.

Before moving on to a discussion of Marx's conception of a cure for capitalism, it's worth summarising the diagnosis his second theory of alienation pioneered. I have argued that Marx's second theory of alienation is a diagnosis of the ways, in which capitalism, by its (relational) nature, thwarts human freedom. It does so by describing how, under capitalism, workers in the process of production produce and reproduce the social relations which keep them in bondage at the same time as they produce the products which are their bearers. This also involves a process of production from which workers are alienated, which in turn entails that workers are alienated from their (human) species-being. Finally, the production and reproduction of capitalist social relations also requires the production and reproduction not only of workers as workers, but also of some other people as capitalists, from whom those workers are alienated. We have thus traced the nature and origins of the four kinds of alienation Marx discusses in his second theory of alienation: alienation from product; alienation from labour process; alienation from species-being; and alienation from others. We have also seen that the basic components of this second theory of alienation are retained throughout Marx's later works all the way through *Capital*. In Chapter 9, we will even see that

---

[80] This becomes an important part of his critique of the utopian socialists, see the *Communist Manifesto*.

it forms the core of one of Marx's most enduring tenets, that capitalism is characterised by two revolutionary contradictions: between the powers and relations of production and between workers and capitalists. With an understanding of Marx's diagnosis of capitalism's ills, it's time to turn to remedy that he proposes: socialism.

References

Primary

Marx, K., & Burns, E. (trans.). (1969). *Theories of surplus value: Part I*. Lawrence & Wishart.
Marx, K., Fowkes, B. (trans.) & Mandel, E. (intro.). (1990). *Capital: A critique of political economy* (Vol. 1). Penguin.
Marx, K., Fowkes, B., (trans.) & Mandel, E. (intro.). 1991. *Capital: A critique of political economy* (Vol. 3). Penguin.
Marx, K., Livingstone, R. (trans.), Benton, G. (trans.) & Colletti, L. (Intro.). (1992). *Karl Marx: Early writings*. Penguin.
Marx, K., & Nicolaus, M. (trans.). (1993). *Grundrisse: Foundations of a critique of political economy*. Penguin.

Secondary

Allen, K. (2011). *Marx and the alternative to capitalism*. Pluto Press.
Arrighi, G., Hopkins, T. K., & Wallerstein, I. (2012). *Anti-systemic movements*. Verso.
Arthur, C. J. (1986). *Dialectics of labour: Marx and his relation to Hegel*. Basil Blackwell.
Avineri, S. (1968). *The social and political thought of Karl Marx*. Cambridge University Press.
Berry, C. J. (1997). *Social theory of the Scottish enlightenment*. Edinburgh University Press.
Bhattacharya, T. (Ed.). (2017). *Social reproduction theory: Remapping class, recentering oppression*. Pluto Press.
Bronfenbrenner, M. (1973). A harder look at alienation. *Ethics, 83*(4), 267–282.
Foster, J. B., Clark, B., & York, R. (2010). *The ecological rift: capitalism's war on the earth*. Monthly Review Press.
Fromm, E. (2004). *Marx's concept of man*. Continuum.
Geras, N. (1983). *Marx and human nature: Refutation of a legend*. Verso.
González-Ricoy, I. (2014). The republican case for workplace democracy. *Social Theory and Practice, 40*(2), 232–254.

Gourevitch, A. (2015). *From slavery to the cooperative commonwealth: Labor and republican liberty in the nineteenth century*. Cambridge University Press.
Gray, J. (1986). Marxian freedom, individual liberty, and the end of alienation. *Social Philosophy and Policy*, 3(2), 160–187.
Hahnel, R. (2015). *Green economics: Confronting the ecological crisis*. Routledge.
Henrich, J., Heine, S. J., & Norenzayan, A. (2010). The weirdest people in the world? *Behavioral and Brain Sciences*, 33(2–3), 61–135.
Holloway, J. (1997). A note on alienation. *Historical Materialism*, 1(1), 146–149.
Holloway, J. (2010). *Crack capitalism*. Pluto Press.
Hudis, P. (2013). *Marx concept of the alternative to capitalism*. Haymarket Books.
Huws, U. (2003). *The making of a cybertariat: Virtual work in the real world*. Monthly Review Press.
Huws, U. (2014). *Labor in the global digital economy: The cybertariat comes of age*. Monthly Review Press.
Israel, J. (1971). *Alienation: From Marx to modern sociology*. Allyn & Bacon Inc.
Jaeggi, R. (2005). *Entfremdung: zur Aktualität eines sosialphilosophischen problems*. Campus.
Kain, P. J. (1988). *Marx and ethics*. Clarendon Press.
Kain, P. J. (1992). Aristotle, Kant, and the ethics of the young Marx. In McCarthy (Ed.), pp. 213–242.
Kamenka, E. (1969). *Marxism and ethics*. Macmillan.
Kamenka, E. (1972). *The ethical foundations of Marxism* (2nd ed.). Routledge & Kegan Paul.
Kropotkin, P. (1997). *The state: Its historic role*. Freedom Press.
Kropotkin, P. (2013). *Mutual aid: A factor in evolution*. Dialectics.
Leopold, D. (2007). *The young Marx: German philosophy, modern politics, and human flourishing*. Cambridge University Press.
Lukács, G., & Livingstone, R. (trans.). (1974). *History and class consciousness: Studies in Marxist dialectics*. Merlin Press.
Mészáros, I. (1972). *Marx's theory of alienation* (3rd ed.). Merlin Press.
Musto, M. (2010). Revisiting Marx's concept of alienation. *Socialism and Democracy*, 24(3), 79–101.
Ollman, B. (1976). *Alienation: Marx's conception of man in capitalist society*. Cambridge University Press.
Padgett, B. L. (2007). *Marx and alienation in contemporary society*. Continuum.
Piven, F. F., & Cloward, R. (1993). *Regulating the poor: The functions of public welfare*. Vintage.
Polanyi, K. (2001). *The great transformation: The political and economic origins of our time*. Beacon Press.
Postone, M. (1996). *Time, labor, and social domination: A reinterpretation of Marx's critical theory*. Cambridge University Press.

Raekstad, P. (2016). Human development and social stratification in Adam Smith. *The Adam Smith Review, 9*, 275–294.
Raekstad, P. (2017). Review of Marx's Inferno: The political theory of capital, by William Clare Roberts. *Disputatio, IX*(44), 127–130.
Raekstad, P. (2020a). Adam Smith: Radical neo-roman and moderate realist. *Archiv für Geschichte der Philosophie, 103*(1), 70–92.
Raekstad, P. (2020b). Realism, utopianism, and human rights. *Political Studies Review, 18*(4), 542–552.
Raekstad, P. (2020c). The present and future of political realism. *Res Publica, 26*(2), 293–297.
Roberts, W. C. (2017). *Marx's Inferno: the political theory of capital*. Princeton University Press.
Saito, K. (2017). *Karl Marx's ecosocialism: Capitalism, nature, and the unfinished critique of political economy*. Monthly Review Press.
Sayers, S. (2007). *Marxism and human nature*. Routledge.
Sayers, S. (2011). *Marx and alienation: Essays in Hegelian themes*. Palgrave Macmillan.
Schacht, R. (1971). *Alienation*. George Allen & Unwin Ltd.
Schweickart, D. (1996). *Against capitalism*. Westview Press.
Smith, A. (1976). *An Inquiry into the nature and causes of the wealth of nations*. Oxford: Oxford University Press.
Swain, D. (2012). *Alienation: An introduction to Marx's theory*. Bookmarks.
Swain, D. (2019). *None so fit to break the chains: Marx's ethics of self-emancipation*. Brill.
Tabak, M. (2012). *Dialectics of human nature in Marx's philosophy*. Palgrave Macmillan.
Wahl, A. (2011). *The rise and fall of the welfare state*. Pluto Press.
Walker, P. (Ed.). (1979). *Between labor and capital*. South End Press.
Walliman, I. (1981). *Estrangement: Marx's conception of human nature and the division of labor*. Greenwood Press.
White, S. (2011). The republican critique of capitalism. *Critical Review of International Social and Political Philosophy, 14*(5), 561–579.
Wolff, J. (1992). Playthings of alien forces. *Cogito, 6*(1), 35–41.
Wolff, J. (2003). *Why read Marx today?* Oxford University Press.
Wood, A. W. (2004). *Karl Marx* (2nd ed.). London: Routledge.
Wood, E. M. (2002). The question of market dependence. *Journal of Agrarian Change, 2*(1), 51–54.
Wright, E. O. (1980). Varieties of Marxist conceptions of class structure. *Politics & Society, 9*(3), 323–370.

CHAPTER 8

The Socialist Alternative

As the previous chapters have shown, Marx's emphasis on human freedom and overcoming alienation remains central throughout his earlier and later works. So too does the importance of freedoms of press etc.,[1] an awareness of both a necessity for some sort of delegation and its potential pitfalls,[2] and a commitment to radical democracy beyond the modern state.[3] However, based on his new understanding of capitalist unfreedom diagnosed in his second theory of alienation he adds three new components. Socialism, or what Marx calls communism, will additionally feature a democratically planned economy, eliminate the capitalist division

---

[1] In fact, as late as 1851 Marx re-published his articles defending freedom of the press without changes. See Draper (1977, p. 59). For more discussion on Marx and Engels' views on freedom of the press, see also Hunt (1974, 1984).

[2] For more on this, see especially Marx's discussion of the Paris Commune in *The Civil War in France*.

[3] It's perhaps worth parenthetically noting that a number of things that might seem anti-democratic to contemporary liberals are in fact just the opposite. For instance, in his text on "The Constitution of the French Republic", Marx writes of "the old constitutional folly. The condition of a 'free government' is not the division, but the UNITY of power. The machinery of government cannot be too simple. It is always the craft of knaves to make it complicated and mysterious" (MECW 10, p. 570/I:10, p. 540). Talk of "UNITY of power" may seem anti-democratic to contemporary liberals, but

of labour, and distribute according to need.[4] These components of a free socialist society all represent ways in which Marx continues to challenge discussions about a free alternative to capitalism. After discussing each component of Marx's socialism in turn, I finish the chapter by defending it against two of its most important and insightful critics: Max Weber and Friedrich Hayek.

Socialism as Emancipation

The fundamental goal of replacing capitalism with a free society remains throughout Marx's works from 1844 onwards. In the *Economic and Philosophical Manuscripts of 1844*, Marx writes that "free conscious activity constitutes the species-character of man"[5] then socialism is "the true *appropriation* of the *human* essence through and for man; it is the complete restoration of man to himself as a *social*, i.e. human, being…".[6] It thus constitutes "the genuine resolution of the conflict between man and nature, and between man and man… It is the solution of the riddle of history and knows itself to be the solution".[7]

Footnote 3 continued

the reality is just the opposite. Recall that the doctrine of the separation of powers is in e.g. Montesquieu (1998), to the US Founding Fathers (Hamilton et al., 2003) and beyond, designed not to achieve democracy, but rather to divide political rule between different powers, limiting the democratic element to one of them and ensuring the others are more monarchical and aristocratic. In other words, the standard doctrine of the separation of powers is an explicitly anti-democratic idea used to *deliberately prevent democracy*. Marx's opposition to this doctrine is thus in reality a radically democratic move in opposition to the anti-democratic tenets of liberalism, past and present. I think it says something important about how subject to liberal ideology we are that we keep confusing anti-democratic liberal ideas with the very essence of democratic governance.

[4] For more detailed discussion, see Ollman (1977), Campbell (2011), and Hudis (2013).

[5] Marx (1992, p. 328/I:2, pp. 240/369).

[6] Marx (1992, p. 348/I:2, pp. 263/389).

[7] Marx (1992, p. 348, pp. 263/389).

Later, Marx and Engels write that "things have now come to such a pass that the individuals must appropriate the existing totality of productive powers, not only to achieve self-activity, but, also, merely to safeguard their very existence".[8] They go on to write that:

> Only at this stage [i.e. of communist/socialist society] does self-activity coincide with material life, which corresponds to the development of individuals into complete individuals and the casting-off of all natural limitations. The transformation of labour into self-activity corresponds to the transformation of the previously limited intercourse into the intercourse of individuals as such. With the appropriation of the total productive powers by the united individuals, private property comes to an end.[9]

In other words, socialist society will be the first to fully realise human freedom as self-direction, which in turn enables greater development among the united individuals. Under these conditions, we will see that in "the real community the individuals obtain their freedom in and through their association".[10] As Marx points out in the *Grundrisse*, socialism enables and generates "[u]niversally developed individuals, whose social relations, as their own communal [*gemeinschaftlich*] relations, are hence also subordinated to their own communal control".[11] This includes social ownership of the means of production, i.e. ownership and control by the associated producers themselves, rather than by states or capitalists.[12]

By restoring full communal control over the social relations that determine their lives, socialism restores the full range of modern social and individual powers to the collective self-rule of its participants.

---

[8] MECW 5, p. 87/I:5, p. 111. Here too I have modified the translation of "productive forces" to "productive powers".

[9] MECW 5, p. 88/I:5, pp. 113–114. Here too I have modified the translation of "productive forces" to "productive powers".

[10] MECW 5, p. 78/I:5, p. 96.

[11] Marx (1993, p. 162/II.1.1, p. 91), square brackets in the translation.

[12] The misunderstanding that socialism amounts to state ownership is nowhere to be found in Marx or Engels. In response to this misunderstanding developing, Engels ridicules the idea e.g. in a note added to the 1892 edition of *Socialism, Utopian and Scientific*. In his *Critique of the Gotha Programme* Marx even argues against states funding workers' cooperatives, arguing that socialist cooperation "has nothing in common with establishing co-operative societies with state aid!" and that cooperatives under capitalism "are only of value if they are independent creations of the workers and not creatures of the government or the bourgeoisie" (Marx 1996, p. 221/I:25, p. 20).

In so doing, it enables them realise their powers for conscious self-direction. Since human social life and its conditions of operation are now controlled completely by the collected social individuals themselves, they can develop their powers and needs freely and universally in accordance with any precepts or measuring rods they themselves choose. Achieving this requires socialism to feature participatory planning, ending the hierarchical division of labour, and distributing according to need.

Participatory Planning

In order to prevent the personal domination of lords and capitalists, as well as the impersonal domination of competitive markets, socialism must be organised through some sort of participatory democratic planning. In the *German Ideology*, Marx and Engels write of socialism as a "society [that] regulates the general production",[13] and of the need for the associated producers to collectively appropriate the totality of society's productive powers. Later in the *Grundrisse*, Marx writes of "[f]ree individuality, based on the universal development of individuals and on the subordination of their communal, social productivity as their social wealth".[14] Nothing, Marx writes, could be more "absurd than to postulate the control by the united individuals of their total production, on the basis of *exchange value*, of *money*".[15] Generalised exchange of the products of labour, and market organisation of social wealth and activity, "stands in antithesis" to the "free exchange among individuals who are associated on the basis of common appropriation and control of the means of production",[16] because these kinds of "private exchange create[s] world trade" and so this particular form of "private independence creates complete dependence on the so-called world market".[17]

In other words, socialist planning must replace capitalist-type markets, because retaining them would keep workers subject to the dependence

---

[13] MECW 5, p. 47/I:5, p. 34.
[14] Marx (1993, p. 158/II.1.1, p. 91).
[15] Marx (1993, p. 159/II.1.1, p. 91).
[16] Marx (1993, p. 159/II.1.1, pp. 91–92).
[17] Marx (1993, p. 159/II.1.1, p. 92).

or domination[18] of the world market. According to Marx, retaining competitive markets between worker-owned firms would retain the kind of impersonal domination that both capitalists and workers are subjected to under capitalism. This entails not only workers' continuing unfreedom, but also the life-threatening pathologies of competitive markets in terms of ecological destruction—more important today than ever before. In Chapter 7, we saw that this continues to pose a challenge to proposals for a free future society that wish to retain competitive markets even with (more) worker-controlled firms, like those put forward by market socialists and various republicans.[19]

The solution can only be participatory democratic planning.

Thus, in *Capital* Marx asks us to "imagine, for a change, an association of free men, working with the means of production held in common, and expending their many different forms of labour-power in full self-awareness as one single social labour force" and regulating labour time "in accordance with a definite social plan", while maintaining the correct relations between "the different functions of labour and the various needs of the associations". In such a situation, he writes, the "social relations of the individual producers, both towards their labour and the products of their labour, are here transparent in their simplicity, in production as well as in distribution".[20] Thus, "[w]hen the worker co-operates in a planned way with others, he strips off the fetters of his individuality, and develops the capabilities of his species".[21]

Of course, planned production will still be subject to certain natural and technical conditions and restrictions, most notably the determination of time and the necessity of organising labour among different branches of production. Marx explains that:

---

[18] Dependence and domination are generally used interchangeably. The German term Marx uses here is Abhängigkeit, which can be translated into either. The translation in question chooses to translate this and its complementary term as dependence and independence, respectively, and which retains Marx's play on Abhängigkeit/Unabhängigkeit in the passage, and I've chosen not to modify this for the same reason.

[19] For one famous example of Marx doing this explicitly, see his critique of Lassallean proposals for economic reform in *Critique of the Gotha Programme*.

[20] Marx (1990, pp. 171–172/II:6, p. 109).

[21] Marx (1990, p. 447/II:6, p. 326).

On the basis of communal production, the determination of time remains, of course, essential. The less time the society requires to produce wheat, cattle, etc., the more time it wins for other production, material or mental. Just as in the case of an individual, the multiplicity of its development, its enjoyment and its activity depends on the economization of time. Economy of time, to this all economy ultimately reduces itself. Society likewise has to distribute its time in a purposeful way, in order to achieve a production adequate to its overall needs; just as the individual has to distribute his time correctly in order to achieve knowledge in proper proportions or in order to satisfy the various demands on his activity. Thus, economy of time, along with the *planned distribution of labour time among the various branches of production, remains the first economic law on the basis of communal production*.[22]

Importantly, the planning Marx advocates is by workers themselves through an association of free people planning and acting in "full self-awareness". It is thus (a) carried out by workers themselves, which (b) enables them to attain conscious self-direction over the distribution of labour time in social production, and (c) enables them to attain conscious self-direction over production as a whole, enabling their entire productive activity to become their own individual and collective self-activity. Marx is therefore *not* advocating a system of planning where a separate board or elite of managers plans on behalf of workers. Such forms of planning—often called central planning and common e.g. in large capitalist corporations—are mediated not through the conscious control of workers themselves, but by a separate organ that workers cannot control and whose power they are subjected to. Such systems retain personal relations of domination and servitude, so we should not be surprised that Marx never advocated such a thing.[23]

---

[22] Marx (1993, pp. 172–173/II.1.1, pp. 103–104), emphases are my own.

[23] Note that this is unaffected by optimistic assessments of the powers and potentials of modern technology like powerful computers (Cockshott & Cottrell, 1993; Phillips & Rozworski, 2019). Current advocates of central planning make a number of important points about how it's prevalent in successful capitalist corporations, about how modern computing power can make all kinds of planning more efficient, and about the value of planning compared to market competition. What they do not do, however, is say anything about the question that Marx focuses on: the question of social power and freedom. Modern computers and technology more broadly can be used to either empower central planners or to enable planning by workers themselves. To empower workers, new technologies must be part of a system of social relations that enable the associated producers

When we speak of planning, we should distinguish between two things. On the one hand, there's the question of workers' councils planning, organising, and overseeing the operations of their own workplace.[24] On the other hand, there's the question of how a large number of workplaces coordinate their activities together and interact to carry out production, reproduction, and allocation. The citations above make clear that for Marx *both* of these forms of planning are necessary for the kind of socialist planning that he envisages. However, in terms of assessing the plausibility of democratic planning of various sorts, these two questions should be distinguished. The plausibility of any system of participatory democratic planning both within and between workplaces is intimately tied up with two other questions: the Weberian question of whether bureaucracy has become a necessary feature of the modern world and the related question of technical divisions of labour.

The Hierarchical Division of Labour

In addition to being democratically structured and planned, Marx thinks that socialism must abolish the division of labour seen under capitalism. In the *German Ideology*, Marx and Engels write that:

> the division of labour offers us the first example of the fact that, as long as man remains in naturally evolved society, that is, as long as a cleavage exists between the particular and the common interest, as long, therefore, as activity is not voluntarily, but naturally, divided, man's own deed becomes an alien power opposed to him, which enslaves him instead of being controlled by him. For as soon as the division of labour comes into being, each man has a particular, exclusive sphere of activity, which is forced upon him and from which he cannot escape.[25]

Note the explicit discussion of the division of labour in terms of alien power and domination. The social division that Marx objects to is thus not about the subdivision of tasks per se. Rather, it's about people being

to take advantage of them. To do that, they must be part of a system of participatory democratic planning rather than subjected to the impersonal domination of competitive markets or the personal domination of bosses and managers. Central planning presupposes exactly the kind of hierarchical division of labour between managers and workers that capitalism develops and that we've seen Marx criticise in the previous chapter and that, as the next sections shows, Marx argues that socialism must do away with.

[24] See Braverman (1998).

[25] MECW 5, p. 47/I:5, p. 34.

forced into particular social roles or spheres, being hindered from leaving them, and how this leads to people being subjected to alien powers that dominate them, making them unfree. Delving further into the political economy of capitalism naturally deepens this analysis.

Perhaps the most extensive collection of Marx's discussion on the division of labour, and the necessity of its overcoming under socialism, is to be found in Volume I of *Capital*, where three distinct but related issues are broached: (a) the hierarchical division of labour and of labour's organisation within workplaces; (b) the division of labour seen under capitalism (especially in factory production); and (c) the necessity of overcoming both of these in a future socialist society. My discussion will move through all three, respectively.

According to Marx, the advent of capitalist manufacture "not only subjects the previously independent worker to the discipline and command of capital, but *creates in addition a hierarchical structure amongst the workers themselves*".[26] We saw in the previous chapter how Marx argues that as capitalist cooperation "extends its scale, this despotism develops the forms that are peculiar to it", by capitalists devolving "the work of direct and constant supervision of the individual workers and groups of workers to" to a dedicated apparatus of managers comparing the "industrial army of workers under the command of a capitalist" to real armies.[27]

Thus, "in the society where the capitalist mode of production prevails, anarchy in the social division of labour and despotism in the manufacturing division of labour mutually condition each other".[28] The effects this has on relations of power and domination between workers and capitalists are clear-cut:

> Division of labour within the workshop implies the undisputed authority of the capitalist over men, who are merely the members of a total mechanism which belongs to him.[29]

---

[26] Marx (1990, p. 481/II:6, p. 354), my emphasis.
[27] Marx (1990, p. 450/II: 6, p. 328).
[28] Marx (1990, p. 477/II:6, p. 351).
[29] Ibid., pp. 476–477/II: 6, pp. 350–321.

In addition to this structural division of labour between workers and a more powerful and privileged layer of managers, manufacture further divides up workers' labour into a number of small, specialised tasks, confining workers to a tiny range of operations. This division of labour "converts the worker into a crippled monstrosity by furthering his particular skill as in a forcing-house, through the suppression of a whole world of productive drives and inclinations".[30] Although this increases the totality of social productive powers, it does so only under the aegis of capital, strengthening its power over the people it commands. It thus both increases "the socially productive power of labour for the benefit of capital" by "crippling the individual worker" and "produces new conditions for the domination of capital over labour".[31]

Factory production extends and exacerbates all of this. Here we have "a lifeless mechanism which is independent of the workers, who are incorporated into it as living appendages".[32]

> The separation of the intellectual faculties of the production process from manual labour, and the transformation of those faculties into powers exercised by capital over labour, is, as we have already shown, finally completed by large-scale industry erected on the foundation of machinery. (...) The technical subordination of the worker to the uniform motion of the instruments of labour, and the peculiar composition of the working group, (...) gives rise to a barrack-like discipline, which is elaborated into a complete system in the factory, and brings the previously mentioned labour of the superintendence to its fullest development, thereby dividing the workers into manual workers and overseers, into the private soldiers and the N.C.O.s of an industrial army.[33]

Here too Marx stresses not only the hierarchical division of labour, but also its effects on workers' development:

> Factory work exhausts the nervous system to the uttermost; at the same time, it does away with the many-sided play of the muscles, and confiscates every atom of freedom, both in bodily and in intellectual activity. Even

---

[30] Ibid., p. 481, II: 6, pp. 354–355.
[31] Ibid., p. 486/II: 6, pp. 358–359.
[32] Ibid., p. 548/II: 6, p. 410.
[33] Ibid., p. 549/II: 6, pp. 410–411.

the lightening of the labour becomes an instrument of torture, since the machine does not free the worker from the work, but rather deprives the work itself of all content.[34]

Summarising this discussion, most of which takes place in Part IV of Volume I of *Capital*, he writes:

> We saw in Part IV (...) that within the capitalist system all methods for raising the social productivity of labour are put into effect at the cost of the individual worker; that all means for the development of production undergo a dialectical inversion so that they become means of domination and exploitation of the producers; they distort the worker into a fragment of a man, they degrade him to the level of an appendage of a machine, they destroy the actual content of his labour by turning it into a torment; they alienate [*entfremden*] from him the intellectual potentialities of the labour process in the same proportion as science is incorporated into it as an independent power; they deform the conditions under which he works, subject him during the labour process to a despotism the more hateful for its meanness; they transform his life-time into working-time... But all methods for the production surplus-value are at the same time methods of accumulation... Accumulation of wealth at one pole is, therefore, at the same time accumulation of misery, the torment of labour, slavery, ignorance, brutalization and moral degradation at the opposite pole, i.e. on the side of the class that produces its own product as capital.[35]

This passage touches on a large number of elements previously discussed, but for now let us note that it encapsulates the two main critical points Marx develops with regard to the nature of the division of labour under capitalism as it developed through manufacture to the factory system. First, the hierarchical division between mental and physical labour and between workers and a middle layer of managers that plan, control, manage, and oversee the labour process, thereby securing the domination and exploitation of workers for capital. Second, the restriction of workers' labour processes to minute and specialised tasks, thwarting their human development, both physical and mental. Note that simply removing managers while retaining subordination to capital cannot solve these problems, since even though e.g. systems of piece work may reduce

---

[34] Ibid., p. 548/II: 6, p. 410.
[35] Marx (1990, p. 798-9/II:6, p. 587-8).

managerial oversight, they remain a "hierarchically organized system of exploitation and oppression".[36]

According to Marx, the solution is to eliminate the hierarchical division of labour altogether. He and Engels write that the "transformation (...) of personal powers into material powers (...) can only be abolished by the individuals again subjecting these material powers to themselves and abolishing the division of labour"[37] and that socialist individuals must therefore "no longer [be] subject to the division of labour".[38] In contrast to previous forms of society, under socialism,

> where nobody has one exclusive sphere of activity but each can become accomplished in any branch he wishes, society regulates the general production and thus makes it possible for me to do one thing today and another tomorrow, to hunt in the morning, fish in the afternoon, rear cattle in the evening, criticise after dinner, just as I have a mind, without ever becoming hunter, fisherman, shepherd or critic.[39]

As he reiterates in the *Grundrisse*, there will of course still be a "planned distribution of labour time among the various branches of production",[40] but, unlike under capitalism, workers under socialism will not be bound and restricted to one activity only, as part of a fixed social structure in which they are compelled to participate either by the force of ruling elites or by the force of material need.

Finally, in Volume I of *Capital*, Marx argues that:

> Th[e] possibility of varying labour [developed by capitalism] must become a general law of social production, and the existing relations must be adapted to permit its realization in practice. That monstrosity, the disposable working population held in reserve, in misery, for the changing requirements of capitalist exploitation, must be replaced by the individual man who is absolutely available for the different kinds of labour required

---

[36] Marx (1990, p. 695/II: 6, p. 514).

[37] MECW 5, p. 78/I:5, p. 95—note that the verb that's been translated to "abolish" here is "aufheben", which is a technical Hegelian term that can both mean to abolish/eliminate and to raise up to a higher level. The translational choice here seems overall correct to me.

[38] MECW 5, p. 88/I:5, p. 114.

[39] MECW 5, p. 47/I:5, pp. 34–35.

[40] Marx (1993, p. 173/II.1.1, p. 104).

of him; the partially developed individual, who is merely the bearer of one specialized social function, must be replaced by the totally developed individual, for whom the different social functions are different modes of activity he takes up in turn.[41]

None of this means an end to modern industry and technology or to the subdivision of tasks in the service of minimising necessary labour time. What it does entail is an end to the exclusion of workers from mental and conceptual tasks, from the planning, management, and overseeing of their individual and collective labour, and allowing their work-week (or year) to consist of any number of specific tasks both within and between industries—subject, of course, to the individual and collective needs of their society, and to their abilities. This would mean that, as G. A. Cohen puts it, "a person does not give himself up to one activity only"; "he does not relate to any of his several activities as to a role in a fixed social structure"; and "what he does is" at least generally speaking, "something he wishes to do".[42]

More precisely, Marx is arguing that socialism must (i) eliminate people's confinement to particular occupations, (ii) eliminate the split between a ruling elite who do all the planning, managing, and overseeing of labour and those who are subject to their power, and (iii) allow people's labouring activities to consist, in principle, of any combination they individually and collectively determine, subject to their abilities and society's needs. This in turn will result in (iv) occupational identities falling away as meaningful social categories altogether.

We can now see how Marx's vision of socialism further challenges a number of current workplace republican proposals for economic freedom. Typically these proposals emphasise, among other things, strengthening exit rights[43] and replacing capitalist firms with worker-owned firms.[44] The same goes for one of the most influential socialist models today, market socialism, which likewise emphasises worker-owned firms within

---

[41] Marx (1990, p. 618/II:6, p. 466).
[42] Cohen (2001, p. 133).
[43] Anderson, Hsieh (2012, 2008).
[44] González-Ricoy (2014) and Gourevitch (2015).

the context of competitive markets with little to no changes in the division of labour.[45] While both aim at economic emancipation, they do so without demanding the elimination of hierarchical divisions of labour.

For Marx, such models cannot secure economic emancipation. First, managers under such systems almost always retain a great deal of uncontrolled power over workers. They monopolise and control important information. They decide which tasks are to be performed, how they are performed, and who by. And they evaluate performance, meting out rewards and punishments. These are all ways in which they have power over workers, which workers themselves cannot control. Simply being able to vote on managers and boards of directors has proven ineffective at preventing this. Even in a formally democratic workplace, in any process of deliberation and decision-making regarding the affairs of that workplace this layer of bureaucrats tends to become the only people with sufficient information, knowledge, and competence to contribute to many vital issues. This renders everyone else in that workplace dependent on them both for their input and goodwill in deliberation and decision-making and for securing the continued smooth operation of the workplace. Over time, this power imbalance undermines any potential for genuine worker self-management. This problem has been noted numerous times throughout the last century, including in market socialist societies such as in Yugoslavia and among numerous cooperatives and recuperated factories which failed to take this issue into consideration. It's also a well-known problem in larger cooperatives, such as the famous Mondragón cooperative. Despite formally democratic decision-making structures, lower wage inequality, and absence of capitalist owners, Mondragón features the very same relations of personal domination between workers and managers as familiar capitalist firms do.[46] This supports Marx's insight that replacing capitalism with a free economy requires not just formal workers' control over workplaces, but also abolishing the hierarchical division of labour.

---

[45] See e.g. Schweickart (1996). Such models are more detailed than I can adequately describe here, including models of banking, taxation, investment, and interaction with familiar types of state institutions.

[46] Kasmir (1996, 2018).

Distributing According to Need

Finally, Marx also believes that socialism requires a criterion for a fully human scheme of remuneration: "from each according to his abilities, to each according to his needs!"[47] This last element enters Marx's writings less as an important component either in its own right or for the purposes of securing the collective appropriation and self-rule of the totality of our social powers. A version of it first appears with some brief discussion in the *German Ideology* and pops up sporadically throughout later works. In fact, compared to many other socialists and much of contemporary political theory, Marx seems strikingly uninterested in devising, comparing, and evaluating principles of distribution for any present or future society. I don't think we should be surprised by this in light of Marx's consistent focus on questions of power, especially questions concerning the structure and presuppositions for collective deliberation and decision-making. It is not clear that anything specific flows from an answer to the question of how to organise a free society to the distinct (though not unconnected) issue of which principles a free society should then go on to distribute everyday consumable goods and services according to. Moreover, whereas we might be able to say something sensible about how a future society should be organised in order to help guide action in the present towards such social change, it's not clear that the same can be said about principles for distributing everyday consumable goods and services. Indeed, in the *Critique of the Gotha Programme* Marx argues that "it was an overall mistake" of the Lassalleans "to make an issue of so-called distribution and to make it the focus of attention",[48] in part due to the fact that principles of distribution result from the relations of production. Throughout his life he consistently rejected moralised conceptions of the labour theory of value and both critiques of capitalism and arguments for socialism based thereon.

Nevertheless, Marx advocates distribution according to need as the one most appropriate to a socialist society. In *Critique of the Gotha Programme*, he writes that:

> In a higher phase of communist society, after the subjection of individuals to the division of labour, and thereby the antithesis between mental

---

[47] Marx (1996, p. 215/I:25, p. 15).
[48] Marx (1996, p. 215/I:25, p. 15).

and physical labour, has disappeared; after labour has become not merely a means to live but the foremost need in life; after the multifarious development of individuals has grown along with their productive powers, and all the springs of cooperative wealth flow more abundantly - only then can the limited horizon of bourgeois right be wholly transcended, and society can inscribe on its banner: from each according to his abilities, to each according to his needs![49]

In other words, need is argued to be the principle of distribution appropriate to socialist relations of production. Rather than simply being about distributing what is produced, we should understand the satisfaction of real social needs—individual and collective—as driving economic production. Socialist production is therefore driven by the satisfaction of real human needs, developed and determined by people themselves, rather than by ruling elites or impersonal market forces. In such a society "the form of a *directly* communal activity and a directly *communal* consumption (...) occur wherever that *direct* expression of sociality *[Gesellschaftlichkeit]* springs from the essential nature of the content of the activity and is appropriate to the nature of the consumption".[50]

Whereas under capitalism, "I have produced for myself and not for you, just as you have produced for yourself and not for me" because "our production is not man's production for man as a man, i.e., it is not social production",[51] under socialism, Marx writes that:

(1) "In my *production* I would have objectified my *individuality*, its *specific character*, and therefore enjoyed not only an individual *manifestation of my life* during the activity, but also when looking at the object I would have the individual pleasure of knowing my personality to be *objective, visible to the senses* and hence a power *beyond all doubt*";
(2) "In your enjoyment or use of my product I would have the *direct* enjoyment both of being conscious of having satisfied a *human* need by my work";
(3) "I would have been for you the *mediator* between you and the species, and therefore would become recognised and felt by you

---

[49] Marx (1996, pp. 214–215/I:25, p. 15).
[50] Marx (1996, p. 350/I:2, pp. 267/391).
[51] MECW 3, p. 225/IV:2, p. 462.

yourself as a completion of your own essential nature and as a necessary part of yourself"; and

(4) "In the individual expression of my life I would have directly created your expression of your life, and therefore in my individual activity I would have directly *confirmed* and *realised* my true nature, my *human* nature, my *communal* nature.[52]

So, under socialist relations of production, we not only realise our freedom through our activities and so enjoy them more fully. We also enjoy our productive activities as actions that help to satisfy real human needs. This helps us to take joy in the good that we're doing, in others' enjoyment of our activities and their products, and in our own nature as social beings who are part of such a society.

However, when socialist relations are first introduced, people will previously have been socialised under capitalism and internalised capitalist norms. As a result, they will not initially distribute according to need, but according to labour. Marx grew to recognise that the majority of socialists around him thought—in his view erroneously—that goods and services should be distributed according to labour under socialism. He thought they did this because they'd internalised the norms of capitalism—after all "[r]ight can never be higher than the economic form of society and the cultural development which is conditioned by it".[53] And he thought that this flaw was both unavoidable and would likely persist for some time "in the first phase of socialist society when it has just emerged from capitalist society after a long and painful birth".[54] In such a society, "just as it emerges from capitalist society, hence in every respect - economically, morally, intellectually - as it comes forth from the womb, it is stamped with the birthmarks of the old society",[55] people will likely distribute according to labour.

This is not because distributing according to labour is appropriate to socialism—quite the opposite. It's because distributing according to labour is a natural outgrowth of capitalism—a moral and ideological imprint of capitalist social relations—which those who introduce socialism

---

[52] MECW 3, p. 228/IV:2, p. 465.
[53] Marx (1996, p. 214/I:25, p. 15).
[54] Marx (1996, p. 214/I:25, p. 15).
[55] Marx (1996, p. 213/I:25, p. 13).

will still, unfortunately, have internalised. In time, however, as the effects of new, socialist relations are felt, people's conceptions of the appropriate principles of distribution will change. Thus, Marx writes that:

> Within a co-operatively organised society based on common ownership in the means of production, the producers do not exchange their products; nor does the labour expended on the products appear any more *as the value* of these products, one of the material properties that they possess, because now in contrast to capitalist society, the labour of individuals will no longer be a constituent part of the total labour in a roundabout way, but will be part of it directly. The term 'return from labour', which is useless even today on account of its ambiguity, thus loses all semblance of meaning.[56]

As the new socialist relations of production take effect, distributing according to labour loses all the meaning it once seemed to have and the form of distribution appropriate to these new social relations, according to need, will blossom forth.

For Marx, these different phases are in no way different modes or relations of production. Dividing the phases of socialism into two separate stages, two separate modes of production, is a later invention by other Marxists, most prominently Lenin in *The State and Revolution*. While Lenin's discussion is much more legally focused and less fleshed-out than many seem to think, many later Lenin*ists* distinguish very firmly between a stage of "socialism" (with a single-party state, state ownership of the means of production, centrally planned economy, distribution according to labour, and so on) and a stage of "communism" (a fully free, stateless society, social (not state) ownership, worker self-organisation, distribution according to need, etc.). This was never Marx's view, and the reconstruction above makes it clear why.

Marx instead speaks of two *phases* of the *very same relations of production*. The first describes how workers, still negatively impacted by the moral and ideological effects of capitalist relations, distribute when they first introduce socialist relations. The second describes how they come to distribute once these new, free socialist relations have made themselves felt. If these two phases of socialism are instead conceptualised as separate

---

[56] Marx (1996, 213/I:25, p. 13).

modes or relations of production, we would completely lose Marx's explanation for why the first phase adopts distribution according to labour. This is not because it's appropriate to that stage, but because it's an unfortunate vestige of capitalism. We would also lose his explanation for the shift from the first to the second phase of socialism, which is due to the effects of new, free socialist relations of production on distributive norms. In other words, for Marx the society that replaces capitalism is a fully free socialist society that, once its new social relations take full effect, distributes according to need. This discussion raises a host of questions about what the transition to a socialist society would look like, e.g. about how to relate to state power, Marx's ideas of a democratic dictatorship of the proletariat, and the two different models of transition offered in the *Communist Manifesto* and *The Civil War in France*. Though interesting, I must leave these for later work.

We have seen that Marx's conception of socialism can be understood as a further development of his vision of democracy. Socialism contains and furthers all the elements to be found in the initial vision of democracy, adding three further components in light of the diagnosis of the ills of modern society that Marx discusses in his second theory of alienation. These three additions are the specification that the economy as a whole must be participatory democratically planned, that the modern division of labour must be done away with, and that people distribute according to need. Marx makes these additions in order to develop a vision of a socialist society intended to realise the same basic commitment to freedom and human development that his conception of democracy attempted to. Universal human emancipation and participatory democracy remain at the heart of Marx's vision of socialism. Having explored this, I turn now to consider two of the most prominent critiques of this project: Max Weber and Friedrich Hayek.

Weber: Socialism Contra Bureaucratic Domination

Let us now consider an important objection to Marx's vision developed by Max Weber. The argument turns on the relations between contemporary industry and technology on the one hand, and the extent to which the elimination of a certain kind of stratification of power, control, and decision-making are compatible with it on the other. Weber's argument is specifically directed against the thoughts expressed in the *Communist Manifesto* and against syndicalism, claiming that de facto rule by an elite bureaucracy is necessary for a contemporary (as of the early twentieth century) industrial and technological economy: "The modern economy cannot be managed in any other way",[57] due to "the necessity for long years of specialist training, for constantly increasing specialisation and for management by specialist officials trained in this way".[58] This "inescapable universal bureaucratisation"[59] is due (1) "partly to purely technical considerations, to the nature of modern means of operation", and (2) "partly simply to the greater efficiency of this kind of human cooperation: to the development of 'discipline', the discipline of the army, office, workshop and business".[60] Weber constantly keeps in mind the import of this claim in his lecture on socialism, which I have been quoting from. Since modern technology necessitates a bureaucracy running the labour process (and other processes of state, the army, etc.), and this bureaucracy and its power will always prevent workers from having meaningful control over the means of production, alienation in the sense I have described it above is impossible to overcome.

Clearly, this supposed need for bureaucratic power and control would render Marx's socialism impossible, since it entails that everyone cannot collectively control the economy—or, for that matter, any other modern large-scale institution. If this is the case, it risks seriously undermining Marx's critique of capitalism, because it implies that we either have to give up collective control over all of society by the associated producers or give up on modern industry and technology. The former route is problematic for methodological reasons. If bureaucratic power and control are unavoidable, then capitalism cannot be criticised on Marx's grounds for being an inferior feasible alternative compared to socialism, since socialism too would share this defect. If, on the other hand, we choose to give up on modern industry and technology, then the comparative assessment between capitalism and socialism becomes much more problematic. If socialism requires us to give up the immense productive powers

---

[57] Weber (1994, p. 279).
[58] Weber (1994, p. 279).
[59] Weber (1994, p. 279).
[60] Weber (1994, p. 281).

of modern industry and technology, how plausible is it to think that it will compare favourably to capitalism, all things considered?

Defusing this sort of objection requires discussing the precise forms through which Marx's vision can be brought about, which will be able to show how it is possible to instantiate Marx's socialism without generating the claimed harms. There are a handful of different proposals for what a society broadly like the one Marx describes might look like, but the one I favour and will consider here is the model of Participatory Economics—ParEcon—developed by Michael Albert and Robin Hahnel.

Participatory Economics is a model of some of the institutional forms that can instantiate much of Marx's vision of socialism.[61] The model has four main components. First, it consists of a federated network of workers' and community/consumers' councils. Every workplace is run by one or more workers' councils, each of around 25–50 members. In these councils, each member is supposed to have roughly equal powers and responsibilities. Both workers' and consumers' councils federate upwards such that, for example, each lower-level council sends one representative to a higher-level council, each in turn consisting of 25–50 such representatives, and so on until the national or international level is reached. The exact number of people in each such council, and the number of levels of such councils, will naturally vary according to any number of factors to do with population, geography, etc. Workers' councils are responsible for the day-to-day operations of the production process, and the workplace in general, as well as being responsible for participating in the formation and implementation of the democratic plan of production. Consumers' councils will federate not according to workplaces, but according to where you live. These, together with the workers' councils, participate in formulating the participatory democratic plans, and are responsible for determining and overseeing relevant public goods and services on relevant levels (things like parks, hospitals, roads, etc.).

Apart from a network of workers' and consumers' councils, participatory economics has three main components: a new way of organising society's division of labour, called Balanced Jobs; a model of democratic

---

[61] For discussion of this model, see Albert (2003), Albert and Hahnel (1978, 1991, 1999), Hahnel (2005, 2012) and Raekstad (2011, 2013). These are also often called "Balanced Job Complexes" rather than "Balanced Jobs". I follow Hahnel (2012) in preferring the latter term, for no other reason than that it's less bulky and conveys its meaning just as well.

planning, called Participatory Planning; and a criterion of remuneration, according to effort and sacrifice. The last component—remuneration according to effort and sacrifice, rather than according to needs—differs from Marx's. Since I also think that this component is much less important than the others, because it deals not with critical issues of power and how to structure deliberation and decision-making but rather on which principles some of these should be done in accordance with, and because it is not important for replying to criticisms of Marx's vision of socialism, I will leave this last component aside for discussion here.

The first port of call is replying to Weber's contention that modern industry and technology make a de facto rule by a distinct layer of bureaucrats unavoidable for future societies. Naturally, in the case of a socialist revolution in the sense Marx envisages, it would be naïve to think that things to do with the organisation of workplaces technologically, spatially, and organisationally would remain the same. Furthermore, many workplaces simply do not require managers with specialist technical competence. In fact, many modern managers come straight from business and management schools and possess less technical knowledge about the workplaces they go into than their workers.

Following István Mészáros,[62] we should also note that Weber just seems to assume that production would cease to function, or at least cease to function well, without bureaucratic management, on the basis of nothing more than a thought experiment. If we hold a certain hierarchical division of labour within some institution constant and remove the personnel at the top, then production will cease to function (properly). Even if we accept this line of reasoning, it does not support the very different thesis that fulfilling the functions of that institution is impossible without someone on the top of a hierarchical division of labour. Why? Since neither Marx nor the syndicalists Weber is criticising assumes, or needs to assume, that the hierarchical division of labour is to be held constant. Quite the contrary: They hold that the social structure should be changed such that there are no hierarchies of that kind, and therefore nobody at the top of them. The fact that removing people from the top of a hierarchical organisation results in chaos for an organisation of that kind—if this really is the case—does not give us reason to think that an

---

[62] Mészáros (1986).

institution structured in a different way cannot perform the functions that the hierarchically structured one can just as well or even better.

On the other hand, in order to challenge Weber's argument at its strongest, I will be ignoring these important considerations and focus purely on the case of factory-type industrial production which typically does feature a layer of managers. I will also further assume, for the sake of meeting Weber's argument in its strongest possible form, that these managers really do possess critical technical knowledge which other current workers in the same workplace or industry at least generally lack (even though this is often demonstrably false).

One specific proposal for addressing just this issue is the idea of Balanced Jobs. Balanced Jobs are a specific way of organising the distribution of tasks within a workplace to ensure that all the members of that workplace can participate properly in their workplace's deliberation and decision-making, as well as develop and flourish as human beings. Balanced Jobs are designed to do this by ensuring two things. First, that everyone in a workplace does both some of the more challenging and rewarding work, as well as some of the heavier and more boring work. This is to ensure that all individuals are strengthened and developed rather than just a few at everyone else's expense. Secondly, that tasks and responsibilities that involve critical knowledge and competence about the way that workplace operates are distributed evenly between those who work there. This is to prevent just the kind of hierarchical division of labour between a separate privileged managers and other workers.[63]

The best argument for Balanced Jobs being possible is the fact that they have actually been implemented in a variety of cooperatives. Some of these are very small indeed, but others are larger. Furthermore, in some cases the balancing has taken some very demanding forms—considerably more demanding than balancing work would be in a normal factory. The "Mondragon Bookshop and Coffeehouse" in Canada, for instance, has succeeded in rotating *every single task* involved in running a bookshop, restaurant, and coffee bar among all of its members. There are also encouraging historical examples of larger-scale plants experimenting with breaking up the division of labour.[64]

---

[63] Apart from the other books on ParEcon already mentioned, see the essays collected in Walker (1979) and also Wright (1980).

[64] See Ness and Azzellini (2011).

A Weberian reply to this might run as follows. Fair enough, it is indeed *possible* to eliminate a distinct bureaucracy within workplaces, but it is still not ultimately *feasible* to do so in the context of modern industry and technology, due to the detrimental effects this would have on efficiency. This claim is sometimes further bolstered by the idea that education is required for certain tasks, which is costly. Ensuring that only a small minority receives such specialised education would therefore be more efficient than an alternative one, at least *all other things being equal*.

The first thing we should point out against this retort is that arguments like it are almost always given with no real supporting evidence whatsoever. What this essentially amounts to is a thinker coming up with something that, if it were true, would support the thing they want to defend, and then strongly asserting that it is true, inevitable, etc. Absent further supporting evidence—which Weber does not provide—there's not much reason to believe that it's plausible.

The second thing we should point out is the importance of the *all other things being equal* assumption. Even if we accept the argument as it stands, there are likely to be countervailing factors affecting the efficiency of workplaces that are worker self-managed. For example, there are workers' cooperatives that are significantly more productive than comparable capitalist firms and worker participation has been found to positively impact efficiency even in capitalist firms. Synthesising over two decades of research on cooperatives in Western Europe, the US, and Latin America, a recent study found that "[w]orker cooperatives are more productive than conventional businesses, with staff working "better and smarter" and production organised more efficiently", while often being larger and not necessarily less capital-intensive than conventional capitalist firms.[65] Famously, a US Department of Health, Welfare and Education study in 1973 concluded its report into the effects of worker participation by stating that "in no instance of which we have evidence has a major effort to increase employee participation resulted in a long-term decline of productivity".[66]

Two possible explanations for this include the psychological finding that higher autonomy leads to greater productivity and the idea that

---

[65] Pérotin, 2018, p. 3. For an older review of relevant literature, see Levine and Tyson (1990) and for two metastudies, see Doucouliagos, 1995 and Doucouliagos, 1997.

[66] Quoted in Schweikart (1996, p. 100).

workers in workplaces have a lot of knowledge and competence of various kinds which they can contribute and implement under various systems of worker management, but not when subject to capitalist or state-imposed managers. A variety of empirical research on human motivation shows satisfying human needs of autonomy as the feeling of self-direction, connectedness, and competence is associated with greater productivity and better results, as well as more intrinsic motivation. Today's capitalist workplaces, by contrast, are much more built around providing extrinsic motivations like rewarding for good results or punishing for failure in various ways. One major downside of this is that adding extrinsic motivation is not only much weaker than intrinsic motivation, it also demonstrably decreases intrinsic motivation—which explains why e.g. praising school-children for good results makes them learn less well, or fining parents for picking their kids up from kindergarten late actually increases lateness. By better being able to satisfy these needs and so supporting intrinsic motivation, it's reasonable to suppose that, all other things being equal, more democratic workplaces would see major forces of increased productivity and so efficiency.

Even under familiar forms of capitalism, there is empirical evidence that gives us reason to doubt Weber's view. In the late 1950s, the Tavistock Institute did a comparative study of methods of work organisation in British coal mines, described as follows:

> This study concerns a group of miners who came together to evolve a new way of working together, planning the type of change they wanted to put through, and testing it in practice. The new type of work organisation which has come to be known in the industry as composite working, has in recent years emerged spontaneously in a number of different pits in the north-west Durham coal field. Its roots go back to an earlier tradition which had been almost completely displaced in the course of the last century by the introduction of work techniques based on task segmentation, differential status and payment, and extrinsic hierarchical control.[67]

This new type of work organisation, dubbed "composite work organization":

---

[67] Herbst (1962, p. 3).

may be described as one in which the group takes over complete responsibility for the total cycle of operations involved in mining the coal-face. No member of the group has a fixed work role. Instead, the men deploy themselves, depending on the requirements of the on-going group task. Within the limits of technological and safety requirements they are free to evolve their own way of organising and carrying out their task. They are not subject to any external authority in this respect, nor is there within the group itself any member who takes over a formal directive leadership function. Whereas in conventional long-wall working the coal-getting task is split into four to eight separate work roles, carried out by different teams, each paid at a different rate, in the composite group members are no longer paid directly for any of the tasks carried out. The all-in wage agreement is, instead, based on the negotiated price per ton of coal produced by the team. The income obtained is divided equally among team members.[68]

In other words, this method of work organisation largely does away with the hierarchical division between mental and manual labour—even while retaining overall capitalist control. How did this affect productivity? Another report on the same case states that the experiment demonstrates "the ability of quite large primary work groups of 40–50 members to act as self-regulating, self-developing social organisms able to maintain themselves in a steady state of high productivity".[69]

Similar findings were made in a comparative study of the production of The Ferguson Tractor by the Standard Motor Company in Coventry in the UK and Detroit in the US, respectively, leading up to and during 1956. Seymour Melman writes that "our attention was attracted to this firm in 1950 following the observation that it was paying the highest wages in the automobile industry and at the same time was operating manufacturing plants that were, by all odds, among the most efficient in the industry".[70] Melman writes that:

> In this firm we will show that at the same time: thousands of workers operated virtually without supervision as conventionally understood, and at high productivity; the highest wage in British industry was paid; high quality products were produced at acceptable prices in extensively mechanised plants; the management conducted its affairs at unusually

---

[68] Herbst (1962, p. 4).

[69] Trist et al. (1963, p. Xiii).

[70] Melman (1958, p. 11).

low costs; also, organised workers had a substantial role in production decision-making.[71]

It was found that "high levels of productivity have been attained with methods of production organization and decision-making that include extensive activity by workers, operating a decision-process of their own".[72] The implications on productivity are clear:

> High levels of rapid growth in industrial productivity can be achieved when industrial workers as well as management do decision-making on production. This implies that unilateral decision-making by hierarchical management groups is not a necessary condition for operation of industrial plants at high productivity levels.[73]

As a result, "[c]hanges in the ways of worker and management decision-making are explicable in terms of the interior mechanisms of particular decision systems, rather than as effects of the methods of production themselves".[74] This, Melman writes, "demonstrate[s] the possibility of managing large and highly mechanized industrial plants by methods that are not part of the preferred doctrine of 'modern' management".[75]

In response to this, it might be argued—again without a shred of supporting evidence—that retaining good productivity without capitalism's hierarchical division of labour is feasible only so long as these remain within a sufficiently competitive market system. In other words, while such different divisions of labour are, *contra* Weber, compatible with modern industry and technology, they are so only in the contexts of competitive markets with the impersonal domination they imply, and not in a planned system of the kind that Marx's socialism and Participatory Economics require. What we need to respond to this are findings specifically about the effects of workers' self-management on productivity that are (at least to some meaningful degree) insulated from the pressures of competitive markets. Here too there is evidence

---

[71] Melman (1958, p. 5).
[72] Melman (1958, p. 5).
[73] Melman (1958, p. 4).
[74] Ibid., p. 5.
[75] Melman (1958, p. 9).

supporting the Marxian view. A study of state-owned, co-determined production units in the Venezuelan economy conducted in 2009, found that workers mentioned that learning "collective management and organisation" helped "in reducing the rigid division between intellectual and manual labour found in traditional capitalist firms", which led to "decreased tension and conflict in the workplace" and "helped to increase productivity".[76] In one instance, due to a government reorganisation, a tomato processing plant was suddenly and unexpectedly left without a coordinator for six months. What happened? The workers effectively took over management and planning themselves, and the plant promptly increased its production from a maximum of 90,000 to 150,000 kgs of tomatoes processed per month.[77]

Put together, these findings suggest three things: Firstly, they show that it seems to be feasible for at least some contemporary workplaces with modern industry and technology (more so than those Weber was discussing) to organise production without bureaucratic control over the labour process. Note that the claim is not that abolishing the hierarchical division of labour will have no negative impacts on productivity as commonly construed. Rather, it is only that there are cases where bureaucratic management, as construed by Weber, has been replaced without the effects that Weber predicted occurring. This shows that the claimed necessity of universal bureaucratisation is incorrect. Secondly, they show that this can lead to overall increases in even standard measures of productivity and that these increases can appear within a short period of time and without a great deal of further re-structuring, other kinds of reorganisation, or new technology. Thirdly, they show that there can be a real drive for this from workers themselves.

This suffices to challenge the Weberian objection, insofar as they show that bureaucratic management does not seem to be universally necessary for production using modern technology. Nevertheless, I think we would be missing out on something important if we simply left the argument here. Our foregoing argument has accepted another important premise which is usually left unexamined: the premise that efficiency is a single, value-neutral concept. By value-neutral I don't mean it is not something

---

[76] Larrabure (2013, p. 188–9.)
[77] Larrabure (2013, p. 188–9).

which may or may not be valued, but that it is, or is taken to be, something which is neutral with respect to other evaluative commitments like freedom and human development. This premise is false. Efficiency is often construed as the value-neutral comparison between the costs and benefits of various inputs and outputs, where one solution is more efficient than another if and only if it has a higher benefit-cost ratio. The very conceptual possibility of imagining such a ratio—ignoring the practical issues of assigning sensible values and using them—presupposes that we have some way of reducing the many qualitatively different inputs and outputs in question to some single quantitative measure; and usually this measure is taken to be that of monetary value as determined by a real or hypothetical capitalist marketplace.

It also ignores the vital question that determines the outcome of any cost-benefit analysis, namely deciding what to count as costs and what to count as benefits. Based on what they considered to be costs and benefits, the Nazis considered gas chambers to be highly efficient (compared to alternatives like shooting and throat-cutting). Based on what they consider to be costs and benefits, the roughly 100 corporations that are responsible for around 71% of CO_2 emissions prefer to keep destroying the conditions for human and other animal life on our planet (which they don't have to pay for) than bearing the much more minor costs of swapping energy sources (which they do have to pay for).[78] Any decent person would make very different assessments, primarily on the basis of what to count as costs and what to count as benefits.

The general point here is that efficiency estimates depend entirely on what we count as costs and benefits, and this is often ignored by critics of socialism. Goods that Marx and many others hold to be important—such as freedom and human development—are often excluded from such estimates entirely.[79] This is important, because some things which are costly in terms of money and time can also be considered as valuable in themselves once we consider human development as a valuable factor. Higher

---

[78] It might be pointed out that a number of these corporations are owned by some state or other, but this is irrelevant to the point being made here, which is about efficiency judgments.

[79] There have been efforts to develop things like the Human Development Index as an alternative to GDP, but this is a different kind of thing altogether from considering inputs and outputs in a process of production.

levels of education, for instance, while they cost money and may not—although this has been challenged—lead to more objects being produced per person, also entail a greater development of human powers. If we consider this to be a valuable output, then it is by no means obvious that the greater time required for educating more people yields a lower total benefit-cost ratio *all other things being equal*. In other words, what counts as efficient or not is completely dependent on what we choose to assign value to when we estimate the costs and benefits of inputs and outputs. This is a point that any critical discussion of Max's critique of capitalism must take into consideration.

Let me make one final point about the division of labour under socialism as Marx conceives of it. If a socialist society can feasibly solve the issue of the structural division of labour, along with being structured by a network of federated councils organising a participatory democratic form of planning, then there is no principled obstacle to spreading individuals' labours across different workplaces. Again, this does not mean that anyone can do whatever they like. It only means that society will now be able to, consistent with its various priorities and the powers and capacities of its members, arrange production in such a way that people who want to, and can, work in various branches or workplaces can do so without additional social hindrances. Having discussed the arguments against replacing the hierarchical division of labour, I turn now to Hayek's challenge to planning.

Participatory Planning and Hayek's Challenge

We have now come to the related question of whether a democratic form of social planning is feasible. For workplaces, the answer is simple. There are and have been a number of cooperatives and recuperated businesses, a handful of which implement Balanced Jobs, and they've generally been able to function well. Democratic planning within workers' councils on the level of individual workplaces exists and has existed, so it's trivially possible. What can we say about the further question regarding the possibility of planning an entire economy democratically, especially in light of the traditional story we're told about how our only options are markets or authoritarian central planning? Obviously, it is impossible to go into any considerable detail on this issue here, but by drawing on the model of Participatory Planning I can make a few points which, I think, convincingly establish the feasibility of participatory democratic planning of a kind which Marx would approve of.[80]

The participants in a participatory planning process are workers' councils, consumers' councils, and something called Iteration Facilitation Boards, or IFBs. IFBs help the planning process by suggesting "indicative prices" which translate a person's work rate—the collected estimate of the quantity and quality of their work's effort and sacrifice—into goods and services. They do not, however, make any actual planning decisions, make any decisions about anyone's consumption, or set rates of exchange of any kind. As such, the "indicative prices" they set to ease the planning process are not prices at all either in Marx's technical sense or in the lay senses of "prices". Briefly put, the planning process is supposed to work roughly as follows:

1. The IFBs estimate the different social costs of various goods and services, taking into account the resources they require, materials, work inputs, as well as things like damages or benefits to people, society, and the environment. These will be based on last year's plan, and will mostly be minor modifications to take into account new developments.
2. Workers' councils meet to suggest what they want their workplace to produce, and what they want to request in order to get this done. Consumers' councils meet to collate their individual consumption proposals, and to decide which public goods and services they want to request. These too are based on modifications of last year's plan, and are suggestions formulated by the individuals and councils who would be carrying them out.
3. In light of this new information, the IFBs calculate the excess supply and demand for all goods and services, labour, investment, and natural resources, and modify their estimates based on what people and councils say they want to consume and produce.
4. Workers' and consumers' councils and federations then send in revised proposals until they deliver one which the other councils in their group can accept, and so on upwards until a final plan is reached.

---

[80] For another interesting model, see Devine (1988).

5. Plans will include necessary margins for the flexibility and revision that people will obviously require throughout the year.
6. In accordance with the plan that is reached, workplaces will be assigned a limited quantity of consumption rights based on their collected work rates. These are then distributed among individual workers in accordance with the specific work rates of the individual tasks that they perform, e.g. monthly or bi-monthly.

This is not, and does not aim to be, a complete account of the planning model, nor will I attempt a proper defence of it here. A few key points from the literature are, however, worth noting. First, all meetings here happen *within* councils, not between them. Proposals are formulated by individuals and councils themselves, and finally have to be accepted by the other individuals and councils within their group. None of this requires anyone else to go into the details of anyone's proposals. All they have to do is look at the relation between the collected costs and benefits of the proposals and vote yes or no. If someone makes an exceptional request, they may have to justify it, or risk having it rejected. Nobody in this model has any interest in voting against someone else's proposal unless it is very unbalanced and deemed to be unjustified, since there are no gains to be had from doing so.

The most important thing, however, is that it is only the individuals and councils involved who themselves make their own activity proposals. Other councils and federations only get to either accept or reject these proposals. Robin Hahnel stresses the importance of this:

> When worker councils make proposals they are asking permission to use particular parts of the productive resources that belong to everyone. In effect their proposals say: "If the rest of you—with whom we are engaged in a cooperative division of labor -- agree to allow us to use productive resources belonging to all of us as inputs, then we promise to deliver the following goods and services as outputs for others to use." When consumer councils make proposals they are asking permission to consume goods and services whose production entails social costs. In effect their proposals say: "We believe the effort ratings we received from our co-workers together with allowances members of households have been granted indicate that we deserve the right to consume goods and services whose production entails an equivalent level of social costs."
>
> The planning procedure is designed to make it clear when a worker council production proposal is inefficient and when a neighbourhood

consumption council proposal is unfair, and allows other worker and consumer councils to deny approval for proposals when they seem to be inefficient or unfair. *But initial self-activity proposals and all revisions of proposals are entirely up to each worker and consumer council itself. In other words, if a worker council production proposal or neighborhood council consumption proposal is disapproved the council that made the proposal revises its own proposal for submission in the next round of the planning procedure. This aspect of the participatory planning procedure distinguishes it from all other planning models and is crucial if workers and consumers are going to enjoy meaningful self-management.*[81]

On the traditional microeconomic assumptions and mathematical modelling traditionally adduced to demonstrate the efficiency of free markets over central planning, the model of ParEcon has been shown to likely be more efficient and hence superior.[82] There is also ongoing computer-based modelling testing the model, and preliminary results are reported to be very encouraging.[83]

From its existence, coherence, and formal promise, it is at least clear that this model gives us a reason to reject any purely theoretical claims that participatory democratic planning is impossible in principle. This gives us an answer to the claimed formal impossibility of democratic planning, but feasibility is about much more than this, which brings us to Friedrich Hayek's critique of planning.

Hayek's critique of planning targets central planning and turns on a claim about human beings' irredeemable epistemological limitations. Human beings' knowledge, he claims, is both imperfect and dispersed among many different individuals, and there's no possibility of ever being able to centralise it into a single (human) mind. Thus, no individual planner will be able to take all the necessary and relevant information into account when formulating economic plans and prices for an entire society. Markets, on the other hand, are, through their pricing mechanism and the information it transmits to firms and consumers, able to collate and transmit a large amount of such relevant information. Because of this, any prices and plans set by centralised planners will, inevitably, be based on, and transmit, less and less reliable information than market

[81] Hahnel (2012, p. 95–6), my emphasis.
[82] For the relevant detail, see Albert and Hahnel (1991); see also Hahnel (2021).
[83] Hahnel, Robin, personal communication and Hahnel (2021).

pricing and firms' individual planning based thereon would, inevitably rendering it comparatively inferior to capitalist markets.[84] If this argument applies also to the kinds of de-centralised democratic planning modelled in Participatory Economics, our model faces a serious challenge which is not answered by its formal coherence and promise, since Hayek's argument asserts that the models' informational inputs would be dramatically inferior to what they would have to be for it to function comparatively well. This is an important challenge for feasibility not because it would show that planning would be impossible (which it doesn't), but because it argues that it's likely to carry other unacceptable costs and consequences which make it unviable as an alternative to capitalism.

The most important point I want to make against this is that Hayek's argument targets the possibility of fulfilling a certain kind of epistemic role that the planning model in ParEcon doesn't have or need. ParEcon does not require that any single individual or board determine a society's prices and economic plan. Instead, it involves individuals formulating their own plans, to be accepted or rejected by their peers, and then compiling these in their lowest-level workers' and consumers' councils. These councils then add the relevant collective goods etc. that they propose; these are then accepted or rejected by the peers within the wider federation (with any revisions made by a council or individual themselves); these are collated into the plan of a higher-level council; and this procedure continues until the final stage is reached. There is a mechanism to simulate the informational role of prices to ease this process, but these have no binding force, don't set rates of exchange of any kind (unlike prices in capitalist societies), and are based on the self-activity proposals of workers and consumers and their councils, with none of the perverse incentives that plague forms of central planning. Now, this is not a complete account of the planning model, nor a defence of it—either of those is beyond our scope here. Rather, it is a (very) brief summary of the flow of information that shows that proposals and plans are all made by individual persons and councils themselves and then collated upwards in such a way that there is no place or need for a single person or council to hold all the information relevant to determining prices and planning. Consequently, Hayek's argument cannot be used as a criticism of Participatory Economics. Since this is one form that a bottom-up planned society that Marx calls socialism

---

[84] Hayek (1945, 1960, 1973, 1976, 1978, 1979, 1988), cf. also Gamble (1996, ch. 3; 2006).

might take, Hayek's argument also cannot be used as a criticism of Marx's vision of socialism in general—although it might well challenge some of the other institutional forms that such a vision could take.

The other point I would like to make on the issue of feasibility is an empirical one. It turns on the premise that forms of democratic planning have existed on societal scales well beyond individual workplaces, and that these have fared rather well in comparison to the capitalisms they have replaced. Remember that the contention of critics like Hayek is *not* that planning will be imperfect and problematic, but that it will be *comparatively worse* than capitalism. From this perspective, there are two reasons to doubt the accuracy of Hayek's claim with respect to participatory democratic planning vs. the type of markets that typify capitalism: one from the perspective of the former; the other from the ecological implications of the latter.

First, we have historical examples which, though none of them implemented a form of participatory planning, provide limited support for it. Perhaps the most prominent is revolutionary Spain in the 1930s. Although revolutionary Spain didn't implement full society-wide planning, and the details of how it worked out are, like all historical experiments with social change, varied and contradictory, the available evidence suggests that the shift towards workers self-rule, federation, and more forms of bottom-up planning were successful and efficient, as well as much freer, than the society they replaced.[85]

Second, Hayek's argument for the comparative efficiency of capitalist-type markets relies on tacit assumptions about what we can and should value. All judgments of efficiency ultimately come down to assessing relationships between costs and benefits, and so in turn depend entirely on what we choose to count as benefits and costs. As I pointed out above with respect to Weber, this means that certain things like securing human emancipation, facilitating human development and flourishing, and not destroying the climate and undermining the conditions for human life on our planet are important things to factor in. Unfortunately, they typically aren't in competitive market exchanges, and this leads to major inefficiencies that Hayek and many other defenders of capitalism fail to consider.

---

[85] On Spain, see e.g. part II of "Objectivity and Liberal Scholarship" in Chomsky (1969, esp. p. 88–92), Broué and Témime (2008), Leval (2018), Mintz (2013) and Peirats (2011, 2012a, 2012b).

This becomes apparent once we consider how capitalism's competitive markets ignore a wide range of real social costs to human and non-human life. It is well-known and recognised that competitive markets externalise benefits and costs that are not borne directly by the buyer and seller in a transaction.[86] When some large powerful corporation sells private jets to billionaires, torture equipment to a dictatorship, or arms to the American Empire, a wide variety of real social costs to human beings and the environment are completely left out—e.g. the millions who are dying and seem likely to die from capitalism's destruction of our biosphere. Of course, they also ignore the myriad harms done to the workers who make these things. In fact, reducing workers' freedom and working conditions often appear as positive ways of reducing labour costs for capitalists. Competitive markets not only incentivise buyers and sellers to ignore these real social costs, they also, as we saw in Chapter 7, force capitalists to ignore them in the service of profit maximisation. As a result, firms are made to produce too much of goods with negative social externalities (e.g. private jets and yachts) and too few goods with positive social externalities (like high-quality public transport). Firms that try to take into account a broader range of harms and benefits are, in time, outcompeted by those that don't. This is not because what they're doing is impossible or contrary to human nature. Rather, the reason firms cannot take these vital considerations into account is because doing so is incompatible with the social structures of capitalism and their inherent dynamics of impersonal domination.

A particularly important aspect of this is of course capitalism's inherent tendency for growth. The slogan that infinite growth on a finite planet is impossible is both true and devastating. Economic growth reliably leads to growing throughputs in matter and energy, which in turn brings with it growing pollution, including emissions of CO_2 and other greenhouse gases.[87] Note that this is a general claim, not a strictly universal one, so the argument that growing pollution isn't strictly inevitable is irrelevant. It's not strictly inevitable that ignoring a pandemic in a major urban centre will lead to lots of people dying, but it generally and predictably will. In both cases, it would be ridiculous to ignore the problem. These

---

[86] For more on everything discussed in this paragraph, see Hahnel (2015, 2021).

[87] See the discussion and sources in Foster, Clark and York (2010, Ch. 5) and Schröder and Storm (2020).

problems can't be solved by e.g. increasing market access or lowering entry costs, since, these do nothing to reduce the impersonal domination of capitalism and its destructive dynamics. Nor can they be adequately solved by government regulation. The variety and complexity of the ecological challenges we face, and the enduring incentives for corporations to ignore, hide, and downplay the harms they cause, as well as work around any attempts at regulation, leave such solutions, though vital in the short term, inadequate in the long run. Of course, governments could take over and direct firms themselves, but this just would be introducing a form of planning.

Once we recognise this, the Hayekian critique of Marx loses all force. It is not reasonable to suppose that, once we take a sufficiently broad view of the relevant costs and benefits, in particular concerns about how capitalism is systematically destroying the planet, the kinds of markets that Hayek prefers are likely to be more efficient than any form of planning, which has the ability to take these concerns into account.[88] If we think that short-term profit-making while destroying our planet and the continued conditions for human life is efficient, while saving the planet, achieving emancipation, and enhancing human development is not, we simply don't have a good conception of efficiency. This Hayekian critique of Marx's vision of socialism is therefore unviable.

In this chapter, we have seen how Marx expands his vision of what a free future society must be like. Based on the diagnosis of capitalism's personal and impersonal forms of domination articulated in his second theory of alienation, he argues that a free socialist society must be fully democratic, feature participatory planning, replace the hierarchical division of labour, and distribute according to need. We saw how this continues to challenge contemporary proposals for free economic institutions and corrected a couple of still-prevalent errors in Marx interpretation. I finished by defending it against the objections of two of its most important critics: Max Weber and Friedrich Hayek.

It's now time to move on to the next chapter, which deals with Marx's conception of his own activities vis-à-vis the agent he holds will bring about a socialist revolution—i.e. his views on the practice of the theorist. This raises two interrelated questions. One is about how the diagnosis of capitalist unfreedom is connected to the driving forces or motivations

---

[88] For details on this in the case of Participatory Economics, see Hahnel (2005).

for socialist revolution as encapsulated in his views on the contradictions between the powers and relations and production and between workers and capitalists. The other is about how Marx understands the connection between theorising and the revolutionary movement. With these last pieces of the puzzle in place we will be able to survey the reconstructed totality of Marx's critique of capitalism.

REFERENCES

PRIMARY

Marx, K., & Carver, T. (ed. and trans.). (1996). *Marx: Later political writings.* Cambridge University Press.
Marx, K., & Nicolaus, M. (trans.). (1993). *Grundrisse: Foundations of a critique of political economy.* Penguin.
Marx, K., Fowkes, B. (trans.) & Mandel, E. (intro.). (1990). *Capital: A critique of political economy* (Vol. 1). Penguin.
Marx, K., Livingstone, R. (trans), Benton, G. (trans) & Colletti, L. (intro.). (1992). *Karl Marx: Early writings.* Penguin.

SECONDARY

Albert, M. (2003). *ParEcon: Life after capitalism.* Verso.
Albert, M., & Hahnel, R. (1978). *Unorthodox Marxism: An essay on capitalism, socialism and revolution.* South End Press.
Albert, M., & Hahnel, R. (1991). *The political economy of participatory economics.* Princeton University Press.
Albert, M., & Hahnel, R. (1999). *Looking forward: Participatory economics for the twenty first century.* South End Press.
Braverman, H. (1998). *Labour and monopoly capitalism: The degradation of work in the twentieth century* (25th Anniversary ed.). Monthly Review Press.
Broué, P. & Témime, E. 2008. *The revolution and the cvil war in Spain.* Chicago, IL: Haymarket Books.
Campbell, A. (2011). *Marx and Engels' vision of building a good society* (pp. 9–32). Marangos.
Chomsky, N. (1969). *American power and the new mandarins.* The New Press.
Cockshott, P. W., & Cottrell, A. (1993). *Towards a new socialism.* Spokesman.
Cohen, G. A. (2001). *Karl Marx's theory of history: A defence* (Expanded Edition). Princeton University Press.
Devine, P. (1988). *Democracy and economic planning: The political economy of a self-governing society.* Polity Press.
Doucouliagos, C. (1995). Worker participation and productivity in labor-managed and participatory capitalist firms: A meta-analysis. *Industrial and Labor Relations Review, 49,* 58–77.

Doucouliagos, C. (1997). The comparative efficiency and productivity of labor-managed and capitalist firms. *Review of Radical Political Economics*, 29, 45–69.
Draper, H. (1977). *Karl Marx's theory of revolution, volume I: State and bureaucracy*. Monthly Review Press.
Foster, J. B., Clark, B., & York, R. (2010). *The ecological rift: Capitalism's war on the earth*. Monthly Review Press.
Gamble, A. (1996). *Hayek: The iron cage of liberty*. Polity Press.
Gamble, A. (2006). Hayek on knowledge, economics, and society. In Feser (Ed.), pp. 111–131.
González-Ricoy, I. (2014). The republican case for workplace democracy. *Social Theory and Practice*, 40(2), 232–254.
Gourevitch, A. (2015). *From slavery to the cooperative commonwealth: Labor and republican liberty in the nineteenth century*. Cambridge University Press.
Hahnel, R. (2005). *Economic justice and democracy: From competition to cooperation*. Routledge.
Hahnel, R. (2012). *Of the people, by the people: The case for a participatory economy*. Soapbox Press.
Hahnel, R. (2015). *Green economics: Confronting the ecological crisis*. Routledge.
Hahnel, R. (2021). *Democratic economic planning*. Routledge.
Hamilton, A., Madison, J., & Jay, J. (2003). *The federalist: With letters of Brutus*. Cambridge University Press.
Hayek, F. (1945). The use of knowledge in society. *American Economic Review*, 35, 519–530.
Hayek, F. (1960). *The constitution of liberty*. University of Chicago Press.
Hayek, F. (1973). *Law, legislation, and liberty* (Vol. 1). University of Chicago Press.
Hayek, F. (1976). *Law, legislation, and liberty* (Vol. 2). University of Chicago Press.
Hayek, F. (1978). Coping with ignorance. *Imprimis*, 7, 1–6.
Hayek, F. (1979). *Law, legislation, and liberty* (Vol. 3). University of Chicago Press.
Hayek, F. (1988). *The fatal conceit: The errors of socialism*. In W. W. Bartley (Ed.), *The collected works of F. A. Hayek* (Vol. 1). University of Chicago Press.
Herbst, P. G. (1962). *Autonomous group functioning: An exploration in behaviour theory and measurement*. Tavistock Publications.
Hsieh, N.-H. (2008). Workplace democracy, workplace republicanism, and economic democracy. *Revue de Philosophie Economique*, 9, 57–78.
Hsieh, N.-H. (2012). Work, ownership, and productive enfranchisement. In M. O'Neill & T. Williamson (Eds.), *Property-owning democracy: Rawls and beyond* (pp. 149–162). Wiley Blackwell.
Hudis, P. (2013). *Marx concept of the alternative to capitalism*. Haymarket Books.

Hunt, R. (1974). *The political ideas of Marx and Engels, volume 1: Marxism and totalitarian democracy, 1818–1850*. Macmillan.
Hunt, R. (1984). *The political ideas of Marx and Engels, volume 2: Classical Marxism 1850–1895*. Macmillan.
Kasmir, S. (1996). *The myth of Mondragon: Cooperatives, politics, and working-class life in a Basque town*. State University of New York Press.
Kasmir, S. (2018). Cooperative democracy or competitiveness? Rethinking Mondragon. *Socialist Register, 54*, 202–223.
Larrabure, M. (2013). Human development and class struggle in Venezuela's popular economy: The paradox of 'twenty-first century socialism.' *Historical Materialism, 21*(4), 177–200.
Leval, G. (2018). *Collectives in the Spanish revolution*. Oakland, CA: PM Press.
Levine, D., & Tyson, L. A. (1990). Participation, productivity and the firm's environment. In A. Blinder (Ed.), *Paying for productivity: A look at the evidence* (pp. 203–214). Brookings Institution.
Melman, S. (1958). *Decision-making and productivity*. Basil Blackwell.
Mészáros, I. (1986). *Philosophy, ideology and social science: Essays in negation and affirmation*. Wheatsheaf Books.
Mintz, F. (2013). *Anarchism and workers' self-management in revolutionary Spain*. AK Press.
Montesquieu, C. (1998). *Montesquieu: The spirit of the laws*. Cambridge University Press.
Ness, I., & Azzellini, D. (Eds.). (2011). *Ours to master and to own: Workers' control from the commune to the present*. Haymarket Books.
Ollman, B. (1977). Marx's vision of communism: A reconstruction. *Critique, 8*(1), 4–41.
Peirats, J. (2011). *The CNT in the Spanish Revolution:* (Vol. 1). PM Press.
Peirats, J. (2012a). *The CNT in the Spanish revolution:* (Vol. 2). PM Press.
Peirats, J. (2012b). *The CNT in the Spanish revolution:* (Vol. 3). PM Press.
Pérotin, V. (2018). *What do we really know about worker co-operatives?* Co-operatives UK.
Phillips, L., & Rozworski, M. (2019). *The people's republic of Walmart: How the world's biggest corporations are laying the foundation for socialism*. Verso.
Raekstad, P. (2011). Deltakende demokrati – en sosialisme for fremtiden. *Rødt!: Marxistisk Tidsskrift, 40*(3), 116–126.
Raekstad, P. (2013, July 30). Review of the people, by the people: The case for a participatory economy. *Marx and Philosophy Review of Books*. Available online at: http://marxandphilosophy.org.uk/reviewofbooks/reviews/2013/792
Schröder, E., & Storm, S. (2020). Economic growth and carbon emissions: The road to "hothouse earth" is paved with good intentions. *International Journal of Political Economy, 49*(2), 153–173.
Schweickart, D. (1996). *Against capitalism*. Westview Press.

Trist, E. L., Higgin, G. W., Murray, H., & Pollock, A. B. (1963). *Organizational choice: Capabilities of groups at the coal face under changing technologies*. Tavistock Publications.

Walker, P. (Ed.). (1979). *Between labor and capital*. South End Press.

Weber, M., Lassman, P. (ed.), & Speirs, R. (ed.). (1994). *Weber: Political writings*. Cambridge University Press.

Wright, E. O. (1980). Varieties of Marxist conceptions of class structure. *Politics & Society, 9*(3), 323–370.

CHAPTER 9

Radical Theory and Revolutionary Practice

Having laid out the diagnosis of capitalism Marx presents in his second theory of alienation and the socialist cure he proposes to it, three questions immediately present themselves. First, what was the role that this critique was to play within his agent-centred approach to political theory? Secondly, why does Marx, in post-1844 works, continue to emphasise and expand greatly on some aspects of alienation (especially alienation from product and alienation from others), while emphasising its more normatively laden aspects less? One answer is that Marx simply abandons alienation and its concerns altogether. This answer cannot be satisfactory, because as we've seen all four kinds of alienation reappear throughout Marx's later discussions of capitalism and feed into his vision of socialism. This leads us to the third question: what role, if any, does the theory of alienation come to play in Marx's later thoughts on human society and social change? I will answer each of these questions in turn, emphasising that Marx's critique of capitalism forms the core of the two revolutionary contradictions of capitalism he does the most to pinpoint in his later works: between the powers and relations of production and between workers and capitalists. This is why Marx keeps returning to the ways in which capitalism thwarts freedom and human development. With this done, I will briefly argue that the reasons Marx seems to have had for thinking that the more normatively laden aspects of his diagnosis were unimportant are partly mistaken. On the basis of his own methodological commitments, there is therefore good reason to pay more attention to these ideas today.

Revolutionary Midwives and the Birth of the Future

The agent-centred position Marx developed in the latter parts of 1843, which formed the basis for the *Economic and Philosophical Manuscripts of 1844*, underwent a significant change during 1844–1845, moving away from a perspective which saw ideas as the active element in social change. On the view that Marx adopts during the writing of the 1844 manuscripts, such ideas would be formulated in some critical political theory and find their (passive) material basis in an agent capable of realising its recommendations. During 1844–1845, this changes to a view where the proletariat is seen as much more active, an agent which can and will tend to generate the powers, needs, and consciousness it requires to bring about a process of socialist revolution.

Accordingly, Marx adopts the *maieutic* or *obstetric* conception of the practice of the theorist. Present capitalist society is in the process of (at least potentially) giving birth to that of the future through the active agency of the working-class movement. The task of the theorist, like that of the midwife, is to help this process unfold and achieve some sort of successful result—e.g. a process of giving birth resulting in a healthy newborn child, or a process of social struggle on the part of the proletariat resulting in a successful transition to a socialist society. It's hard to pin down all of the decisive factors of this shift, but they almost certainly include his enduring contacts with French communist/socialist workers' organisations, interactions with thinkers like Moses Hess and Friedrich Engels, and, crucially, the revolt by the Silesian weavers. Michael Löwy has summed this development up as follows:

> Between the weavers' revolt (June 1844) and the *Theses on Feuerbach* (about March 1845), the process of formation of the Marxist *Weltanschauung* was completed. This was *the* great ideological turning point in the evolution of the young Marx. The Silesian rising, together with the communist movement he encountered in Paris, faced him concretely with the problem of the revolutionary praxis of the proletarian masses. In the *Vorwärts* article, Marx discovers the proletariat as the *active* element in

emancipation, but he does not yet draw the philosophical conclusions from this discovery. A few weeks later, he sketches, in *The Holy Family*, a first attempt at a theoretical solution of the problem. He believes he can grasp revolutionary activity—which is evidently outside the Young Hegelians' world of thought—through the categories of the French materialism of the eighteenth century. Soon, however, he perceives that the revolutionary praxis of the *masses* cannot be fitted into the narrow framework of the "theory of circumstances": this is his break with "the old materialism", which at once spreads to all levels. The *Theses on Feuerbach* expose the "practical essence" of history and of social life, of "sensuousness" and of theory, of the relations of men with nature and among themselves, and, finally, outline a coherent set of ideas, a significant global structure: the *philosophy of praxis*, the general theoretical foundation for the idea of revolutionary self-emancipation of the proletariat.[1]

This is later accompanied by a critique of the authoritarian approaches to theorising he identifies in enlightenment, utopian socialist, and Feuerbachian materialist works[2]—and that, as we saw in Chapter 6, Marx himself endorsed while a radical democrat. The simplistic "old materialist" view that we can change human beings and society simply by following the right educators or leaders forgets that "it is essential to educate the educator himself. This doctrine must, therefore, divide society into two parts, one of which is superior to society", something Marx clearly thinks is nonsensical.[3]

Marx finds the source of this mistake in the old materialism's "standpoint" of civil society; by contrast, "the standpoint of the new is human society, or social humanity".[4] Marx's alternative approach builds on the belief that "the coincidence of the changing of circumstances

---

[1] Löwy (2005, p. 109).

[2] The connection between the philosophy of Feuerbach's materialism and French and English socialism, in particular Robert Owen's, is made explicit in *The Holy Family* (MECW 4, p. 124–32/MEGA$_1$ I:3, pp. 300–309, see also Engels' discussion of the role of Feuerbach in their development in *Ludwig Feuerbach and the End of Classical German Philosophy*). For this critique applied to utopian socialists, see the *Communist Manifesto*.

[3] Marx (1992, p. 422/IV:3, p. 20).

[4] Ibid., p. 423/IV:3, p. 21.

and of human activity or self-changing can be conceived and rationally understood only as *revolutionary practice*".[5] Accordingly, there can be no enlightened intellectuals standing above society, developing and bestowing the right ideas upon the masses. Nor can any elite organisation wielding the immortal principles of some radical theory take power and give freedom to the people. The only way to secure universal human emancipation is through struggles for self-emancipation that develop our powers, needs, and consciousness for ourselves—this is why "the emancipation of the working classes must be conquered by the working classes themselves".[6]

According to Marx, the old materialist approaches fail to do justice to the nature of human conscious powers and ideas; the ways they change and respond to different natural, social, and historical contexts; and their role in changing society. He thus argues that Feuerbach doesn't see the experienced world as a "historical product, the result of the activity of a whole succession of generations (…) developing its industry and its intercourse, and modifying its social system according to the changed needs".[7] These ideas grew out Marx's reflections not only on the activity of socialist workers, but also out of the ideas in the *Economic and Philosophical Manuscripts of 1844* that prefigured them, e.g. when Marx writes that "*[i]ndustry* is the *real* historical relationship of nature", that it has "transformed human life all the more *practically* through industry and has prepared the conditions for human emancipation".[8]

In this way, Marx's growing emphasis on both the lived experiences of workers under capitalism and on the importance of changing social relations in response to human needs that Marx embarked upon in developing his theory of alienation led him to overhaul his outlook. Far from rejecting his theory of alienation, this new outlook is premised on the centrality of the relations of production and the implications thereof for thinking about human beings, society, and social change more broadly. Nowhere is this clearer than in Marx's discussion of the revolutionary contradictions of capitalism.

---

[5] Ibid., p. 422/IV:3, p. 20.
[6] MESW 2, p. 19/I:20, p. 13.
[7] MECW 5, p. 39/I:5, p. 20.
[8] Marx (1992, p. 355/I:2, pp. 272/396).

Alienation and the Revolutionary Contradictions of Capitalism

Marx consistently identifies two key revolutionary contradictions of capitalism: the contradiction between the powers and relations of production and the contradiction between workers and capitalists.[9] He writes that:

> These various conditions [the natural, social and historical conditions under which individuals interact, especially the relations of production], which appear first as conditions of self-activity, later as fetters upon it, form in the whole development of history a coherent series of forms of intercourse, the coherence of which consists in this: an earlier form of intercourse, which has become a fetter, is replaced by a new one corresponding to the more developed productive powers and, hence, to the advanced mode of the self-activity of individuals—a form which in its turn becomes a fetter and is then replaced by another. Since these conditions correspond at every stage to the simultaneous development of the productive powers, their history is at the same time the history of the evolving productive powers taken over by each new generation, and is therefore the history of the development of the powers of the individuals themselves.[10]

These contradictions between productive powers on the one hand, and forms of social intercourse on the other, are claimed to be the source of "all collisions in history".[11] Similarly, in his *Preface to A Contribution to the Critique of Political Economy*, Marx famously wrote that at "a certain stage of development, the material productive powers of society come into conflict with the existing relations of production... From forms of development of the productive powers these relations turn into their fetters.

---

[9] Of course, Marx talks about a number of other contradictions of capitalism, e.g. in his analyses of its various crisis tendencies. However, it is well-known that he never argues that these are the driving forces of socialist revolution (on their own), on which see Lebowitz (2020, Ch. 4).

[10] MECW 5, p. 82/I:5, pp. 103–4. I have modified the translation of "Kräfte" from "forces" to "powers" so that it's more in line with how this term is translated throughout this book and in other contexts. This preserves the important conceptual link to its role in Marx's discussion of human development and the important conceptual link between "powers" in general and "productive powers" in particular.

[11] MECW 5, p. 74/I:5, p. 90.

Then begins an era of revolution".[12] This is at once one of Marx's most important and most misunderstood ideas, and can only be properly understood by careful attention to the precise nature of the conflict between the powers of production and the relations of production.

We'll shortly see how these play out in Marx's later writings, but a pre-emptive summary will be helpful. The contradiction between powers and relations of production consists in the fact that, on the one hand, capitalism's development of the powers of production has made socialism possible, and with it universal human emancipation and greater human development, while, on the other hand, capitalism's inherent social relations prevent workers from realising those potentials. The theory of alienation from the product of labour, from productive activity, and from species-being is Marx's diagnosis of how capitalist social relations do the latter. Building on this, the contradiction between workers and capitalists is provided by alienation from others. Capitalist social relations necessarily include at least two classes—workers and capitalists. Proletarians are rendered inherently unfree by the social relations that define capitalism; experience their condition as one of domination, oppression, impoverishment, and misery relative to the potentials they rightly perceive to be available; and so become interested in, and driven to, fight to improve their conditions in the short term and replace unfree capitalist relations with free, socialist relations in the long term. At the same, capitalist social relations also entail a class of capitalists. They have a great deal of wealth, power, and privilege, and hence feel empowered and at ease in their situation,[13] and so will struggle to maintain capitalism and prevent a transition to socialism. Note that this is not simply an effect of capitalists having certain goods or amounts of money, but due to their structural relations of power, which the former may or may not (but typically do) flow from. As such, the contradiction between workers and capitalists springs from the power relations of capitalism, not from their more contingent distributive effects.

---

[12] Marx (1992, pp. 425–426/II:2, pp. 100–1). Here too I have modified the translation from "forces" to "powers", for the aforementioned reasons.

[13] MECW 4, p. 36/MEGA$_1$ I:3, p. 206.

Let's see how this plays out in Volume I of *Capital*, where Marx writes[14]:

> This expropriation is accomplished through the action of the immanent laws of capitalist production itself, through the centralization of capitals. One capitalist always strikes down many others. Hand in hand with this centralization, or this expropriation of many capitalists by a few, other developments take place on an ever-increasing scale, such as the growth of the co-operative form of the labour process, the conscious technical application of science, the planned exploitation of the soil, the transformation of the means of labour into forms in which they can only be used in common, the economizing of all means of production by their use as the means of production of combined, socialized labour, the entanglement of all peoples in the net of the world market, and, with this, the growth of the international character of the capitalist regime. Along with the constant decrease in the number of capitalist magnates, who usurp and monopolize all the advantages of this process of transformation, the mass of misery, oppression, slavery, degradation and exploitation grows; but with this there also grows the revolt of the working class, a class constantly increasing in numbers, and trained, united and organized by the very mechanism of the capitalist process of production. The monopoly of capital becomes a fetter upon the mode of production which has flourished alongside and under it. The centralization of the means of production and the socialization of labour reach a point at which they become incompatible with their capitalist integument. This integument is burst asunder. The knell of capitalist private property sounds. The expropriators are expropriated.[15]

Earlier on in the same work, Marx writes that;

> As the number of the co-operating workers increases, so too does their resistance to the domination of capital, and, necessarily, the pressure put on by capital to overcome this resistance. (...) Similarly, as the means of production extend, the necessity increases for some effective control over the proper application of them, because they confront the wage-labourer as the property of another *[fremdes Eigentum]*.[16]

---

[14] For reasons of time and space, I've restricted the sources discussed below to Volume I of *Capital* only, but the same claims can be found throughout his published and unpublished works until the end of Marx's life.

[15] Marx (1990, p. 929/II: 6, p. 682).

[16] Marx (1990, p. 449/II:8, p. 329).

There's a lot going on here, all of which, I will show, builds upon Marx's critique of capitalism, in particular the theory of alienation. By productive powers, Marx means the collected real possibilities that a given human society has for producing things (in the broadest possible sense) to satisfy human needs. This includes all forms of land, machinery, labour, technology, levels of scientific achievement, and even forms of social organisation or intercourse. By forms of social intercourse, Marx means the relational structures within and through which human beings work on and with one another and the natural world to secure the production and reproduction of their societies—including, but not limited to, economic production. The totality of the available means for satisfying human needs, as expressed in the idea of a society's productive powers, both restrict and enable changes in these relational structures.

Powers and relations of production come into contradiction when and only when the totality of productive powers available enables a much greater development of human powers—including, but not limited to, powers of production—than is possible within the constraints of the current relations of production. As we've seen, Marx thinks that capitalism has developed the powers of production—especially the kinds of machinery, technology, and socialised forms of production—in ways that have made socialism possible—not just in societies that have gone through this process, but any society thereafter.[17] He also thinks that our ability to make full use of these powers is fettered by the continued existence of capitalist relations of production. The contradiction between the powers and relations of production thus consists in the fact that the same capitalist social relations both enable human emancipation (by developing the powers of production in the right ways) and prevent human emancipation (until they are abolished/replaced by socialist ones).

A real movement towards socialism begins, Marx believes, when this contradiction has developed. Ironically, by developing the powers of production in ways that enrich themselves, capitalists spur "the creation of those material conditions of production which alone can form the real

---

[17] That is, to any society thereafter that can acquire them. Marx clearly points out in both his letter to Vera Zasulich and in the 1872 preface to the *Communist Manifesto* that it is *not* necessary for each society to first reach the stage of capitalism before transitioning to socialism, only that capitalism must have evolved in some society and developed the means of production. In fact, in both places he argues the exact opposite, that e.g. Russia may be able to transition to socialism without first introducing capitalism.

basis of a higher form of society, a society in which the full and free development of every individual forms the ruling principle".[18] Capitalism has also brought workers together into collective workplaces; improved their means of communication and thus organisation; and unified them under common interests against the dominating social relations of capitalism. As a result, workers also come to perceive the powers of production that are available, the potentials for emancipation and further human development they entail, and how the personal and impersonal domination of capitalism prevents them from realising these potentials.

This explains why, in his *Preface to A Contribution to the Critique of Political Economy*, Marx writes that "[m]ankind thus inevitably sets itself only such tasks as it is able to solve, since closer examination will always show that the problem itself arises only when the material conditions for its solution are already present or at least in the course of formation".[19] Applied to socialist revolution, the point here is that it's only when the material conditions for socialism have developed that the potential inherent in them can be perceived. It's only when these potentials are perceived that we can begin to ask questions about how we can change relations of production to better take advantage of the potentials we're aware of. And it's only when we do that that we can form a revolutionary movement seeking to realise these potentials by replacing the relations of production.

It's clear how this results in the contradiction between workers and capitalists. Capitalists, being in a position of greater power, wealth, and privilege, will fight to retain their position, which in turn entails that they work to maintain capitalism and suppress any attempted socialist revolution. Workers not only experience their situation as alienated, unfree, and impoverished. They also rightly perceive that the development of the powers of production has made it possible to change these conditions, replacing the unfree capitalist relations with free socialist ones that better enable their development and flourishing—hence Marx's point in Volume I of Capital that capitalism uses workers "to satisfy the need of the existing values for valorization" instead of employing its resources to "satisfy the worker's own need for development".[20] In other words, workers' need

---

[18] Marx (1990, p. 739/II:6, p. 543).
[19] Marx (1992, p. 426/II:2, p. 101).
[20] Marx (1990, p. 772/II:6, p. 567).

for development, for expanding their powers to do and to be, leads them to develop an interest in replacing capitalism with socialism. Note that for Marx, as he writes in the *Grundrisse*, even "private interest is itself already a socially determined interest, which can be achieved only within the conditions laid down by society and with the means provided by society", as a result of which "its content, as well as the form and means of its realization, is given by social conditions".[21] In this way, workers' interest in socialist revolution is rooted in the contrast between the emancipatory potentials capitalism has enabled and how its alienating, dominating, and unfree social relations prevent workers from taking advantage of them.[22] The contradiction between workers and capitalists consists in the fact that the same conditions, the same social relations of capitalism, generate both a social force interested in and seeking to replace capitalism with socialism and a social force interested in and seeking to retain capitalism and prevent socialism.

Where Chapter 7 showed that Marx retains all the ideas expressed in his four kinds of alienation throughout his later works, here we have seen that they form the core of his understanding of the revolutionary contradictions of capitalism. If [c]ommunism is "the real movement which abolishes the present state of things", the theory of alienation and the revolutionary contradictions of capitalism explain how the "conditions of this movement result from the premises now in existence".[23]

There's thus no incompatibility between Marx's theory of alienation and his later theories of society and social change. Quite the contrary: the theory of alienation essentially grows into his understanding of capitalism's contradictions as the basis for socialist revolution. Alienation thus

---

[21] Marx (1993, p. 156/II.1.1, p. 89).

[22] Though often identified only with the later Marx, the earliest prefigurations of these ideas can, as I pointed out above, be found as early as the *Economic and Philosophical Manuscripts of 1844*. Here Marx writes that "*[i]ndustry* is the *real* historical relationship of nature, and hence of natural science, to man" and that it has "transformed human life all the more *practically* through industry and has prepared the conditions for human emancipation", even though, at the same time "immediate effect was to complete the process of dehumanization" (Marx 1992, p. 355/I:2, pp. 272/396). As you'd expect from my reading, he rapidly moves on to talk about how if this is "conceived as the *exoteric* revelation of man's *essential powers*, the *human* essence of nature or the *natural* essence of man can also be understood" (ibid., both) and to discuss the meaning of freedom in connection to consciousness (Marx 1992, pp. 355–356/I:2, pp. 272–273/396–397).

[23] MECW 5, p. 49/I:5, p. 37.

remains the core of Marx's diagnosis of the revolutionary contradictions of capitalism, providing the basis for his understanding of how capitalism both generates the real movement for proletarian self-emancipation and imposes obstacles thereto.

The Revolutionary Theorist as Midwife

If the proletariat is the class which is already beginning to actively put the wheels of socialist revolution in motion, then the role of the theorist is not, as Marx wrote in 1843, to develop the philosophy or critique which will provide its active head, since no such thing is needed. The proletariat is already politically active and developing its own needs, powers, and consciousness.

What the theorist should do instead is help this active process of consciousness-raising and self-emancipation along. Some things will be relevant for this and others will not. A proper understanding of the nature of capitalism—its tendencies and laws of motion—and of how it dominates and subjugates the working class will no doubt be vital. So too will an understanding of capitalism's class structure and its contradictory character—revealing its inherently historical character and potential for revolutionary transformation. One part of this will involve critiquing and overcoming what Marx calls "Commodity Fetishism": the phenomenon by which the social characteristics that certain objects have by virtue of their role in capitalist social relations (being commodities, money, capital) are misperceived as natural properties inhering in the objects themselves.[24] By revealing the socially generated and in key ways contingent character of these properties, Marx's political economy helps to unmask the real nature of capitalism and empower workers to overthrow it.

A correct understanding of capitalism's political economy is important for overthrowing it in a number of more specific ways as well. For instance, a central early debate Marx had with other socialists centres on what is often called the Iron Law of Wages. Briefly put, the Iron Law of Wages refers to the idea that workers' real wages inevitably tend towards the bare minimum required for survival and/or reproduction. If this is correct, then organising the working class to fight for reforms—e.g. for better real wages and working conditions—in the present in order to

---

[24] See esp. Heinrich (2012, Ch. 3, section 8 and Ch. 10).

build a revolutionary socialist movement is unviable. Why? Because if the Iron Law of Wages holds, then no lasting improvements to real wages is possible, and this means that so too is fighting for lasting piecemeal wage increases under capitalism. Thus, no such process can be expected to build a revolutionary movement in the long run. We can thus see why Marx turned to focus on political economy: it was vital for helping the proletariat to raise its consciousness and stake out a viable socialist strategy. Politically speaking, Marx's purpose for writing *Capital* was to make reading it pointless.

But if Marx retains his theory of alienation, why does he emphasise its more normative aspects less in later works? I think it is because he thinks that it is unhelpful, compared to the other things a theorist could be doing, to keep developing and putting forth these normatively laden components. The task of agent-centred political theorists is *not* to develop normatively laden political theory for its own sake, but to help influence political agents in ways that help them bring about the alternative(s) the theorists support. The first and fourth kinds of alienation have obvious virtues in this regard. The fourth kind is important for a wide variety of practical issues. If capitalists wield capital, are empowered by it and dominate and exploit workers by means of it, it is obvious that it is in their interests to retain capitalism, why they can be relied upon to defend it as an economic system, why they cannot be accepted as important powers within proletarian organisations (as funders, leaders, etc.), and so on. The first kind of alienation is important because it lays out how, and in which ways, capitalism dominates, oppresses, and subjugates workers. In so doing, one can see how certain proposed solutions to the problems inherent in capitalism, such as a return to small-scale craft production, will be ineffective in the long run: they will only modify capitalist social relations in minor and temporary ways; and over time capitalism, with all its vices, will inevitably reappear. In a sense, we can understand a great deal of Marx's later political economy as fleshing out the first kind of alienation.

Marx seems to think otherwise about further developing and emphasising the second and third kinds of capitalist alienation—alienation from the process of production and from species-being. Arguably, workers already know that capitalists dominate and oppress them, and this can easily be confirmed by looking at the theory produced by workers themselves at the time. Perhaps they don't need an additional argument to the effect that this is indeed so or to the effect that its vices are particularly harmful for their freedom and human development. The second and third kinds of alienation thus seem less valuable for helping to guide working-class movements in ways that better enable them to carry out socialist revolution, so there's little value in harping on about them. While "[p]hilosophers have only *interpreted* the world, in various ways; the point is to *change* it".[25]

This hinges on the efficacy of normative argumentation for motivating and guiding political agents. Marx de-emphasises the second and third kinds of alienation because he believes them not to be very useful contributions that a theorist can make to the struggle to replace capitalism with socialism. What use could these more normative aspects of Marx's thought have for the kind of agent-centred realism that Marx advocates?

One major virtue of returning to Marx's ideas about freedom, its value, and its obstruction by capitalism, is that they are at least in principle amenable to empirical testing. It is in principle possible to try to discover whether human beings have some powers of conscious self-directed activity; whether or not conscious self-directed activity is important and significant for the development of human beings; whether or not capitalist and other labour processes do thwart conscious self-direction; and whether or not labour processes are particularly important, for whichever reasons, in this regard. Marx is a realist, and his arguments are consciously highly descriptive in character. At no point does he try to retreat from the descriptive and contingent to the necessary and normative in order to insulate his normative political thought from possible refutation. This is important, because it makes it possible to gather various kinds of evidence which we can use to either accept or reject his argument for good reasons. If conscious self-directed activity turns out not to be important for human development, then we should not, in Marx's view, value it. Explicit attention to the nature and value of self-directed activity can enable us to gather evidence either for or against Marx's central contention that capitalism thwarts human development, supporting or undermining his claims for good reasons. But what positive purpose could this have for the agency of the existing working-class struggle that Marx intends to address?

A focus on Marx's conception of freedom as self-direction, its importance, and its thwarting by capitalist domination, can contribute to

---

[25] Marx (1992, p. 423/IV:3, p. 21).

working-class political agency for at least three reasons. It can help to focus that agent's conception on what capitalist unfreedom consists in and why it matters; guide theoretical and practical efforts to replace capitalism; and play an important motivational role to the participants in revolutionary struggle.

Firstly, it's no doubt important to diagnose how capitalism generates certain kinds of domination and unfreedom; but it's also important to understand what this unfreedom consists of and why it matters. The latter helps us to organise our thoughts about which problems are important, which problems are more important than others, and why they are so. For instance, from the discussion of the second and third kinds of alienation it is clear that and why, the relations of production are so important for human freedom. That discussion likewise makes it clear why these relations are more important than many others, e.g. one's leisure pursuits.

Secondly, this focus on the nature of the problem of capitalist unfreedom and its importance should further aid us in thinking about how to overcome its causes, both theoretically and practically. The focus on self-directing the labour process can help us both discuss the necessary kinds of institutional substance we need for a free society. It can also help guide the institutional forms which we try to institute, since it allows us a reasonably well-specified criterion—one among others—according to which we can formulate and evaluate proposals for institutional forms and assess their foreseeable consequences and implications.

Thirdly, attending to the nature of proletarian unfreedom under capitalism can play an important motivational role for participants in revolutionary struggle. One component of social struggle is, and has always been, normative argumentation, minimally for purposes of justification and legitimation, but also for wider purposes of motivating groups and individuals. The frequent use of, and changes in, normative arguments in all kinds of social struggles bears witness to this. We see it in arguments from justice, freedom, protagonism, and self-management among contemporary Latin American movements; in anarchist, syndicalist, and democratic confederalist movements from values of freedom, equality, and mutual aid; in feminist movements from principles of equality, justice, and the elimination of hierarchies and oppression; and many more besides. These are more than mere rhetorical appeals, they have a very real motive force, and some effort in articulating, reforming, and arguing from such normative notions can be a useful contribution to the social struggle itself.

By focusing less on these issues in his published works, Marx succeeded in doing a great deal of very valuable work with regard to developing his economics, particular historical analyses, journalism, and so forth—all of which was important and rightly influential. However, neglecting its normative aspects not only led to a great deal of confusion among later Marxists, including leading many of his followers to look to other, and inferior, normative views, such as moralist Kantian theory. From the perspective of a Marxian agent-centred realism, this can be viewed as a distraction which has been harmful in terms of wasting a great deal of time, energy, and intelligence of a fairly large number of highly capable people. It has also led to a diversion of focus to issues which are more amenable to being dealt with by such inferior approaches, rather than the more important and practical concerns that a realist approach to political theory deals with much better.[26] It also means that those who have made and sought to act upon various kinds of normative appeals and arguments within proletarian movements have not had the benefit of Marx's thoughts on the subject. If we take such arguments to be influential within movements and believe that normative arguments can play an important motivational role, then re-emphasising these aspects of Marx's thought might make a useful contribution to the actions of the potentially revolutionary subject that his thought is organised around.

Finally, re-emphasising the normatively laden aspects of Marx's critique of capitalism can help motivate revolutionary activity. One of the things that hinders people from engaging in revolutionary struggle is arguments against replacing capitalist with socialist economic institution. Insofar as reconstructing and defending Marx's critique of capitalism allows us to respond to and disarm some of these arguments, we can expect it to play this additional motivational role too. Take the following very simplistic argument as an example: Freedom requires private and personal property; socialism does away with private property. Therefore, socialism makes everyone less free (or, even if it only makes some less free, it makes them less free with no corresponding increase in freedom for anyone else). It might seem unconvincing to many, and it is definitely presented here in an overly simplistic form, but similar kinds of arguments are advanced by right-libertarians and their followers, especially in less formal political debates. Note, however, that the distinction Marx and Engels make

---

[26] See Raekstad (2015).

between personal and private property in the *Communist Manifesto* will not work to answer this objection; a good answer requires recourse to an explicit conception of freedom.

Marx's notion of self-directed activity can furnish the basis for a very straightforward answer to this kind of argument. Private property is not necessary for the conscious self-direction of human activities and therefore not necessary for human freedom. For example, a factory or farm in which all productive activity is jointly consciously self-directed by those who work there need not be formally owned by anyone. Someone might object to this that some individual or person would have to own the land or factory in order for any systematic use and production to take place on it. Such an argument obviously neglects the fact that what we term "property" is a historically contingent set of social practices, which vary a great deal across human history and human societies, many of which organised complex forms of agriculture, horticulture, and herding with nothing like the kinds of systems of private property in land that many modern thinkers take for granted. In any case, refuting arguments such as these requires some appeal to normative concepts, such as Marx's concept of freedom. Given that these arguments are convincing to at least some workers, being able to refute them is another valuable way in which re-emphasising the normative aspects of Marx's theory of alienation can contribute to the actions of the potentially revolutionary subject or agent Marx is concerned with, causing them to e.g. support or less oppose revolutionary practices.

I have summarised the shift in Marx's methodology from 1843 and the part of 1844 during which he wrote the *Economic and Philosophical Manuscripts of 1844* to the view he lays out in the 1845–6 *German Ideology* onwards. In so doing, I have shown how Marx moved towards an understanding of the proletariat as an active revolutionary subject and with that formulated a critique of earlier revolutionary theorists and modified his own approach to theorising. Complementing this, I have shown how the theory of alienation not only continues (as we saw throughout Chapter 7) to appear throughout his later works, but that it even forms the core of his mature account of capitalism's two main revolutionary contradictions, between productive powers/relations and between workers/capitalists. Although all four kinds of alienation reappear throughout his later works, Marx dedicates much more time and energy to exploring and expanding upon its more descriptive aspects. I've argued that one of the main reasons he does so is that he no longer thinks they are as important contributions to the revolutionary movement. Against this, I have argued that these normative elements of the theory of alienation can indeed play a useful role for three reasons: they can help focus that subject or agent's conception of what capitalist unfreedom consists in and why it matters; they can help to guide theoretical and practical contributions to capitalism's replacement; and they can play an important motivational role to the participants in revolutionary struggle.

REFERENCES

PRIMARY

Heinrich, M. (2012). *An introduction to the three volumes of Karl Marx's capital*. Monthly Review Press.
Marx, K., & Nicolaus, M. (trans.). (1993). *Grundrisse: Foundations of a critique of political economy*. Penguin.
Marx, K., Fowkes, B. (trans.) & Mandel, E. (intro.). (1990). *Capital: A critique of political economy* (Vol. 1). Penguin.
Marx, K., Livingstone, R. (trans), Benton, G. (trans) & Colletti, L. (intro.). (1992). *Karl Marx: Early writings*. Penguin.
Lebowitz, M. (2020). *Between capitalism and community*. Monthly Review Press.
Löwy, M. (2005). *The theory of revolution in the young Marx*. Haymarket Books.
Raekstad, P. (2015). Two contemporary approaches to political theory. *International Critical Thought, 5*(2), 226–240.

CHAPTER 10

Towards a New World

I have shown that Marx's political theory was realist in nature, that it presents a critique of capitalism for thwarting human freedom and thereby human development, and that this critique remains defensible in light of the findings of the contemporary human sciences. After a brief recap, I will here offer some pointers on how Marx's critique of capitalism remains important for opening up new and important avenues in theorising both the expanding ills of capitalism and the necessities of emancipation.

Part I laid out Marx's rich and neglected theory of human development in terms of powers and needs, and showed how he uses it to articulate a positive concept of freedom as self-direction. On this view, freedom is valuable both in itself as the realisation of a particularly important human power and for positively impacting a wide range of other human powers.

Next, Part II detailed Marx's first critique of modern society, showing one of the ways in which he critiques both capitalism and the state for thwarting human freedom and thereby human development. There we saw that Marx advocates a radical idea of democracy to replace capitalism and the state in ways that go beyond merely democratic states and prefigure his later socialist ideas. The discussion of Marx's shift from a realisation-oriented to an agent-centred approach to political theory explained not only how Marx's approach to political theory differs in the two theories of alienation, but also how added descriptive content rightly altered his realist method of political theorising.

Building on this, Part III reconstructed the second theory of alienation as a diagnosis of specifically how capitalism thwarts human freedom and thereby human development, his expanded conception of its cure in socialism, and, finally, his conception of the (correct or best) practice of the theorist. There we saw his theory of alienation being employed to diagnose capitalism's interconnected forms of personal and impersonal domination and how he recommends a socialism to cure it that includes the full democratisation of social life, replacing competitive markets with democratic planning, abolishing the hierarchical division of labour, and distributing according to need. Finally, we saw how this theory not only is retained throughout Marx's later works, including *Capital*, but also constitutes the core of his analysis of capitalism's revolutionary contradictions. While Marx turned to focus more on the descriptive side of this critique, I've argued that we have good reason to revive it today. Now, what does this do for contemporary political theory and practice?

This contributes to contemporary methodological debates in political theory by showing two detailed ways in which a critical political theory was developed along realist lines. Despite the growing interest in realism in recent years, there has been little work that can compare to the radical critical endeavour of thinkers like Marx. The work of such thinkers has played an important role in influencing recent human history, so their approaches to the subject deserve considerable attention in their own right. There is also good reason to think that political theorists who wish to influence real politics today would do well to understand the methods and approaches which have proven effective in the past—whether they wish to follow them or not.

One way this can be done would be to open up a research programme that seeks to do realist political theory in an empirically well-informed and interdisciplinary way. This could draw on recent advances in history, anthropology, archaeology, and psychology, as well as the sociology of social movements and on the ideas of non-Western forms of political theorising. Such a programme could explore our foundational political concepts, values, and commitments, including through forms of genealogy and ideology critique; it could use these lessons to assess the relations and institutions we are subject to; it could develop models of future relations and institutions and strategies for reaching them; and it could help to provide us with some general orientation in navigating the world we face.

There are a variety of other ways in which Marx's diagnosis of the ills of capitalism can contribute to political theory, of which I will briefly mention three. One is how it can account for the kinds of power exerted over people in contemporary financial capitalism. It's often difficult to understand the nature of the powers wielded by today's financialised capitalism over individuals and institutions. The power of financial markets inheres not in single individuals (like kings, emperors, or popes) or specific decision-making bodies or organisations (like parliaments, senates, or trade organisations). Although the powers of individuals, bodies, and organisations remain real and important components of financialised capitalism, the powers wielded by financial markets themselves are not controlled by any of them. This raises major conceptual challenges, including: when people and institutions are subjected to the power of financial capitalism, *what* if anything, is it that has power over them and *how* does it render them unfree? Marx's thought provides us with a place to start to answer these questions. *What* has power over people under contemporary financial capitalism is still the socially constituted *capitalist social relations* which come to constitute a power outside and seemingly independent of those subject to them, and which control their economic lives and institutions. By controlling people's economic lives, these social relations render people unfree by thwarting their powers for consciously self-directing their own activity. Just as Marx's theory of alienation was only the starting-point for his research into political economy, so too this provides only the starting point for an analysis and critique of contemporary financialised capitalism—its precise powers and laws of motion require much further specific investigations, which some Marx-influenced thinkers have already begun.[1] What is clear, however, is that no matter how much more complicated contemporary financialised capitalism has become, it remains subject to the critical diagnosis offered by Marx's theory of alienation.

In addition to this, Marx's critique of capitalism remains useful for diagnosing the lived reality of many people worldwide. Oddly, Marx's thought is sometimes thought passé for its focus and reliance on the industrial working class, which many argue no longer reflects the lived

---

[1] For example Foster and Magdoff (2009), Foster and McChesney (2012), and Harvey (2011, 2015).

experiences of most people. There are many things wrong with this critique, but the main problem is that it's wrong in both of the main ways that it needs to be right. First, as Immanuel Ness points out, from 1980 to 2007 the standard industrially defined working class has actually grown "from 1.9 billion to 3.1 billion workers—far more working people than at any time in the history of capitalism", mostly in the Global South and in large part in "response to the restructuring of financial capital".[2] He goes on to argue that "Marx's depiction of an alienated and estranged workforce in the nineteenth century can be applied to the condition of workers in the Global South today",[3] including living in the margins of major cities, lacking many citizenship and residency rights with resulting lack of access to public services, thorough-going casualisation and precarity, and much more. Furthermore, the Marxist proletariat was always defined not in terms of any industrial character, but in terms of its social relations. It therefore includes service sector workers just as much as it does factory workers, and their conditions, whether in the Global North or the Global South, remain alienated and unfree. From the perspective of global humanity, Marx's critique of capitalism has never been more relevant.

The diagnosis of impersonal forms of domination can also help us make sense of the subtle forms of power involved in a variety of current high-technology transformations our capitalism is undergoing. New dynamics of surveillance capitalism, the rule of algorithms in managing platform workers and other office workers, and the subtle forms of manipulation exercised by automated systems in various different ways all demand a more sophisticated way of thinking about freedom than current liberals, or their concepts of freedom, can provide. Marx's concept of freedom as self-direction, and his understanding that it can be undermined by either personal or impersonal forms of domination, can provide a starting point for understanding how many of these new socio-technical systems exercise power over those subject to them regardless of whether they're controlled by particular nefarious bosses or not.

Perhaps most importantly, Marx's critique also leaves us with a number of resources for thinking about human emancipation in more positive terms. Indeed, nothing could be more obvious than the growing importance of Marx to movements fighting for universal emancipation. A

---

[2] Ness (2016, p. 14).

[3] Ness (2016, p. 183).

proper understanding of what his political theory consists in, the vision of a future it includes, and the nature of the critique it levels against capitalism, can provide such movements with a greater understanding of what it is that they're up against, which institutions need replacement or reform, and how one might go about doing so.

First, a renewed understanding of Marx's critique should help us to re-frame how we think about Marx's work as fundamentally a project of universal human emancipation through intersectional working-class self-emancipation. For Marx, this entails the democratisation of all aspects of social life. We've seen that for Marx, this requires replacing both capitalism and the state with a network of bottom-up democratic councils, restoring the powers of society to the collective control of the totality of its participants. He also argues that such a socialist society must be organised through participatory democratic planning; replace capitalism's hierarchical division of labour; and distribute goods and services according to need, while members will contribute according to ability. I've also argued that these commitments call us to think about which specific institutional forms they can be realised through. How exactly can we go about participatory democratic planning on large, medium, and small scales? How can we reorganise the division of labour in ways that best serve the free self-development of all? And how do we make distribution according to need a concrete reality? These questions should be central to thinking about the socialist alternative to capitalism going forwards.

Second, this should be accompanied by an honest and ruthless criticism of proposed alternatives to capitalism that fail to address the forms of unfreedom Marx discusses. Contemporary academics, even many who call themselves socialists, tend to favour either some renewed form of social democracy or a form of market socialism. The problem with these models is that neither of them can seriously address Marx's diagnoses of the forms of domination between managers and workers, embodied in the division between mental and manual labour; the impersonal forms of domination entailed by the kinds of competitive markets they include; or the latter's inherent dynamics of ecological devastation. A renewed socialism cannot settle for such half-measures, nor can anyone who wants our species to survive.

Third, Marx's focus on democratisation and his theory of human development can inform the way we think about social change and especially collective emancipation. If capitalism is alienating and a socialist society is its unalienated cure, any transition to socialism requires a process of de-alienation. Marx's theory of human development gives us the nuts and bolts needed to make sense of this process. Introducing free socialist institutions presupposes revolutionaries who have developed the need to realise these institutions and the powers and consciousness that enable them to do so. How, given that we are starting from a capitalist society, can we develop people with the powers, needs, and consciousness necessary for them to take us to a free socialist society? Like socialism itself, the revolutionary subjectivity required for bringing it about is not something that can be handed down by some benevolent leaders or secret revolutionary elite—as for the Lassalleans that Marx opposed. Socialism can only be introduced by the working classes themselves within their mass organisations which will lead both the resistance to capitalism and the transition beyond it.

It follows from this that those committed to replacing capitalism with socialism should pay very close attention to the social relations within our organisations and movements, especially the ways in which they structure deliberation and decision-making. The best way to ensure the development of the revolutionary subjectivity required for a free socialist society is for the structures and relations within organisations of struggle and transition to reflect those of the socialist society aimed at. Arguably, only experience of and experiments with these things will help participants teach themselves how to live and organise social life in these ways, develop a need for doing so, and becoming conscious of what such society is and entails. This connects to both past and present debates about prefigurative politics, a question which is increasingly debated both in the academy and a plethora of popular movements, by both Marxists and non-Marxists alike.[4] Marx's theory of human development can be put to work in thinking about how to structure deliberation, decision-making, and wider culture within anti-capitalist organisations and movements, by being used to assess the impacts of these things on developing participants' powers, needs, and consciousness. Do we structure organisations in ways that enable and promote the free or self-directed activity of all of their participants? Are our organisations really collectively self-governed by all of their members? Does power within them really and consistently

---

[4] For example Dixon (2014), Gordon (2018), Raekstad (2018), Raekstad and Gradin (2020), Swain (2019b), and van de Sande (2015).

flow from the bottom up, rather than from the top down? Do our movements and organisations develop their participants' powers, needs, and consciousness in the ways required for them to replace capitalism and the state with a free socialist society, if and when the opportunity arises? This demands not only that we more systematically begin to study the forms and substance of prefigurative politics, but also that we work to bring together the best parts of different socialist traditions that have worked much more on these questions than many Marxist theorists.[5] In my view this demands that we develop a non-sectarian, new synthesis of the best parts of Marxist, anarchist, decolonial, antiracist, feminist, and syndicalist ideas.

These questions and more are being asked and beginning to be answered by a plethora of organisations and movements worldwide. Through them, Marx's thought is once again a living element in political struggles, and one which we're beginning to understand better than was possible before. If this is correct, then it seems that philosophy is again becoming a material force in social and political struggles—a force not only for understanding the world, but also for changing it.

REFERENCES

SECONDARY

Dixon, C. (2014). *Another politics: Talking across today's transformative movements*. University of California Press.

Foster, J. B., & Magdoff, F. (2009). *The great financial crisis: Causes and consequences*. Monthly Review Press.

Foster, J. B., & McChesney, R. (2012). *The endless crisis: How monopoly-finance capital produces stagnation and upheaval from the USA to China*. Monthly Review Press.

Gordon, U. (2018). Prefigurative politics between ethical practice and absent promise. *Political Studies, 66*(2), 521–537.

Harvey, D. (2011). *The enigma of capital: And the crises of capitalism* (2nd ed.). Oxford University Press.

Harvey, D. (2015). *Seventeen contradictions and the end of capitalism* (Reprint ed.). Oxford University Press.

Ness, I. (2016). *Southern insurgency: The coming of the global working class*. Pluto Press.

---

[5] Raekstad and Gradin (2020).

Raekstad, P., & Gradin, S. (2020). *Prefigurative politics: Building tomorrow today.* Polity Press.
Raekstad, P. (2018). Revolutionary practice and prefigurative politics: A clarification and defence. *Constellations, 25*(3), 359–372.
Swain, D. (2019a). *None so fit to break the chains: Marx's ethics of self-emancipation.* Brill.
Swain, D. (2019b). Not not but not yet: Present and future in prefigurative politics. *Political Studies, 67*(1), 47–62.
Van de Sande, M. (2015). Fighting with tools: Prefiguration and radical politics in the twenty-first century. *Rethinking Marxism, 27*(2), 177–194.

Appendix: A Brief Overview of the (Other) Principal Interpretations of Marx's Normative Commitments

Different interpreters disagree not only about the nature of Marx's critique of capitalism, but also about the normative components that this critique builds on. The contemporary literature contains a large number of positions on these two questions. Some believe that Marx's critique rests on human development and/or freedom; others that it builds on certain principles of distributive justice that are violated by exploitation; while others believe his critique is based on an ethical view of human nature. This appendix will provide a brief overview of the other principal approaches to understanding the normative components of Marx's critique of capitalism and why I think they should be rejected as plausible readings of Marx. After laying out some necessary terminology, I will examine and reject four main alternatives to the one I've explained and defended in Part I of this book. First (A), there is the "amoralist" position, advocated especially by Allen Wood, according to which Marx does not appeal to straightforwardly ethical principles at all, but rather, if anything, to some other kinds of general-purpose wants, needs, or interests. Secondly (B), there is what is often called the "moralist" reading, advocated by commentators such as G. A. Cohen and Norman Geras, according to which Marx is committed to some number of ethical principles like a theory of justice, or ethical ideals such as freedom, community, etc., and capitalism is criticised for violating or failing to live up to the evaluative terms in question. Thirdly (C), there is the approach that understands Marx's critique of capitalism as one based on an ethical ideal of human nature—often cashed out in terms of an (at least partially) ethical ideal of human species-essence. Fourthly (D), there is a kind of internal critique which begins from the normative principles or ideals developed within a given society, in terms of which that society justifies things like its own existence (either in part or *in toto*), its various institutions, policies, actions, etc. This society is then critiqued for failing to follow, live up to, or realise its own principles or ideals.[1] I shall outline each of these positions in turn, arguing that they all fail to do justice to what Marx himself says—and/or needs to say—about the normative components of his political theory as embodied in his critique of capitalism, from the *Economic and Philosophical Manuscripts of 1844* all the way through to the *Grundrisse* and *Capital*.

Before I move on, however, two preliminary points are in order. First, my discussion will leave aside the numerous details and variations involved in the separate cottage-industry on "Marx and Justice". Strictly speaking, any appeal to a Marxian critique of capitalism founded on a notion of justice necessarily implies a prior conception of the normative elements of that critique and their status[2]—either a moralist position or the first kind of internal critique—which I will reject in (B) and (D), respectively, as a result of which this subsequent concern is rendered moot. For another, the following overview is not meant to provide a detailed survey of all the different writers and arguments within the "Marx and Morality" debates. Many individual writers have highly complex views which interpret, combine, and hybridise Marx's many and varied normatively charged statements about capitalism in a number of different ways. In light of this fact, the reconstructive purpose of this appendix, and the further fact that I believe these individual positions to build mostly on erroneous normative components anyway, their additional details are not strictly relevant here. It would thus make little sense to examine them all in detail. To do so adequately would, moreover, require much more time and space than is presently available. Instead, I first aim to summarise the four main kinds of normative foundations Marx's critique(s) or capitalism can be said to

---

[1] Unfortunately, there are interesting commentators on this issue that fall outside of this typology, such as MacIntyre (2009), Martin (2008), and Blackledge (2012). Their positions are too unique, and require a much too detailed and lengthy treatment than it is possible to provide here.

[2] See for instance Geras (1985, p. 47).

rest on which are not my own, in their most plausible formulations, and briefly present the reasons why I find them to be implausible.

It is difficult to get a simple overview of the state of the discussion concerning the normative components of Marx's theory, partly because many of the various participants proceed from very different ethical and political assumptions, and partly because the participants use different, and sometimes inconsistent, terminology. Different writers read Marx's critique in terms of concepts such as the "normative", the "ethical", the "moral", the "amoral", and many more, and they often do not take care to use these in the same way, or to clarify or compare their uses to those of other writers. In light of this fact, I will begin my discussion by outlining the terminology it will employ. In this way, my account of the different positions and their vocabularies can be made commensurable, hopefully rendering the subsequent discussion more comprehensible.

The word "normative" employed can be taken in a few different ways. "Normative" here does not simply mean something being of, or pertaining to, a norm. Nor does it mean a separate kind of thing distinct from, and necessarily opposed to, the descriptive *tout court*. To use the term in this way would be implicitly to commit Marx to a substantive kind of meta-ethical dualism which I do not believe he holds. "Normative" is, however, used to denote that aspect of a theory—Marx's or others'—which deals with all matters concerning what's good or bad, better or worse, and how, very broadly speaking, things should or ought to be. This includes the realm of concerns about ethical rules and norms, conceptions of the good life, etc., but also other realms such as the correct or incorrect use of language, aesthetics, considerations to do with rationality and reasonableness, and so on. For the purposes of this appendix, the "normative" and the evaluative will be used synonymously to denote this class of considerations.

There is a common way of thinking about the "normative" which contrasts it with the "descriptive" in such a way that the two are wholly separate categories. I leave aside the question of whether or not this is a correct or a useful way of thinking about things, noting only that this is not how the term "normative" will be employed here. For one, there is no reason whatsoever to believe Marx adhered to a dualism of this kind and for another, there are a number of things which fall within the scope of the normative as just construed which are clearly also descriptive entities. For example, it is perfectly possible to hold up an existing society or individual as an ideal of ethical, aesthetic, or rational perfection (e.g.

Socrates, Jesus, Muhammad) and then proceed to evaluate all others in comparison to that ideal. Such a postulated ideal would then be both a descriptive entity and a normative one. The same is even clearer with the correct or incorrect uses of words and grammatical constructions. It is a matter of descriptive fact that at least some such things are not permitted or acceptable—like, in English, using the word "cat" to refer to an ocean. The word "normative", then, is here not used to distinguish some elements of Marx's thought from the descriptive *tout court*, but to distinguish these former kinds of components of his theories—whatever we take them to be—from these theories' *merely* descriptive components, such as Marx's accounts of how the capitalist economy works as a matter of fact.

The "normative", however, should be distinguished from the narrower concept of the "ethical". "Ethical" is here used to denote that which belongs to the more traditional—yet still broadly construed—scope of inquiry into a more limited set of values, including the realms of ethical rules and norms; conceptions of the good life; conceptions of human growth, development, and flourishing; questions about the good, the right, and the just; as well as other concerns about individual and collective ends. I am unable to formulate a clear distinction between the ethical and the normative in terms of necessary and sufficient conditions. I can, however, point to a number of things which fall within the scope of the latter, but outside that of the former. The realm of the ethical does not, unlike that of the normative, include certain distinct kinds of concerns such as concerns of a purely aesthetic nature or of the correct and incorrect uses of language. Thus, a concern with the injustice of U.S. foreign policy is an ethical and therefore also a normative concern, while correcting someone's erroneous spelling or clearly incorrect utterances of the word "literally" is a normative matter, but not an ethical one.[3]

This still broad sense of the "ethical" can be contrasted with the even narrower realm of "morality". In what follows, "morality" will refer to matters of individual and collective action and decision-making relative

---

[3] This example may be controversial, insofar as it abstracts away from the harms caused to listeners upon experiencing the horror of "literally" used in the sense of figuratively+emphasis. Insofar as the action of doing so causes harm, it would indeed fall under the category of the ethical as well.

to ethical rules or norms[4] of whatever kind. A concern to live one's life without violating another person's human rights or without violating the ten commandments is thus a moral concern (and therefore also an ethical and a normative one), while a person's attempt at achieving what they take to be a good human life (assuming this consists not merely in following a set of prescribed ethical rules and norms) is an ethical concern, but not necessarily a moral one.

The ethical rules and norms in question can be thought of in a number of different ways. In the following, ethical rules and norms will be approached, understood, or conceived of either "concretely" and "contextually" or "abstractly" and "ahistorically". Here a "concrete" and "contextual" understanding of a concept or an ethical rule or norm is one which proceeds, or attempts to proceed, from how a concept, rule, or norm functions in a certain context (in a particular group, for a particular slice of time, etc.), how it is or is not acted upon within that context, and how it is formulated and deliberated upon in that context. This kind of approach then proceeds to develop an account of the concept, rule, or norm from this starting point.

In contrast to the emphasis on the practical embeddedness of the terms under analysis found in the contextual approach, an "abstract" understanding proceeds, or attempts to proceed, from a general definition or description of a concept, rule, or norm rather than its practical use within one or more particular contexts. In contrast to the importance attributed to the historical location, change, and variability emphasised in a contextual approach, an "ahistorical" understanding of concepts, rules, and norms is one which proceeds, or attempts to proceed,[5] in an abstract way to analyse and utilise these without regard for their historical location, function, and change over time. It is, at least in principle, possible to analyse concepts concretely while taking an ahistorical approach to their

---

[4] I write "ethical" rules and norms to distinguish those rules and norms which are ethical from those rules and norms that are purely pragmatic conventions, rules of aesthetics (e.g. rules of musical composition), and so on.

[5] If one believes, as I do, that everything formulated by a human being is significantly sensitive to, and in part dependent on, the context within which it is formulated, then there can be no such thing as an abstract formulation of the kind shortly to be discussed, only attempts at doing so which are doomed to fail. In order to simplify the discussion, I term those approaches which attempt to proceed abstractly in the above sense as "abstract" approaches—even though, if I and its other critics are correct in the basic premise of its factual impossibility, there is, strictly speaking, no such thing.

study, or to seek to analyse concepts abstractly but to understand them historically. However, as far as our discussion below is concerned it must be borne in mind that the concrete and contextual on the one hand, and the abstract and ahistorical on the other, tend to come together as part of a package. This is particularly evident in the theorists discussed in sections (A) and (B) of this appendix. Ethical rules and norms are not, however, the only things that can be concrete, contextual, abstract, and/or ahistorical in these senses; so too can principles, ideals, notions of right and justice, etc.

It should now be clear that, on the account just given, everything moral is also ethical, but not vice versa, and that everything ethical is also normative, but not vice versa. In other words, the normative contains the ethical and much more besides, and the ethical contains the moral and, at least potentially, much more besides. None of these things are necessarily distinct from the descriptive, factual, and empirical in that they lack any such content, but they are distinct from the *merely* descriptive, factual, and empirical.

The preceding discussion about the normative, the ethical, and the moral has shifted from one about the realms or domains of these categories to the entities which appear within them—to wit, ethical rules and norms, and how these are thought of and with. It will thus be instructive, before moving on, to say something about the terms I will be using to denote some of these entities, namely what "principles" and "ideals" are taken to be. A "principle" can mean many different things, but here it will be taken to mean a standard of, or rule or norm for, individual or collective action and decision-making. Principles may be ethical—"do not steal"—or non-ethical—"don't eat the yellow snow", "don't annoy the big men with sharp bits of metal"—in nature. Ethical rules and norms are thus all principles of a particular kind, but not all principles are ethical. An "ideal", on the other hand, is here a conception of, or standard for, perfection, an instance of perfection—say, a perfect human being or a perfect society—or an instance of either of the former serving as a goal which a person or society ought, in some sense, to strive towards.

With some basic terminology in order, I can now proceed to the available views on the normative components of Marx's critique of capitalism.

(A) The Amoralist Reading

There are two principal versions of the "amoralist" reading of the normative components of Marx's critique of capitalism. According to the simple version of amoralism, Marx's work has no ethical—and perhaps no normative—content whatsoever. The details of this claim can be cashed out in different ways. One way of cashing out the details of a simple amoralist position, which we find in writers such as Plekhanov and Bukharin, is the orthodox view that Marx appeals only to the desires, needs, and interests of the working class, and should not burden itself with anything beyond understanding and perhaps manipulating "merely" superstructural elements such as justice and morality[6] in the interests of satisfying these desires, needs, and interests. We may presume that the latter is fairly clear insofar as it involves the claims that morality, and ethics more widely, are largely, if not completely, epiphenomenal vis-à-vis the economic base; that such concerns play no important role in any of Marx's thought; and that it is irrelevant, if not potentially distracting and therefore pernicious, to revolutionary practise to pursue them.

An amoralist position and critique of capitalism can appeal only to people's individual or group desires, preferences, and/or interests, without employing or requiring any specifically ethical content. For instance, one does not need things like moral principles to tell someone standing at the edge of a cliff not to take another step forward. At most it is sufficient to point out that doing so would get one killed, with an implicit premise about how such an outcome is undesirable and/or contrary to one's interests. Similarly, demonstrating that capitalism fetters the development of productive powers and results in avoidable evils for the proletariat, in conjunction with an assertion of a viable and more satisfactory alternative, can, at least in principle, suffice to convince them that capitalism is somehow inadequate and thereby motivate them to organise to replace it.[7]

---

[6] E.g. Bukharin (1925), Hodges (1964, 1966), Leiter (2015), and Plekhanov (1898). The names cited make it obvious why this position is labelled an "orthodox" one.

[7] There is another version of simple amoralism developed by Tucker (1970, 1972) which argues that the extremely partisan nature of Marx's quasi-religious world-view supposedly rules out any genuinely ethical or moral components. Since this is no longer accepted by virtually anyone, I leave discussion of it aside for our purposes here.

Such simple amoralist positions were, however, challenged by the discovery of, and in particular by later commentary on, Marx's early writings of 1844, which prompted readings of Marx on which he held a normative conception of human nature,[8] was involved in a project of redefining man from which different sets of moral principles derive,[9] and others. Although the early amoralists correctly note the absence of a fully developed and articulated normative theory in much of Marx's work, his rejection of any notions of right and justice, and his subsequent harsh criticism of other thinkers who attempt to base a rejection or critique of capitalism thereon, they nevertheless run into a series of problems.

One of the major weaknesses of simple amoralist interpretations, which in fact has gone on to plague many of the subsequent debates on Marx, morality, and justice, is the tendency to conflate and collapse conceptions of morality, of right and justice, of ethics, and of normativity in general. An absence or rejection of either or both of the former does not, and certainly need not, entail the absence or rejection of either of the latter two. By conflating and collapsing any and all notions of normativity, ethics, morality, right, and justice in such a way that they form a single undifferentiated "blob", early amoralists were able to support their conclusions by utilising a couple of quotations of Marx repudiating one or more of these (especially right or justice, but also morality), explaining their nature and emergence wholly in terms of the contexts within which they arose and subsequently sustain themselves, and thereafter arguing that all normative considerations worthy of the name are unnecessary (because revolutionaries can appeal to workers' wants and needs just as easily, if not easier), undesirable (because work in ethics will both divert attention and energy from real revolutionary activities and risk perverting the enterprise itself, insofar as the capitalist mode of production succeeds in adversely influencing it), and contrary to the teachings of Marx. However, the evidence adduced by those attempting to argue that Marx altogether rejected any normative or ethical position from which to critique capitalism, especially among the early amoralists, amounts only to support the much weaker claim that he rejects the much more restricted normative positions founded on conceptions of right, justice, and morality.

[8] E.g. Fromm (2004).
[9] Allen (1974).

In addition to this significant underdetermination of simple amoralism in Marx's work, this family of readings also runs into a number of other problems. One of these is that the diagnoses and subsequent critiques of capitalism that Marx offers in his early writings—e.g. the early Hegel critiques, *On the Jewish Question,* and the *Economic and Philosophical Manuscripts of 1844*—clearly have a normative, in fact an ethical, foundation and focus, with notions of freedom, self-direction, and human development playing important roles. Furthermore, as we've seen throughout Parts I and III of this book, explicit commitments to human development and freedom, and critically diagnosing how capitalism restricts freedom and human development relative to the achievable alternative of socialism, reappear throughout Marx's later works, including *Capital*. The early development and later persistence of these normatively laden concepts in Marx's later work render any simple amoralist position highly implausible. Consequently, we should look for any other available alternative before giving in to such a conclusion.

Despite the problems which beset these simpler forms of amoralism, it has been ably argued that a more sophisticated version of it would be able to meet the above challenges while articulating an interesting thesis consistent with a viable interpretation of Marx's writings. The strongest sophisticated amoralist reading of Marx has been articulated by Allen Wood. According to Wood's sophisticated amoralism, Marx's critique of capitalism can be grounded in supposedly non-ethical[10] goods such as "self-actualization, security, physical health, comfort, community, freedom".[11] Wood argues that although Marx is clearly opposed to capitalism for its failures to provide these goods for the proletariat, he "never claims that these goods ought to be provided to people because they have the *right* to them, or because *justice* (or some other moral norm)

---

[10] Wood and others use the term "non-moral" here, leaving it unclear what "moral" means in this particular context. In our terms outlined above, however, it seems clear that what these writers term "non-moral" is what I would term non-ethical.

[11] Wood (2004, p. 129). This view was developed by Wood (1972a, 1972b, 1979, 2004). A sufficiently similar position reading Marx in amoralistic terms is that of Acton (1955) and Miller (1983, 1984). Relatedly, Buchanan (1982) reads needs in the sense of undistorted preferences, although he would probably reject identifying Marx's position as "amoral".

demands it".[12] Wood adds to this an analysis of Marx's explicit rejection of morality and theories of justice, asserting their status as ideologies limited in relevance to, as well as critically restricted by, the forms of society within which they develop. As a result of the distinction between ethical and non-ethical goods, Wood claims that, despite his explicit rejection of criticisms of capitalism in terms of morality, right, and justice, Marx is nevertheless able to provide a viable evaluative foundation on which to base a critique of capitalism.

Wood's account of Marx's critique of justice can be summarised as follows:

(1) Principles of justice are conceived of in terms of their function within a given mode of production, i.e. in terms of whether or not, and the extent to which, they "fit" it; thus
(2) such principles are not abstract and ahistorical ones in terms of which actions, institutions, and so on, are evaluated, but instead they are standards generated within, and, at least in part, by a mode of production in terms of which various social actions and interactions within that mode of production are subsequently evaluated;
(3) Marx followed Hegel in rejecting a formal conception of justice supposedly generated by, or deducible from, abstract forms or universal principles, as a result of which;
(4) the justice of institutions' acts does not depend on their consequences, but, as mentioned in (1), on their functional relationship with and within a given mode of production.

In short, Wood holds that Marx viewed notions of right (*Recht*) and justice (*Gerechtigkeit*) in politico-juridical terms, i.e. as normatively laden rules governing and regulating individual and social actions and interactions, which may or may not be adequately embodied in the institutions—particularly the legal institutions—of the societies within which they arise. Since the demands on individual and social actions and interactions vary signifcantly across different contexts—especially across different modes of production—so too must the rules according to which they are

---

[12] Wood (2004, p. 129).

best regulated. As such, modern private property laws and normal[13] wage labour exchanges are just in capitalist societies because they constitute, regulate, and/or reinforce a well-functioning aspect of capitalist societies; in a hunter-gatherer society, by contrast, they would likely be both pointless and harmful.[14]

Moving on from right and justice to morality, Wood argues that since what we normally call everyday morality is similarly concerned with regulating and directing the actions and interactions of individuals and groups within and only within the context of a given mode of production—stipulating what we should do in certain situations, banning certain courses of action or ways of treating others, and so on—it follows that these notions are completely unsuited to making recommendations of one such mode of production over another. Furthermore, Wood argues, a shift from one mode of production to another—e.g. by means of social revolution—likely entails that the rules (morality, right, justice, law) of the former mode of production must not only change, but also be violated in the very act of change itself. Not only can a revolutionary critique of capitalism not base itself on such notions, it plausibly has to violate them in order even to get off the ground.[15]

As a reading of Marx, Wood's sophisticated amoralist position has some major virtues. First, it can explain Marx's own silence on the subject of justice, both distributive and commutative, in his critical discussions of capitalism. Secondly, it can make sense of Marx's repeated insistence that

---

[13] "Normal" in the sense that they do not involve what are taken to be untoward elements such as direct coercion, slave-like contracts or contractual conditions, do not involve illicit transfers such as bribes, etc.

[14] There is of course another, merely descriptive, sense in which the terms "right" and "justice" are used by others and, occasionally, by Marx himself. This is the purely descriptive sense in which a given legal system, state, or whatever, recognises or upholds certain principles as people's rights or certain arrangements as being just simply as a matter of fact. There is, in other words, a sense in which a principle X can be a principle of justice in a given kind of society because it is one which is well-suited to the proper functioning of that society and thus ought to be implemented and adhered to in some way, and a distinct sense in which X can be a principle of justice in a given society in that it simply is a principle which as a matter of fact is adhered to in that society. Wood's sophisticated amoralist reading holds that Marx discusses politico-juridical terms in both senses—though Marx himself, especially in his earlier writings, is often far from clear about when he is employing these terms in their normative or in the merely descriptive senses.

[15] Wood (1972b).

capitalist exchanges and distributions[16] are in fact just (within a capitalist mode of production). For instance, in Volume I of *Capital* Marx writes that the normal capitalist purchase of labour-power to produce surplus value is "by no means an injustice towards the seller",[17] i.e. the labourer. Thirdly, it readily accounts for his criticism of theorists who do in fact attack capitalism on the basis of its alleged injustices. Also in Volume I of Capital, Marx explicitly rejects Proudhon's creation of an "ideal of justice" from the "juridical relations that correspond to the production of commodities" and his attempting to turn this ideal back upon itself to reform "the actual production of commodities, and the corresponding legal system, in accordance with this ideal",[18] and in the *Critique of the Gotha Programme* he harshly criticises Lasalleans for employing a notion of the just proceeds of labour:

> What is a 'just' distribution?
> Don't the bourgeoisie claim that the present distribution is 'just'? And on the basis of the present mode of production, isn't it in fact the only 'just' distribution? (...) Don't sectarian socialists have the most varied ideas about 'just' distribution?[19]

He goes on to argue that "it was an overall mistake" of the Lassalleans "to make an issue of so-called distribution and to make it the focus of attention".[20]

But if Marx does not rest his critique of capitalism on the foundations of right and justice, and if he must rest his critique of capitalism on something, what is it? Having already rejected readings attributing to Marx a normative conception of human nature,[21] Wood turns instead to what he terms "non-moral"—in our terminology non-ethical—values. Now, some of these supposedly non-ethical values can plausibly be described as such. Things like the preservation of self and essential institutions, stability, efficiency, and productivity may be valued for moral or ethical

---

[16] The legalistic conception of justice and the distributive conception of justice are often not clearly delineated in this literature.

[17] Marx (1990, p. 301/II:6, p. 207).

[18] Marx (1990, p. 178n2/ II:6, p. 114).

[19] Marx (1996, p. 211/I:25, p. 12).

[20] Marx (1996, p. 215/I:25, p. 15).

[21] See Wood (1972a).

reasons, but it is also equally clear that they can be valued for purely amoral reasons—that is, by appeal only to someone's desires, preferences, and interests. So far so good. However, Marx's critique of capitalism rests on, and Wood's account consequently includes, many other concepts— concepts like freedom and human development—which do not, or at least not immediately, appear to have the same structure. Wood's early comments on this are too vague to be of any use, initially amounting simply to a claim that the normative foundations for Marx's critique lie in the developing desires and needs of the proletariat which are satisfiable by the means of production, but are fettered by capitalistic relations of production.[22] The reason this account is too vague to be useful is that it fails to specify any distinction between putatively ethical and non-ethical goods which can account for why the more contentious goods Wood discusses are *bona fide* instances of non-ethical goods.

Wood's later account[23] does much better and provides a fuller distinction according to which ethical—what he calls "moral"—goods are those things we value or want because our conscience or moral law tells us to, whereas non-ethical goods are things we value because they satisfy our own conceptions about our wants, needs, or the good life. On this view, Marx criticises capitalism because it "frustrates many important *nonmoral* [in our terminology non-ethical] goods: self-actualization, security, physical health, comfort, community, freedom", but he "never claims that these goods ought to be provided to people because they have the *right* to them, or because *justice* (or some other moral norm) demands it".[24]

But how do we make sense of the idea of non-ethical goods? If the critique of capitalism in terms of freedom, self-direction, etc., is cashed out in terms of one kind of ethics versus an ethics centred on notions of right and justice, then it either becomes a moralist or internal-critique position—depending on how the principles or ideals for action are conceived. On the other hand, the non-ethical goods in question could be derived in some way from a normative conception of human nature or a notion of human development, but neither of these preserves an interesting distinction between an amoralist position and these other

---

[22] Wood (1972b).

[23] I.e. Wood (2004), but some less developed discussion is also to be found in Wood (1979).

[24] Wood (2004, p. 129).

two kinds. If, however, these options are to be avoided, as Wood wants, then we must ask whether or not it is possible to make sense of his distinction in a way which manages to preserve an interestingly non-ethical character of the goods involved, while at the same time being able to ground a critique of capitalism.

The best way I believe that Wood's conception of non-ethical goods can be re-cast is by formulating the notion of non-ethical goods in terms of objective interests. If we define a person's objective interests as the wants or preferences they would have under conditions of perfect (complete and correct) information, perfect clarity of cognition, and under ideal conditions of reflection and deliberation, then non-ethical goods can be conceived as those general-purpose goods which everybody would want under such (and perhaps also under less strict) conditions. This construal allows us both to preserve the "amoral" character of the goods in question—they are clearly normative, not obviously ethical, and certainly not moral—while at the same time managing to make sense of that category of goods as something valuable, on the basis of which a critique of social relations and institutions may be mounted. On such a construal, Marx's critique of capitalism would appeal specifically to the objective interests of the proletariat, in the sense of giving one or more arguments for it being in their objective interests, *qua* members of the proletarian class, to overthrow capitalism.

This last point raises an obvious question: Why should others who are not proletarians care about such a critique of capitalism? Consider one of the more straightforward cases of a non-ethical good, efficiency, and consider two possible forms of society, S_1 and S_2, that differ only in that S_1 is more efficient than S_2, and that the benefits of this greater efficiency accrue entirely to the proletariat—all things remaining equal for non-proletarians. In such a case, why should or might non-proletarians, like Marx himself, care? This is a complicated question to answer, but we can mention the three most obvious lines of reply an amoralist like Wood might make. First, he might argue that this is a relatively unimportant issue. Since proletarians are by far the majority of society, and since their interests can be appealed to in a straightforward way that is all that is needed for Marx's critique to be able to motivate a revolutionary change, and that's all that it attempts and needs to do.

A second line of reply could argue that even though *Marx's critique* of capitalism appeals only to non-ethical goods, non-proletarians may well have good ethical reasons to care about the non-ethical goods of proletarians. For instance, a wealthy capitalist might, in principle, care about the individual well-being and preference-satisfaction of proletarians because they adhere to certain ethical commitments which they believe require it of them. They may, for instance, be a utilitarian of some sort, committed to whichever social, economic, and political institutions maximise overall utility and believe that capitalism does a worse job than socialism would of providing proletarians with non-moral goods essential to maximising (their) utility. As a result, a capitalist utilitarian of this sort might come to adhere to socialist revolution on moral grounds, based on its shortcomings with respect to providing non-moral goods to the proletariat. In this case, Marx's critique of capitalism, despite appealing only to the non-ethical objective interests of the proletariat, would nevertheless be able to appeal indirectly to non-proletarians via their ethical commitments. Obviously, this could also very well happen for proletarians. They too could find Marx's amoralist critique of capitalism appealing not just by reflecting on their own objective interests, but also indirectly because their ethical commitments require that they care about the relevant non-ethical goods and/or their effects, e.g. on utility.

A third possible line of reply would be that non-proletarians could be brought to care about Marx's critique of capitalism through various kinds of non-ethical concerns about the non-ethical goods available to the proletariat, for instance through simple sentiment (e.g. an emotional reaction of compassion or concern) or through strategic instrumental thinking (e.g. through thinking the proletariat's well-being is essential for carrying out victorious military campaigns in the future, and thus, indirectly, for one's own future well-being), but this reply is likely to be far less interesting or satisfactory to most Marxists, so I won't elaborate on it further.

These replies can be expanded in a number of different ways, but there is insufficient space to do so here. All I've attempted to show with them is that reading Marx as basing his critique of capitalism on non-ethical goods such as the objective interests of the proletariat—as amoralists such as Wood do—is not inherently contradictory or ridiculous, and that it still leaves space to argue for additional ethical or moral considerations to play a role among both proletarians and non-proletarians.[25]

---

[25] As we see in Chapter 9, Marx doubts at least some of the efficacy of these things, but that is a distinct issue.

It is by no means clear, however, that Wood's distinction between ethical and non-ethical goods can find enough support in Marx's works. The distinction between ethical and non-ethical goods is not one that Marx ever makes. Nor is it clear that he relies on, or takes himself to rely on, any such distinction between normative categories—assuming we may call non-ethical goods normative in the weak sense outlined above. In Wood's defence it should be said that such a distinction at least can make sense of Marx's own numerous statements against notions of right, justice, etc. (see above), while at the same time providing a fairly clear and interesting manner in which Marx's criticisms of capitalism can be cashed out in a plausibly non-ethical sense. As far as rational reconstruction goes, then, this may be a necessary, and therefore in some minimal sense justified, way to proceed.

In line with this, Wood's account in general makes an important point I wish to preserve, namely Marx's own insistence on appealing to the wants and needs of the proletariat rather than getting bogged down in more abstract normative questions. Marx is concerned with social revolution, he believes that the best way of doing so is by direct appeal to the wants and interests of the working class as revolutionary agent, as a result of which his explicit focus—especially in his mature works intended for a potentially revolutionary audience—is on such appeals. If we thus distinguish the strategic reasons for Marx's largely non-moral criticisms of capitalism from the actual normative components his rejection and critique in fact rest upon, then we can preserve the value of this insight without rendering Marx's thought non-ethical in the strict sense of being devoid of ethical content. As far as Wood's reading goes, however, such a position would no longer be amoral—that is, non-ethical—in any interesting sense. Wood could, as I do, reject the notion that Marx's critique of capitalism rests on any notion of morality, right, or justice as construed by moralist commentators (see section (B) of this appendix below), but there is no interesting sense in which such normative content, once accepted, can still be considered non-ethical; it necessarily invokes something of ethical force or value beyond mere wants and interests.

Furthermore, as I argue throughout this book (especially Part I), there is a clear focus in Marx's work on certain concerns—i.e. concerns with human development, from which concerns with freedom as self-direction derive—from 1844 and all the way through to his latest works. As I show in Chapters 7 and 8, these components continue to play key roles throughout Marx's mature discussions of capitalism and its envisioned cure of socialism. The typical and most plausibly non-ethical goods that Wood mentions, such as health, security, efficiency, and so on, are simply not among them. These other needs (health, security, etc.) are, of course, important to any plausible conception of human development. *Pace* Wood's amoralism, however, they do not play the critical role of providing the normative components for either of Marx's two theories of alienation. Wood, though he notes the connections between Marx's evaluative concerns and his theories of alienation,[26] is unable to come to grips with them. True to the limitations of his amoralism, Wood reads alienation principally in terms of workers' desires for a "sense of meaning" and "self-worth", which are thwarted by their not being able to meet their needs for self-actualisation and self-development, in turn necessary consequences of capitalism.[27] Since a sense of meaning and self-worth are things that (so the claim goes) everyone wants, or would want under the right ideal circumstances, such a view coheres with an amoralist reading. Unfortunately for Wood's thesis, it has no positive textual basis in Marx's writings.

If, for pragmatic reasons, we limit ourselves to the four main components of Marx's critique of capitalism that reappear throughout his writings on political economy, his four kinds of alienation, the problems with Wood's reading are immediately apparent. Of the four kinds of alienation that Marx discusses—from (social-relational) product, from the labour process, from one's species-being, and from others[28]—the first and third have nothing to do with consciousness at all and the fourth is about relations with other human beings. If we grant that alienation from the labour process is a result of alienation from the social-relational product, we still lack anything like an adequate account of how the latter two kinds fit into the picture. Alienation from the labour process is an important point, but there is no reason to believe that it is best or most plausibly explicable in terms of feelings of meaning and self-worth. To Marx, alienation is a category of objective states of affairs, not of psychological experiences. Of course, the experiences of these states of affairs will be experiences of alienation, and, as we have seen in Chapter 3, they are

---

[26] See Wood (2004, esp. ch. 4).
[27] Ibid., p. 23.
[28] See Chapter 7.

clearly not enjoyable, but these are the inherent results and implications of conditions of alienation, not what alienation consists in. In defending Wood, we could allow that the various forms of alienation Marx discusses are general-purpose obstacles to attaining other things everyone wants or would want because of their corrosive impacts on things like freedom, solidarity, community, and so on, which in fact seems to be Wood's position. This, however, leads us back to the initial criticism, which was that the key underlying concerns of Marx's theories of alienation are not properly accounted for by such an appeal to an unconnected multiplicity of bad things.

In summary, then, simple amoralism is rejected due to the fallacious account it entails about the nature and development of Marx's theories and the fact that there is at least one more plausible account available. Sophisticated amoralism, however, succeeds in capturing some of Marx's insights and beliefs about the nature of right, justice, and so on, as well as his views on revolutionary theoretical advocacy—principally by appeal to wants and interests rather than the articulation and application of abstract ethical principles and theories. However, this position too should be rejected. It cannot make sense of the clear persistence of different and seemingly unrelated normative concerns in Marx's writings and it cannot give a satisfactory account of the linchpin of Marx's life work developed in his second theory of alienation, which, as I show in Part I, rests on other normative commitments.

(B) The Moralist Reading

It is easy to forget that the moralist readings of Marx[29] in fact arose from a critique and rejection of the amoralist positions widespread among many Marxist and non-Marxist commentators. The simple form of amoralism held basically that Marx's theories had, or was supposed to have, no genuine ethical components whatsoever. Relatedly, the sophisticated

---

[29] This paradigmatically includes both the category of writers who view Marx as criticising capitalism for its injustice, such as Arneson (1981), Cohen (1981, 1983, 1989), DeGoyler (1992), Elster (1983, 1985), Geras (1985, 1992), Green (1983), Husami (1978), Nielsen (1988), Riley (1983), Ryan (1980), van de Veer (1973), van der Linden (1984), and Young (1978, 1981), as well as others such as Allen's (1974) utilitarian reading and Gregor's (1968) interpretation in terms of nomic redefinition of man from which different sets of abstract ethical principles follow, and other readings in terms of (moral) principles of freedom, individuality, etc.

amoralism developed by Wood held that Marx's critique of capitalism rests on two legs: first the rejection of traditional morality couched in terms of right and justice; instead, secondly, building on the supposedly non-ethical values of freedom, emancipation, community, and so on. In contrast to these, a moralist position is one of a family of positions which hold that Marx's critique of capitalism rests on one or more of the following:

(1) One or a set of abstract and ahistorical principles—whether principles of justice or otherwise—delimiting or determining what ought to, or what may or what may not, be done to a person by other individuals and/or by social institutions. The principles in question may include maxims like "people have a right to the full proceeds from their labour-power", "it is wrong to steal from others", "exploitation is wrong", and so on, where these are construed as ethical principles rather than, say, mere descriptions of reigning legal or customary rules and norms.

(2) One or a set of abstract principles specifying the necessary and/or sufficient criteria for a society to have a certain ethical status ("decent", "just", "well-ordered", and so on), and according to which social relations, structures and institutions, and/or constitutional, and legal arrangements are to be ordered and/or reformed.

(3) One or a set of abstract and ahistorical principles specifying goals for individuals and/or societies which they ought to act in order to bring about or realise to the greatest extent possible, such as "one should maximise overall utility", but also other abstract principles or ideals of freedom, autonomy, community, etc.

Examples of such approaches abound in contemporary political theory, e.g. Nozick's postulation of natural "rights" as the foundations for his political thought (1),[30] Rawls' two principles of justice specifying the conditions for a just society (2),[31] and Cohen's ideal of community (3).[32] If Marx is supposed to have held something like a moralist position, we

---

[30] See Nozick (1974).

[31] See Rawls (1999, 2001, 2005). Note the absence of "ahistorical" here, since Rawls' principles of justice are not ahistorical in the required sense.

[32] Cohen (2008, 2009), cf. Vrousalis (2010, 2012).

would expect him to first articulate, presumably with some clarity, the abstract principles on which his critique of capitalism was based, demonstrate how capitalism both fails and is likely to keep failing to meet them, and critique capitalism in one way or another on those grounds. It is therefore absolutely vital for a moralist reading that it can demonstrate either that Marx had, or that he must have had, some principles of the required kind that he in fact uses in a critique of capitalism. I will argue that no such principles are to be found.

Before moving on, we should note that the normative principles in (1), (2), and (3) above are held, on moralist readings of Marx, to be abstract and ahistorical in nature, and thus not properly subject to variance across different natural, social, and historical contexts. By this I mean that the contextual variance in question is believed to be in some way ethically legitimate or salutary. If, on the contrary, one holds the view that the principles in terms of which Marx critiques capitalism are of such a nature that they rightly vary across different contexts, then one's position collapses into a variant of internal critique. Why? Because the first kind of internal critique discussed in (D) below is one which draws its principles from a particular context, in terms of which actions, institutions, etc. within that context are then critiqued. On such an account, capitalism is critiqued in terms of the principles which arise in capitalist societies and in terms of which those societies tend to legitimate themselves. If the principles in question properly vary across contexts as a result of being generated only within and in part by such contexts, then they are, in a sense, principles internal to that context (or range of relevantly similar contexts). A critique in terms of such internal principles can then, logically, be one of two kinds. Either an action, institution, or whatnot can be critiqued in terms of principles external to the context in which that action, institution, or whatnot appears—external critique—or it can be critiqued in terms of principles internal to that context or range of contexts—internal critique. It is hard to see how an external critique of capitalism in this sense can make any sense of Marx's work. It seems wildly implausible to suppose that any of the principles in question are not valued in the context of capitalist societies and there is no clear way that such a critique, in light of the global spread of capitalism, can serve to bring about any change in human societies—a concern central to Marx's work. Since external critique in this sense is completely implausible, an internal critique is the only coherent alternative. As such, if the normative foundations of Marx's critique of capitalism along the lines of the kinds of principles in (1), (2), and (3) are to avoid collapsing into a variant of internal critique, they must be analysed and formulated abstractly and ahistorically.

Of the three kinds of principles mentioned above, the vast majority of moralist readings of Marx fall into one of two camps. Either they are readers, such as Cohen and Geras, who accept the proposition that Marx had a theory of justice, in terms of which he rejected capitalism. In this case the principles in question will be abstract and ahistorical principles of kinds (1) and (2) above. This is often coupled with a reconstructed theory of exploitation as the centre-point of Marx's critique of capitalism, according to which capital appropriation violates the principles of justice in question.[33] In the other camp are readers who believe that Marx rested his rejection of capitalism not on a theory of right, justice, etc., but in terms of ethical principles or ideals of freedom, emancipation, community, and so on. I will briefly discuss each variant in turn. In my view, the best and most exhaustive list of arguments for the justice-theoretical reading of Marx is that provided by Norman Geras,[34] who admirably synthesises, clarifies, and adds to those of many other justice-theorists. I cannot do these arguments full justice in an overview such as this, but I can and will provide a brief outline of each of them, followed by a brief outline of why I find them to be ultimately unconvincing as arguments establishing that Marx had, and/or must have had, a theory of justice (understood as one or more abstract and ahistorical ethical principles) on which he based his critique of capitalism. Geras' arguments can be summarised as follows:

---

[33] I should perhaps note that I take my rejection of all alternative ethical components—especially those based on ethical principle of various kinds—also to give good grounds for rejecting the idea that Marx's theory of "exploitation" is an ethical critique of capitalism. Any remotely plausible textual interpretation of this idea as one with ethical content must presuppose one or another of these alternative conceptions of Marx's ethical views, all of which I argue we have good reason to reject. I should also point out that Marx never says he is doing anything at all ethical with his theory of exploitation, that given the actual definition of exploitation and its rate in his economics it can only occur in capitalist society (since it presupposes the production of value, which is the hallmark of capitalism), that he explicitly points out that capitalist exchange is not unjust in *Capital*, and that Marx consistently says he does not mean anything ethically loaded by it—and, as we have seen, he criticises those who, like Proudhon and the Lasalleans, attempt to critique capitalism on these grounds (e.g. in the *Critique of the Gotha Programme*). The reader will note that these points have been discussed in section (A) of this appendix, as important aspects of the amoralist position that, unlike its analysis of Marx's critique of capitalism, I wish to preserve (both because they're correct interpretations of Marx and because I find them compelling).

[34] Especially Geras (1985).

(i) Justice consists, in some sense, in the exchange of equivalents. Under capitalism this seems to be the case in the sphere of exchange, but is not in fact so in the sphere of production, where surplus value is extracted. *Prima facie*, this seems a good basis on which to believe that capitalism is unjust.[35]

(ii) Although Marx claims that capitalism is not unjust, he nevertheless uses terms such as "theft", "plunder", and "robbery" to describe the capitalist appropriation of surplus value, thereby implicitly employing a language of injustice.

(iii) "From what Marx says about capitalist robbery", Geras argues that "we can infer a commitment to independent and transcendent [I take this to mean at least abstract and ahistorical – otherwise I am unsure what 'independent and transcendent' is supposed to mean here] standards of justice, and further evidence of the same thing is provided by his way of characterizing the two principles of distribution that he anticipates for post-capitalist society".[36]

(iv) Marx's seemingly relativist statements about right and justice are not in fact relativist, but realist, expressing his awareness of the different prospects for realising or meeting these principles in different historical contexts. When Marx speaks of "higher standards" of right in socialist societies, he must implicitly be relying on some kind of abstract and ahistorical criteria in terms of which these supposedly higher standards are evaluated.

(v) There is nothing reformist or necessarily in conflict with Marx's thought about a focus on distribution as such, only about those cases where this is not accompanied by an understanding and critique of the relations of production from which such distributions flow.

(vi) Although Marx finds it unimportant, there is nothing inherently anti-revolutionary, from a Marxian point of view, about criticising capitalism on the basis of right or justice, and such criticism can happily work alongside other, amoral, critiques and appeals.

---

[35] The relevant consideration must be in the sphere of capitalist production, not exchange, since Marx repeatedly writes—and justice-theorists acknowledge that he repeatedly and coherently writes—that capitalist exchange is an exchange of equals and is not unjust.

[36] Geras (1985, p. 85).

(vii) Right and justice cannot rightly be categorised as *merely* juridical principles; minimally, Geras argues, right and justice can also be distributive principles.[37] Merely juridical principles and conceptions of right and justice Marx does criticise.[38] It is also possible to have, and in fact Marx must have had, in order to mount a critique of capitalism at all, some kind of abstract and ahistorical principles of right or justice in terms of which different social arrangements can be evaluated.

(viii) That is what, for instance, the principle "from each according to his abilities, to each according to his needs"[39] amounts to: a principle of distributive justice.

(ix) Claims that Marx rests his critique on ethical principles of freedom, community, emancipation, and so on, instead of a proper theory of justice, rely on an inconsistent usage of texts whereby a distinction is made between one kind of ethics and another, which is not to be found in any of Marx's works. "Marx does, of course, condemn capitalism for its unfreedom, oppression, coercion, but so does he in substance condemn it for its injustice. And just as, conversely, he does indeed identify principles of justice that are internal to and functional for the capitalist mode of production, so also does he identify conceptions of freedom and of self-development historically relative in exactly the same way".[40] To pick one such category over another is arbitrary and unjustified as far as Marx's own texts are concerned. It should thus be rejected.

(x) To the amoralist counter-argument that Marx himself repeatedly repudiates any notion of a critique of capitalism founded on justice, it was suggested by Cohen,[41] and repeated by many others since, that Marx both genuinely believed that he did not

---

[37] Recall that Wood's (1972a, 1972b, 2004), and some others', early work, to which Geras' arguments are in part responses, tended to conflate these two distinct kinds of concerns. This point is largely a rejection of that conflation.

[38] Marx also rejected distributive principles, to which moralists generally reply with points (viii) and (x) below.

[39] Marx (1996, p. 215/I:25, 15).

[40] Geras (1985, p. 62).

[41] Cohen (1983).

have a theory of justice and that he nevertheless did in fact have a theory of justice upon which his critique of capitalism rests.[42]

I will now examine each of these arguments, point by point. Point (x) is simply an ad hoc stipulation to account for the painfully obvious fact that the reading of the justice-theorists flatly contradicts every single explicit statement on the matter that Marx himself ever made—some of which have been cited above in section (A) of this appendix. (I consider it unnecessary to supply further quotations to back this up, since absolutely everyone in these debates agrees on this point.) Given Marx's impressive intellectual feats, absence of obvious cognitive pathologies, etc., this alone gives us good reason to look for any other available reading before accepting an interpretation with this implication.

The remaining points seem to construct a strong case, at least prima facie, but closer inspection reveals that this is not in fact so. Point (i) is not directly about Marx, and there is no independent reason to believe he either held it or that it did significant work in any of his thinking about the normative status of capitalism per se. Demonstrating that the value the labourer receives is less than the value their labour creates is important to Marx's economics in that it allows him to explain the origin of surplus value and thereby the origin of profits. However, he never uses this point to criticise capitalism, he certainly never says he is doing any such thing, and the only argument otherwise proceeds from the normatively laden descriptions of this process of appropriation which will be dealt with below. Similarly, points (v) and (vi) add nothing by way of positive argumentation for the justice-theorist. Point (iv) makes something like a plausible claim, but a justice-theoretical conclusion does not necessarily follow. Its argument for abstract and ahistorical "criteria" of assessment is equally consistent with numerous other alternative kinds of standards or criteria, including an ethics based on a normative notion of human nature or an evaluative metric of human development. Consequently, it too does no meaningful work for the justice-theorist in this

---

[42] These points summarise in particular the excellent work in Geras (1985). It should be noted that (x), unlike the others, is not formulated by Geras as a proposition in the defence of the justice-theoretical interpretation. Instead, it is defended as the only viable way of reconciling Marx's explicit statements with what he takes to be the overwhelming case made for that interpretation by points (i)–(ix).

context. And this has further implications for the consideration of points (vii) and (viii).

Starting with (vii), there is no reason to assume that right and justice cannot be categorised in merely politico-juridical terms. In fact, there is a good argument for saying, as amoralists like Wood do, that this was precisely how those terms were understood by Marx. On this reading, when Marx criticises politico-juridical conceptions of right and justice he was criticising precisely what he understood "justice" in general to be. As far as reconstructing what Marx took himself to be doing, then, the justice-theoretical claim Geras makes in (vii) has no force unless it can demonstrate that Marx in fact held a conception of justice which goes beyond merely politico-juridical concerns. Such a demonstration remains outstanding. Naturally, our concepts of right and justice may differ from Marx's, in which case one can argue that Marx held something which we would, and he would not, recognise as falling under the terms of right and justice. If this is indeed the case, then the weight of the argument falls on whether (ii) and (iii) enables the justice-theorist to excavate such a principle or set thereof. I shall shortly argue that they do not.

Moving on to (viii), it seems correct to say that "from each according to his ability, to each according to his needs" can rightly be called a principle of distributive justice—or at least a principle of distribution—in the sense that it is an abstract principle which is supposed to guide the distribution of goods and services in a society. There is, however, no independent reason to believe that this in any way conflicts with the amoralist reading[43] of principles of distribution, along with other principles guiding and constraining the interactions between groups and individuals, as appropriate or not only to certain contexts and not others, and therefore good/bad or better/worse only relative to those contexts. When Marx mentions this distributive maxim, it is in the context of describing socialist society, and this maxim is offered precisely as the one most appropriate to that kind of society (for more on which see Chapter 8). There is no independent reason to believe that this distributive maxim is a stand-alone, abstract, and ahistorical principle of justice by which capitalism is judged and found wanting by Marx. If anything, it is part of a package—socialist society—which is held, as a whole, to be superior to capitalism. Because the distributive principle in question only appears as part of this wider

---

[43] Again, see Wood (1972a, 1972b, 2004).

package which is valued as a totality, it is unable to do the independent normative work of recommending one such package over the other that a justice-theorist like Geras wants it to do. It can of course be recommended in terms of other evaluative criteria, but that entails giving up any justificatory force it would have had as an independent principle of distributive justice.

This is further bolstered by the fact that the supposed distributive maxim does not appear in any of Marx's early works in which he first develops his ideas on socialism and its normative foundations, such as the *Economic and Philosophical Manuscripts of 1844*, *Notes on James Mill*, and *The Holy Family*. It is discussed, briefly, in the *German Ideology*, but only from the point of view of socialism, not in any discussion of capitalism. If the principle in question were of real importance to Marx's critique of capitalism, we would certainly expect it to be discussed in that context, which it never is, and to do some significant work in Marx's thought on capitalism, which it never seems to do. On the other hand, notions of human species-being and human development appear numerous times, receive at least some significant discussion, and definitely seem to do important work for Marx both in the early writings and in his later works when discussing capitalism, shown in Part I. These are therefore much better candidates for the normative components of Marx's critique of capitalism

As concerns (ix), the first point to make is that such a distinction between principles of justice and other principles is, *pace* Geras, *not* arbitrary. Given Marx's explicit, repeated, and consistent rejection of founding a critique of capitalism on right, justice, or distributive concerns—a point recognised, incidentally, by justice-theorists, along with all the other participants in these debates—this distinction allows those who believe that Marx appeals to some kind of normative principles to distinguish one category of such principles which is not subject to the criticisms that Marx levels against those of morality, right, and justice. The distinction between principles of justice and other ethical principles can be considered arbitrary only if we already hold that there is an extremely good reason to believe that Marx has and/or needs principles of justice in the first place. As such, this claim too rests entirely on the arguments for the justice-theoretical view that Geras presents in (ii) and (iii). If their case is not entirely watertight, then (ix) is simply false, since a distinction along the lines proposed provides one way in which we can account both for Marx's normative commitments and his rejection of morality, right, and justice. Since it is now clear that (ii) and (iii) must shoulder the entire burden of Geras' justice-theoretical interpretation, it is to these that I now turn.

If the foregoing is correct, then Geras' entire remaining case for supposing that Marx had some principle(s) or a theory of justice rests on nothing more than the claim that the language of "theft", "robbery", etc., that he employs must imply a prior conception of justice which is violated by the capitalist appropriation of surplus value. Since the distributive maxim mentioned in (iii) has already been dealt with, I shall focus now on this sole remaining argument. It can be presented in syllogistic form as follows:

(a) Descriptions in terms of "robbery", "theft", "plunder", etc., presuppose some principle(s) or theory of justice, the stipulations of which are violated by the object, process, or whatever that is described in this manner.
(b) Marx describes capitalist appropriation of surplus value using terms like "robbery", "theft", "plunder", etc.
Therefore:
(c) Marx presupposes, or must presuppose, some principle(s) or theory of justice.

There are at least three reasons to be suspicious of (c) which should motivate a rejection of one or both of its premises. No principle of the required sort is ever formulated by Marx (cf. the discussion of (viii) above); there is no consensus among justice-theorists about what principles are required for the critical work to which Marx is supposed to be putting them; and, as we have seen in section (A) above, Marx himself repeatedly denies having any such principles, and criticises those who do repeatedly, consistently, and vociferously. Given his clarity and consistency on this point, it would be extremely implausible to think that Marx managed to be so completely wrong about his own view as to both have such a theory and keep thinking that he doesn't.

Since (b) is incontrovertible, those who, like me, wish to reject (c) must find something wrong with (a). Numerous arguments have been offered in favour of rejecting or explaining away (a), many of which fail.[44] The

---

[44] The most thorough treatment available are those of Geras (1985, pp. 65–69; 1992).

strongest reasons why I believe (a) should be rejected are the following. First, using the descriptive cognates mentioned need not be taken to presuppose a principle of justice being violated. Rather than necessarily relying on an antecedent conception of justice of a very particular kind, Marx may be read as engaging in an attempt to reform existing conceptions and/or usages of "theft" and its cognates in line with what he takes to be their core meanings and centres of normative force, in order in turn to help reform popular judgements about the nature of capitalist appropriation for political purposes. The core meanings in question may consist in, for instance, that in both capitalist appropriation and in more familiar cases of theft, something is being appropriated from someone else without their acceptance, that in (at least some of instances of) both cases something is being so appropriated without the "losers'" awareness and knowledge, and so on. By shifting the way in which this kind of normatively laden language is used, certain actions and processes which are normally thought of as morally salutary *per definitionem*—such as the everyday purchase of labour-power in a capitalist economy—now come to be described in terms which are more negatively laden. Even if no new facts are added, such a shift in how these concepts are used may nevertheless help bring about a change in the way the process of capitalist appropriation is thought of and evaluated—one which better suits the political needs and interests of the proletariat *qua* revolutionary class.

Another possible interpretation of the relevant passages—again, at least as well-founded as Geras' justice-theoretical reading thereof—is that by describing the process of capitalist appropriation in terms of unequal exchange, theft, plunder, and so on, Marx is re-describing a familiar process—a description buttressed by his economic theory and its problem-solving power (e.g. its ability to explain the origin of profits under equal exchange, or its ability to explain the possibility of economic crises)—in a new way such that certain elements which were previously obscured or unknown now come to be illuminated. These elements turn out in fact to be the opposite of what they look like—viz. what looked like free and equal exchange is shown in fact to be coerced and unequal exchange and thus, in some sense, "theft", "robbery", etc.—and this in turn causes, or at least is supposed to cause, the addressees to change their conceptions and assessments of the object(s) of this re-description. In this case no new concepts need to be added and no familiar concepts need to shift either their meanings or their general usage. Instead, what changes here is the way in which a familiar process is described or re-described as a matter of fact.

Whereas the first alternative interpretation just outlined was concerned with the reform of the terms of a language (or at least of their usage), the second alternative interpretation first and foremost concerns the cognitive grasp of the process in question through its re-description. In the latter case, new descriptive knowledge is added which, in some way, leads to a subversion of how a familiar process is thought of—with downstream effects on how that process must now be evaluated. It remains an entirely open question whether the terms or concepts used in this re-description are, strictly speaking, accurately applied, and whether or not these terms should be reformed in light of the new light shone upon the process of capitalist appropriation. In the former case, by contrast, it need not be the case that any further descriptive knowledge of the nature of capitalist appropriation has been revealed; the question is purely one of whether the terms in question could or should legitimately be shifted in meaning and/or use. The two are not by any means exclusive: Marx may well have been attempting both to illuminate the nature of capitalism and simultaneously to reform the relevant normatively laden language in a unified manner, thereby reforming both our cognitive grasp of capitalist appropriation and the normatively laden language in terms of which we think about, reflect on, and deliberate upon it.

It seems clear that both of the proposed alternative readings proceed from the premise that Marx's practise concerning, and perhaps also his conception of, language, or at least of language-use, is a different one from that implied by premise (a) of Geras' justice-theoretical argument above. Geras' justice-theoretical premise (a) seems to rely on, at least *inter alia*, the assumption that "theft" and its cognates necessarily presuppose a violation of some principle of justice,[45] that this principle must have some clear, coherent, and determinate content, and that this clear, coherent, and determinate content must be specified antecedently to its application—whether by a theorist or by lay users. Geras' justice-theoretical premise (a), then, holds that only with a principle of justice specified antecedently such that it has clear, coherent, and determinate content could Marx have been able to characterise capitalist appropriation in terms

---

[45] I shall henceforth stick to the singular for the sake of simplicity.

of "theft" and its cognates. I shall henceforth call this conception of language and language-use the "justice-theoretical conception".

There are at least four reasons to doubt that Marx's practice with regard to concepts and their usage was of the kind that Geras presupposes, or needs to presuppose, for premise (a). Firstly, there is no direct evidence in Marx's writings or elsewhere to suggest that he adhered to, or took himself to adhere to, the justice-theoretical conception of language and language-use. Secondly, Marx's practice with regard to the concepts he uses to describe and evaluate capitalism is hard to square with the strictures of the justice-theoretical conception of language and its use. For instance, Marx's usages of the terms for "alienation" (Entäusserung and Entfremdung) simply do not have any one single, clear, coherent, and determinate meaning in their various appearances throughout Marx's *oeuvre*. This is particularly clear in the *Economic and Philosophical Manuscripts of 1844*, where he distinguishes between four distinct kinds of "alienation". Although they are connected in important ways, there is, as we saw in Chapter 7, no one single, clear, coherent, and determinate meaning that they all share. Admittedly, this is an unusually dramatic instance, but it is not the only one. In the interests of reconstructing Marx's theories and their presuppositions in the most plausible manner possible, this consideration militates against reading Marx in terms of the justice-theoretical conception of language and language-use that Geras presupposes, in favour of a more fluid, open-ended, and pragmatic one more in line with the alternative readings I have proposed.

Thirdly, the justice-theoretical view of language and language-use that Geras relies on does not seem to cohere as well with Marx's theory of practice, or with his general conception of the connections between concepts, modes of thought, and their natural, social, and historical contexts as mine does. One of the central components of this aspect of Marx's thought is precisely that the ways in which human beings conceptualise and make sense of their natural, social, and historical environment are themselves ongoing human practices which are, in important ways and to a significant extent, influenced by the context within which their human creators are situated. On such a conception, it is plausible to suppose that language and language-use is a rather fluid and indeterminate sort of thing: one whose elements are generally not tied down to clear definitions; are sensitive to the needs and interests of those who use them; and which, in turn, tend to shift and change, more or less explicitly and more or less consciously, with the altering needs and interests of their users. If we grant this, and if we further accept that concepts can influence political practice in a significant way, then it follows that language and language-use is itself something which can be, at least in principle, something which it is worth trying to change in order better to further one's political purposes. Again, this coheres much better with the alternative readings suggested than it does with that of the justice-theorists.

Fourthly, the more fluid and indeterminate conception of language and language-use, its connections to human practical activity and the needs and interests inherent therein, and the resulting thesis about the pragmatic revisability of language, all seem to cohere better with Marx's consistent emphasis—throughout his life—on developing the concepts one employs to understand an aspect of reality such that they are best able to match the "real movements" of the object of study, rather than setting up an antecedently defined framework which the objects of study are then subsequently analysed and/or evaluated in terms of. This includes not only Marx's discussions and analyses of straightforwardly descriptive matters, such as in his critique of the classical political economists' superficial analysis of capitalist social relations in the *Economic and Philosophical Manuscripts of 1844*[46] and or his critique of Proudhon in the *Poverty of Philosophy* for setting up a scheme of abstract and ahistorical concepts prior to detailed empirical study—badly compromising the latter as a result. It also occurs in at least one context, namely in the 1837 letter to his father, in which Marx has both normative and descriptive concerns in one and the same investigation—namely his projected study of law and legal systems.[47] In this letter, one of Marx's main stated concerns is, as in the other instances just mentioned, that the concepts needed to understand and evaluate something need to be developed alongside, and in response to, the object of study. He contrasts this with his own earlier idealistic attempts—as well as those of Kant and Fichte—at proceeding from antecedently defined concepts and categories which are then subsequently applied to the objects of study. Not only does this further underscore that such concepts are malleable and should, when appropriate, be altered or further developed in response to the needs and interests of their users; it also explicitly presents an approach to language and its use precisely in line with the alternative conception I have outlined

---

[46] See for instance I/2:234–235.
[47] III/1:9–18, esp. 10–11 and 15–16.

from the point of view of a critique of the justice-theoretical conception. Note that none of these four reasons constitute anything like a knock-down argument against the justice-theoretical conception of language and language-use that Geras needs to presuppose for his argument to hold water. What they do provide is very good reason to prefer the more fluid, indeterminate, and pragmatic conception over Geras' justice-theoretical one, which, *in lieu* of further evidence on the matter, renders the former position the more plausible of the two.

If, then, it is plausible to believe that Marx held a view of language and language-use which is fluid, indeterminate, and pragmatic in nature, responsive to the needs and interests of its users, and capable of contributing to social change, the two alternative readings proposed above make a lot of sense. In the case of one of the alternative readings, Marx can be interpreted as trying to shift the meanings and/or uses of familiar normatively loaded terms such that they better suit the needs and interests of the proletariat *qua* revolutionary class. In the case of the more cognitive reading, Marx can be read as exploiting the fluidity and indeterminacy of the relevant normatively laden concepts in order to highlight certain previously unseen—now revealed, thanks to their re-description—aspects of the process of capitalist appropriation and accumulation as in fact, at least in crucial respects, the opposite of what they are normally taken to be. Since Geras' justice-theoretical view implied in premise (a) is such a particularly strong one—and, furthermore, is used to support a highly speculative conclusion—the burden of proof lies on Geras to find decent support for such a claim if his argument as per (a)–(c) is to go through. Unfortunately for moralist readings, such evidence is nowhere to be found. The alternative readings proposed, and the view of language and language-use which underlies them, have significant advantages, though they too remain speculative. They cohere better with Marx's actual practice with concepts and conceptual development; they cohere better with his general account of practice, base and superstructure, and so on; and they cohere far better with what Marx himself has to say about the relationship between contexts, the objects of study, and the language to be employed for making sense of them. Perhaps most importantly, the alternative readings are in general less speculative in nature, insofar as they do not demand that Marx must have had some vitally important theoretical components of a kind which he both never develops and explicitly, repeatedly, and vociferously rejects.

In summary, then, I have argued that a close look at the evidence and arguments that Geras offers in favour of the justice-theoretical reading of Marx reveals that his case is extremely flimsy, resting, at best, solely on the syllogism (a)–(c). Furthermore, I have argued that there is little reason to accept the major premise (a) in light of the availability of competing and more plausible interpretations of what Marx is doing with the normatively charged concepts in question—interpretations which need not rely on implicit conceptions of justice. This, together with other good reasons to reject the conclusion in (c), means that the interpretation in (a) ought to be rejected. However, even if (a)–(c) is not rejected, the non-existent principle(s) of justice required to make sense of these claims still do not deserve serious consideration as the normative foundations of Marx's critique of capitalism, if only because the only diagnostic critiques he does develop and retain rest on other foundations altogether.

One moralistic way in which these other grounds can be understood is in terms of abstract and ahistorical principles or ideals of freedom, equality, community, rationality, and so on.[48] I believe that this position carries a major and important insight—namely that Marx's chief objections to capitalism were made in terms of its detrimental effects on human freedom, self-rule, or self-direction, as diagnosed in his critique of capitalism that I've discussed throughout this book. Where this account goes wrong, however, is in the way it posits these principles or ideals without sufficient attention to the way they are grounded in Marx's accounts of human development, human beings, and human society. This is what I have tried to provide throughout Part I, setting the stage for the later chapters' accounts of alienation, democracy, and socialism. Furthermore, the way this other moralist kind of approach posits values externally— either from the point of view of another society, or from some supposed

---

[48] Brenkert (1979), Comninel (2010), arguably DeGoyler (1992) and Kamenka (1972) (Kamenka 1969, by contrast, seems to claim these commitments in turn derive from a normative conception of human nature or species-being), Lukes (1985), Mcbride (1975), Peffer (1990), Sichel (1972), Soper (1987) and Sowell (1963). Allen's (1974) appeal to utility may also, arguably, fit into this category. There is a version of this claim according to which Marx criticises capitalism in terms of the socialist and/or communist distributive maxims as higher forms of society (cf. Lukes 1985; McBride 1975; Miller 1983; Nielsen 1988; Riley 1983; Sayers 1989, 1994, 2007a). Such a view, it seems to me, must in turn rest on some other kind of normative foundations in terms of which the "higher" and "lower" forms of society are determined as such. As a result of this they collapse, ultimately, into more familiar variants (an argument Geras advances against Sayers in the former's 1992).

neutral or "God's-eye" point of view—further neglects Marx's fundamentally realist (and thus contextual) approach, premised as it is on the evaluation of competing, achievable alternatives in light of their differing social realisations. In Marx's social theory, moral values and beliefs form part of the superstructure which arises and is, at least in part, generated, conditioned, and constrained by the material base upon and within which it does so. An acceptable account of the normative components of Marx's critique of capitalism must not only say something about the surface commitments to, e.g. freedom, but must explicate them within the deeper accounts of human nature, history, politics, and social change they are embedded within.

There are three principal ways in which these surface commitments to things like freedom can be so explicated: by grounding them in a normative conception of human nature; by grounding them in the social and historical contexts within which they arise; and by grounding them jointly in a conception of human development and their relevant contexts. In the remainder of this appendix, I will briefly discuss and reject the first two; the last is examined and defended in Part I.

(C) An Ethical Human Nature

One of the ways that Marx's adherence to notions of, e.g. freedom can be understood, without moralistic appeals to ahistorical and abstract normative principles, is by grounding it in an ethical[49] conception of human nature. There are basically two ways in which this can be done.[50] On the one hand, the human "nature" or "essence" in question can be cashed out in terms of distinctly human capacities for rational thought and deliberation, self-directed and other-directed activity, capacities for sociality

---

[49] It is logically possible to propose a normative conception of human nature which is, for instance, aesthetically or rationally normative, but not ethical. Positing such a conception as a reading of Marx is neither textually plausible, nor does it seem to have been pursued by anyone grouped together in this section. Arguably, a normative conception of rationality does play a part in those approaches which read Marx's critique in terms of objective interests or amoral goods, as discussed above.

[50] I deliberately exclude, for obvious reasons, those who believe Marx to have an Aristotelian account of human nature, but which holds this not to do any important ethical work, e.g. Wood (2004) and Buchanan (1982) for the later, but not the earlier (from 1844 onwards) Marx, since these reduce to some other (e.g. moralist or amoralist) interpretation.

and community, etc., which are important as conditions for, and/or constituents of, human development, and valued as such.[51] So long as this development of human nature is valued for the fact that it is such a development and flourishing, it is this latter (i.e. human development) evaluative conception that does the work of providing the normative components on which Marx's critique of capitalism is held to be based. As such, this approach collapses into the second kind of internal critique discussed in Part I. To the extent that such a conception differs from the approach I advocate, my objections are that my approach can make better sense of how these commitments (freedom, self-direction, a conception of human nature, etc.) hang together, how they cohere with Marx's other statements about human needs, wealth, etc., and as a result my reading can muster greater textual plausibility and depth of analysis.

On the other hand, a normative conception of human nature can be cashed out in terms of a more detailed account of human nature with a particular essence of *telos*, the ethical content of which is either basic in some way or underwritten by an *ergon*-argument. We see this kind of argument most prominently in the work of Nasser and Kain, the general form of which can be sketched as follows[52]:

1. There is a natural function, essence, or *telos* distinctive of the human species and all members thereof (presumably barring pathology).
2. This function, essence, or *telos* constitutes the ethical good for human beings.
3. This function, essence, or *telos* consists in one or more of the following: rational thought and deliberation; freedom; self-directed activity; autonomy; other-directed activity (in the sense of having as its intentional goal the satisfaction also of other humans' needs); and/or the formation of healthy human relationships and communities.

---

[51] Aronovitch (1980), Avineri (1968), Booth (1992) and Buchanan (1982) (for the young Marx of 1844, but not the later one). Fromm (2004), Gilbert (1992), Leopold (2007), probably Miller (1992) and Wilde (1998), see also McMurty (1978).

[52] Kain (1988, 1992), Kamenka (1969), and Nasser (1975). Wood (2004) has interesting points when it comes to the connection between Aristotle's and Marx's view of human nature, but denies that this plays any non-amoralist normative role in Marx.

4. In order to achieve the human ethical good, it is therefore necessary to ensure that these constituents of the human function, essence, or *telos*, as per 3, are developed, nurtured, or realised.

This argument is then typically coupled with a reading of Marx's theory of history and critique of capitalism according to which these normative foundations require freedom from both natural and socially imposed necessity or compulsion, that capitalism by its industrial and technological advances has made such liberation possible in principle, but that capitalist relations of production prevent this potential from being realised by the nature of the social forms of necessity it imposes—a critique expressed in especially the theory of alienation in the *Economic and Philosophical Manuscripts of 1844*. This view can affirm the aforementioned points regarding the absence and repudiation of abstract principles in Marx's works traditionally advanced against moralist readings, while retaining a genuinely normative basis for Marx's critique of capitalism. In contrast to the previous version discussed, this conception of an ethical human nature rests not on a deeper commitment to human development. Instead, it requires a much more limited account of which human essence or *telos* is valuable in itself, as a result of which it does not have the same breadth and open-endedness of the view that I advocate.

The account of a normative human nature in terms of a human essence or *telos*, however, is not particularly plausible as a reading of Marx. First, there is little explicit talk of a human "essence" in Marx's later works. This is not due to any substantial change from a "humanist" to an "antihumanist" position on Marx's part—as is shown when one compares Marx's discussion of the difference between human beings and animals from the *Economic and Philosophical Manuscripts of 1844* to Volume I of *Capital* (see Chapters 3, 4, and 7). Rather, as we have seen, the shift is one of terminology only.[53] Even though the very young Marx operates with a conception of human "essence", this has a very different structure from that of the static and ahistorical essences in, e.g. Aristotle and Feuerbach. To take just one example, in the 6th of the *Theses on Feuerbach* Marx criticises Feuerbach for resolving the "religious essence into

---

[53] For discussion of the use of the term "alienation" in the older Marx, see Cowling 2006.

the *human* essence". "But", he writes, "the human essence is no abstraction inherent in each single individual. In its reality it is the ensemble of the social relations"; on Marx's view, this conception drives Feuerbach to abstract from the historical process and fix religious ideas in the isolated human individual, rendering "essence" something which "can be comprehended only as 'genus', as an internal, dumb generality which *naturally* unites the many individuals".[54] I discuss some of the positive implications of this discussion for how Marx thinks about human nature or essence in Chapters 3, 4, and 7. Here, I want only to draw one important point from it. Any Aristotelian conception of human essence or *telos* as well as (in particular premise 1 of) the *ergon*-argument sketched above, clearly presupposes, and needs to presuppose, a human essence as an abstraction inherent in every single human individual, as a kind of "genus" generality which somehow "naturally" unites all the individuals falling within it. As such, it is a position which Marx explicitly rejects, at least from 1845 onwards. Furthermore, as I show in the section on "The Nature of Alienation" in Chapter 7, since after these criticisms Marx continues to write about human nature in essentially the same way as he does before (e.g. in 1844), the Aristotelian reading of Marx's supposed ethical conception of human nature is implausible even as a reading of Marx's views prior to 1845. It should therefore be rejected.

Secondly, Marx himself never formulates anything like a kind of *ergon*-argument anywhere in his writings. If he in fact had a view that was so close to Aristotle's in this manner, it seems highly implausible that he would both (a) fail to provide this crucial foundation, and (b) fail to acknowledge his debts to the master—especially in light of the fact that he readily acknowledges his significant debts to Aristotle elsewhere.

Third and last, since, as I show in Part I, there is a viable alternative which allows us both to account for the normative significance of the kinds of human needs and capacities this approach rightly highlights, without having to posit either an implausible notion of human "essence" or a non-existent argument or argumentative structure, we have further reason to look elsewhere to the foundations provided by a metric of human development. With this reading out of the way, I turn to the last remaining alternative reading of the normative foundations of Marx's

---

[54] Marx (1992, p. 423/IV:3, p. 21).

critique of capitalism, namely that which reads that critique as an internal critique formulated in terms of principles.

(D) Internal Critique Based on Ethical Principles

Fourthly, there is the kind of "internal critique" or "immanent critique"[55] advocated by, among others, Seyla Benhabib and Steven Lukes, which, while still being one that primarily employs normative principles of some kind for its critical purposes, seeks to analyse and develop the normative principles which are generated within, and also in part by, the various contexts within which they arise, and analysing the various inconsistencies, contradictions, and ideological perversions to which the normative fabric of a given social context is subject. The principles in question may be ethical or more narrowly moral in nature, but they can also belong to wider normative concerns to do with, e.g. rationality or aesthetic considerations. This kind of internal analysis is performed in order to criticise things like a society's—and other relevantly similar societies'—empirical beliefs, normative goals and ideals, as well as practices, social relations, institutions, legislation, policy, or whatever. Instead of criticising a society in terms of normative principles assumed or imposed abstractly and ahistorically, such critique is "internal" in the sense that it criticises a form of society in terms of that society's own internal evaluative standards.

Not all variants of internal critique—or readings of Marx in terms thereof—fit into this category, however; many rest on normative foundations which are not internal in the required sense. We must thus distinguish at least two senses in which a given critique can be internal. The first, normative, sense is the one just given, and it is in this sense and in this sense only, that internal critique can be said to be based on normative foundations interestingly different from, e.g. moralist readings or readings based on an ethical human nature. Internal readings in this normative sense include, *inter alia*, those who read Marx in terms of an emancipatory *telos* of liberation from natural necessity, in turn derived from a descriptive analysis of human historical development,[56] those who

---

[55] Some writers who read Marx's work in part or in whole in terms of such a notion (to be clarified below) include Antonio (1981), Benhabib (1984), Buchanan (1981), Buchwalter (1991), Chitty (1997), Geuss (1981), Lohmann (1986), Lukes (1985) and Sayers (1989, 1994, and possibly 2007a).

[56] Antonio (1981).

read Marx as criticising capitalism in terms of the Lockean natural rights theory it generates,[57] or more broadly those who read Marx as in some way critiquing capitalist society in terms of the values and normative standards it, in part or in whole, generates[58] In addition to these, there are also positions which appeal more broadly to people's ends and ideals, at least in part determined by the contexts within which these develop, and hold that various forms of descriptive investigation (e.g. into political economy) can rightly lead to the revision of these principles, with downstream effects on individual and collective action.[59]

There is another, methodological, sense in which the terms "internal critique" and "immanent critique" are sometimes used without appealing to the same kind of normative components. One such reading would be one that interprets Marx as critiquing capitalism for failing to live up to the achievable potentials available at a given stage of development—be these potentials for human emancipation, human development, maximising productive outputs of goods and services, or whatever. Such critique is internal insofar as capitalism is critiqued only in light of certain contextual parameters, such as a certain level of development of the productive powers. However, to the extent that such critique invokes evaluative criteria which are not principles internal to a given context, its normative components collapse into one of the other options discussed elsewhere in this appendix or in Part I.[60]

As is the case with many readings of Marx and the normative foundations for his critique of capitalism, there are elements worth preserving in the principles-based internal reading as well, particularly in terms of its ability to elucidate the elements of *ideologikritik* in Marx's works and his love of demonstrating the hypocrisy and illusory nature of appeals to the supposed freedom and equality inherent in capitalist exchange and production. However, it is not clear that Marx's own rejection and

---

[57] Lohmann (1986).

[58] Benhabib (1984), Buchanan (1981) and Geuss (1981).

[59] This seems to be, at least part of, Geuss (1981), McCarney (1990) and Chitty (1997).

[60] Lohmann (1986), for instance, reads Marx as both engaged in immanent critique of the kind just discussed, but also developing a (rather unclear) form of abstract and ahistorical critique as well. Buchwalter (1991) believes Marx must rest on some abstract and ahistorical values of rationality, self-realisation, and so on. Lukes (1985) holds Marx to mix forms of internal and a more moralistic form of critique.

critique of capitalism in fact rests on any of the above-mentioned internal, or any relevantly similar, normative principles. While delighting in demonstrating the illusory nature of equality under capitalism, for instance, he never uses these principles or ideals for any further positive purpose in terms of mounting a critique of capitalism or for envisioning a future socialist society.

Furthermore, it is not clear that this kind of internal critique reading can account for Marx's numerous statements, some of which we have discussed in section (A) of this appendix, rejecting ethical principles for these purposes. In principle, it seems an account of the origins of a society's conceptions of right, justice, and morality in which these arise within, and are at least in part determined by, their contexts could be combined with an exposition of capitalism showing it to in fact violate such principles and on that basis, recommend revolutionary action—this seems to be exactly what the internal critique reading wants to establish. If successful, this would offer a way in which Marx's views (as discussed in particular by Wood and others) on right, justice, and morality can be squared with a normatively grounded critique of capitalism without requiring problematic appeals to a normative conception of human nature. However, any view which takes Marx to be relying on principles of some kind, as this approach must, seems to run into the following cluster of general problems:

1. Marx nowhere devotes significant time or space to elaborating such principles or sets thereof in their own right (with the partial exception of freedom, which I examine in Chapter 3).
2. As we have seen in our discussion of the justice-theoretical readings in section (A) of this appendix, Marx explicitly denies relying on any notions of right, justice, distributive maxims, or morality whatsoever.
3. As we have also seen, Marx explicitly, consistently, and vociferously criticises all those who do rely on such notions to criticise capitalism.
4. It is not clear that a notion of right, justice, morality, and/or any distributive maxims either (a) play a significant role in the formulation and deployment of, or (b) are required to make sense of the normative grounds for, Marx's linchpin critical diagnosis of capitalist society as expressed in his two respective theories of alienation.

There seems to be no way in which this cluster of objections can be addressed without appealing to alternative normative components such as amoralism or a human development-based view. Having rejected the former in section (A) above, I advocate the latter in Part I.

Bibliography

Primary

Engels, F., & Henderson, W. O. (Ed.). (1967). *Engels: Selected writings*. Penguin.
Marx, K., & Carver, T. (ed. and trans.). (1996). *Marx: Later political writings*. Cambridge University Press.
Marx, K., & Engels, F. (1969). *Karl Marx and Frederick Engels: Selected works in three volumes* (MESW). Progress Publishers.
Marx, K., & Engels, F. (1975–2004). *Marx Engels Collected Works* (MECW). Lawrence & Wishart.
Marx, K., & Engels, F. (1975). *Karl Marx Friedrich Engels Gesamtausgabe* ($MEGA_2$). Dietz/Akademie Verlag.
Marx, K., & Engels, F. (1927–1932, 1935). *Karl Marx-Friedrich Engels-Historische-kritische Gesamtausgabe: Werke, Schriften, Briefe* ($MEGA_1$). Marx-Engels Verlag.
Marx, K., & Nicolaus, M. (trans.). (1993). *Grundrisse: Foundations of a critique of political economy*. Penguin.
Marx, K., & Burns, E. (trans.). (1969). *Theories of surplus value: Part I*. Lawrence & Wishart.
Marx, K., Fowkes, B. (trans.) & Mandel, E. (intro.). (1990). *Capital: A critique of political economy* (Vol. 1). Penguin.
Marx, K., Fowkes, B., (trans.) & Mandel, E. (intro.). 1991. *Capital: A critique of political economy* (Vol. 3). Penguin.
Marx, K., Livingstone, R. (trans.), Benton, G. (trans.) & Colletti, L. (Intro.). (1992). *Karl Marx: Early writings*. Penguin.

Secondary

Abensour, M. (2004). *La Démocratie contre l'État: Marx et le moment machiavélien* (2nd ed.). Éditions du Félin.
Acton, H. B. (1955). *The illusion of the epoch.* Cohen & West Ltd.
Adams, W. (1991). Aesthetics: Liberating the senses. In Carver (ed.), pp. 246–274.
Albert, M. (2003). *ParEcon: Life after capitalism.* Verso.
Albert, M., & Hahnel, R. (1978). *Unorthodox Marxism: An essay on capitalism, socialism and revolution.* Boston: South End Press.
Albert, M., & Hahnel, R. (1991). *The political economy of participatory economics.* Princeton University Press.
Albert, M., & Hahnel, R. (1999). *Looking forward: Participatory economics for the twenty first century.* South End Press.
Allen, D. P. H. (1974). Is Marxism a philosophy? *The Journal of Philosophy, 71*(17), 601–612.
Allen, K. (2011). *Marx and the alternative to capitalism.* Pluto Press.
Alexander, R. J. (1999). *The anarchists in the Spanish Civil War* (2 Vols.). Janus.
Anderson, E. (2017). *Private government: How employers rule our lives (and why we don't talk about it).* Princeton University Press.
Antonio, R. J. (1981). Immanent critique as the core of critical theory: Its origins and developments in Hegel, Marx and contemporary thought. *The British Journal of Sociology, 32*(3), 330–345.
Arneson, R. J. (1981). What's wrong with alienation? *Ethics, 91*(2), 202–227.
Aronovitch, H. (1980). Marxian morality. *Canadian Journal of Philosophy, 10*(3), 357–376.
Arrighi, G., Hopkins, T. K., & Wallerstein, I. (2012). *Anti-systemic movements.* Verso.
Arthur, C. J. (1986). *Dialectics of labour: Marx and his relation to Hegel.* Basil Blackwell.
Avineri, S. (1968). *The social and political thought of Karl Marx.* Cambridge University Press.
Baderin, A. (2014). Two forms of realism in political theory. *European Journal of Political Theory, 13*(2), 132–153.
Balibar, E. (2008). *Spinoza and politics.* Verso.
Bavister-Gould, A. (2013). Bernard Williams: Political realism and the limits of legitimacy. *European Journal of Philosophy, 21*(4), 593–610.
Bhattacharya, T. (Ed.). (2017). *Social reproduction theory: Remapping class, recentering oppression.* Pluto Press.
Benhabib, S. (1984). The Marxian method of critique: Normative presuppositions. *PRAXIS International, 4*(3), 284–298.
Berki, R. N. (1990). Through and through Hegel: Marx road to communism. *Political Studies, 38*(4), 654–671.

Berlin, I. (2002). *Liberty: Incorporating four essays on liberty*. Oxford University Press.
Berry, C. J. (1997). *Social theory of the Scottish enlightenment*. Edinburgh University Press.
Blackledge, P. (2012). *Marxism and ethics: Freedom, desire, and revolution*. State University of New York Press.
Bookchin, M. (1974). *Post-scarcity anarchism*. Wildwood House.
Booth, W. J. (1992). Households, markets, and firms. In McCarthy (Ed.), pp. 243–271.
Braverman, H. (1998). *Labour and monopoly capitalism: The degradation of work in the twentieth century* (25th Anniversary ed.). Monthly Review Press.
Bray, M. (2013). *Translating anarchy: The anarchism of occupy wall street*. Zero Books.
Breckman, W. (1999). *Marx, the Young Hegelians, and the origins of radical social theory*. Cambridge University Press.
Breen, K. (2015). Freedom, republicanism, and workplace democracy. *Critical Review of International Social and Political Philosophy, 18*(4), 470–485.
Brenkert, G. J. (1979). Freedom and private property in Marx. *Philosophy & Public Affairs, 8*(2), 122–147.
Brinn, G. (2019). Smashing the state gently: Radical realism and realist anarchism. *European Journal of Political Theory, 19*(2), 206–227.
Bronfenbrenner, M. (1973). A harder look at alienation. *Ethics, 83*(4), 267–282.
Buchanan, A. E. (1981). The Marxian critique of justice and rights. *Canadian Journal of Philosophy, Supplementary, 7*, 269–306.
Buchanan, A. E. (1982). *Marx and justice: The radical critique of liberalism*. Methuen.
Buchwalter, A. (1991). Hegel, Marx, and the concept of immanent critique. *Journal of the History of Philosophy, 29*(2), 253–279.
Bukharin, N. (1925). *Historical materialism: A system of sociology*. International Publishers.
Campbell, A. (2011). *Marx and Engels' vision of building a good society* (pp. 9–32). Marangos.
Carver, T. (Ed.). (1991). *The Cambridge companion to Marx*. Cambridge University Press.
Carver, T. (2010). The German ideology never took place. *History of Political Thought, 31*(1), 107–127.
Chattopadhyay, P. (2018). *Marx's associated mode of production: A critique of Marxism*. Palgrave Macmillan.
Chen, B., Vansteenkiste, M., Beyers, W., Boone, L., Deci, E. L., Van der Kaap-Deeder, J., Duriez, B., Lens, W., Matos, L., Mouratidis, A., Ryan, R. M., Sheldon, K. M., Soenens, B., Van Petegem, S., & Verstuyf, J. (2015). Basic

psychological need satisfaction, need frustration, and need strength across four cultures. *Motivation and Emotion, 39*(2), 216–236.

Chirkov, V., Ryan, R. M., Kim, Y., & Kaplan, U. (2003). Differentiating autonomy from individualism and independence: A self-determination theory perspective on internalization of cultural orientations and well-being. *Journal of Personality and Social Psychology, 84*, 97–109.

Chirkov, V., Ryan, R. M., & Willness, C. (2005). Cultural context and psychological needs in Canada and Brazil: Testing a self-determination approach to the internalization of cultural practices, identity, and well-being. *Journal of Cross-Cultural Psychology, 36*, 423–443.

Chitty, A. (1993). The early Marx on needs. *Radical Philosophy, 64*, 23–31.

Chitty, A. (1997). Introduction: The direction of contemporary capitalism and the relevance of theory. *Review of International Political Economy, 4*(3), 435–447.

Chitty, A. (2006). The basis of the state in the Marx of 1842. In Moggach (Ed.), pp. 220–241.

Chitty, A., & McIvor, M. (Eds.). (2009). *Karl Marx and contemporary philosophy*. Palgrave Macmillan.

Chomsky, N. (1969). *American power and the new mandarins*. The New Press.

Cockshott, P. W., & Cottrell, A. (1993). *Towards a new socialism*. Spokesman.

Cohen, G. A. (1981). Freedom, justice and capitalism. *New Left Review, 126*, 3–16.

Cohen, G. A. (1983). Review of Karl Marx by Allen W. Wood. *Mind, 92*(367), 440–445.

Cohen, G. A. (1989). *History, labour and freedom: Themes from Marx*. Clarendon Press.

Cohen, G. A. (2001). *Karl Marx's theory of history: A defence* (Expanded Edition). Princeton University Press.

Cohen, G. A. (2008). *Rescuing justice and equality*. Harvard University Press.

Cohen, G. A. (2009). *Why not socialism?* Princeton University Press.

Colletti, L. (1992). Introduction to Marx 1992, pp. 7–56.

Collier, A. (2009). Marx and conservatism. In A. Chitty & M. McIvor (Eds.), pp. 99–104.

Comninel, G. (2010). Emancipation in Marx's early work. *Socialism and Democracy, 24*(3), 60–78.

Cowling, M. (2006). Alienation in the older Marx. *Contemporary Political Theory, 5*(3), 319–339.

Deci, E. L., & Ryan, R. M. (2000). The "what" and "why" of goal pursuits: Human needs and the self-determination of behavior. *Psychological Inquiry, 11*(4), 227–268.

Deci, E. L., & Ryan, R. M. (Ed.). (2002a). *Handbook of self-determination research*. University of Rochester Press.

Deci, E. L., & Ryan, R. M. (2002b). Overview of self-determination theory: An organismic dialectical perspective. In E. L. Deci & R. M. Ryan (Eds.), pp. 3–33.

Deci, E. L., & Vansteenkiste, M. (2004). Self-determination theory and basic need satisfaction: Understanding human development in positive psychology. *Ricerche di Psicologia, 27*(1), 23–40.

Deci, E. L., Ryan, R. M., Gagné, M., Leone, D. R., Usunov, J., & Kornazheva, B. (2001). Need satisfaction, motivation, and well-being in the work organizations of a former eastern bloc country: A cross-cultural study of self-determination. *Personality and Social Psychology Bulletin, 27*(8), 930–942.

DeGoyler, M. (1992). The Greek accent of the Marxian matrix. In McCarthy (Ed.), pp. 107–153.

Devine, P. (1988). *Democracy and economic planning: The political economy of a self-governing society*. Polity Press.

Di Domenico, S. I., & Ryan, R. M. (2017). The emerging neuroscience of intrinsic motivation: A new frontier in self-determination research. *Frontiers in Human Neuroscience, 11*(145).

Dixon, C. (2014). *Another politics: Talking across today's transformative movements*. University of California Press.

Doyal, L., & Gough, I. (1991). *A theory of human need*. Palgrave Macmillan.

Draper, H. (1977). *Karl Marx's theory of revolution, Volume I: State and bureaucracy*. Monthly Review Press.

Duff, K. (2017). The criminal is political: Policing politics in real existing liberalism. *Journal of the American Philosophical Association, 3*(4), 485–502.

Duquette, D. A. (1989). Marx's idealist critique of Hegel's theory of society and politics. *Review of Politics, 51*(2), 218–240.

Elster, J. (1983). Exploitation, freedom and justice. *Nomos, 26*, 277–304.

Elster, J. (1985). *Making sense of Marx*. Cambridge University Press.

Feser, E. (Ed.). (2006). *The Cambridge companion to Hayek*. Cambridge University Press.

Finlayson, L. (2015). *The political is political: Conformity and the illusion of dissent in contemporary political philosophy*. Rowman & Littlefield International.

Fischer, N. (2015). *Marxist ethics within Marxist ethics within western political theory: A dialogue with republicanism, communitarianism, and liberalism*. Palgrave Macmillan.

Floyd, J., & Stears, M. (Eds.). (2011). *Political philosophy versus history?: Contextualism and real politics in contemporary political thought*. Cambridge University Press.

Foster, J. B., & Magdoff, F. (2009). *The great financial crisis: Causes and consequences*. Monthly Review Press.

Foster, J. B., Clark, B., & York, R. (2010). *The ecological rift: capitalism's war on the earth*. Monthly Review Press.
Foster, J. B., & McChesney, R. (2012). *The endless crisis: How monopoly-finance capital produces stagnation and upheaval from the USA to China*. Monthly Review Press.
Forrester, K. (2012). Judith Shklar, Bernard Williams, and political realism. *European Journal of Political Theory*, *11*(3), 247–272.
Foucault, M. (1988). *The history of sexuality, volume 3: The use of pleasure*. Vintage.
Foucault, M. (1990a). *The history of sexuality, volume 1: An introduction*. Vintage.
Foucault, M. (1990b). *The history of sexuality, volume 2: The care of the self*. Vintage.
Foucault, M. (1995). *Discipline and punish: The birth of the prison* (2nd ed.). Vintage.
Frazer, E. (2008). Political theory and the boundaries of politics. In D. Leopold & M. Stears (Eds.), *Political theory: Methods and approaches*. Oxford University Press.
Frazer, E. (2010). What's real in political philosophy? *Contemporary Political Theory*, *9*(4), 490–507.
Fromm, E. (2004). *Marx's concept of man*. Continuum.
Furner, J. (2011). Marx's sketch of communist society in *The German ideology* and the problems of occupational confinement and occupational identity. *Philosophy and Social Criticism*, *37*(2), 189–215.
Galston, W. A. (2010). Realism in political theory. *European Journal of Political Theory*, *9*(4), 385–411.
Gamble, A. (1996). *Hayek: The iron cage of liberty*. Polity Press.
Gamble, A. (2006). Hayek on knowledge, economics, and society. In E. Feser (Ed.), pp. 111–131.
Geras, N. (1983). *Marx and human nature: Refutation of a legend*. Verso.
Geras, N. (1985). The controversy about Marx and justice. *New Left Review*, *150*, 47–85.
Geras, N. (1992). Bringing Marx to justice: An addendum to a rejoinder. *New Left Review*, *195*, 37–69.
Geuss, R. (1981). *The idea of a critical theory: Habermas and the Frankfurt school*. Cambridge University Press.
Geuss, R. (2001). *History and illusion in politics*. Cambridge University Press.
Geuss, R. (2003). *Public goods, private goods*. Princeton University Press.
Geuss, R. (2005). *Outside ethics*. Princeton University Press.
Geuss, R. (2008). *Philosophy and real politics*. Princeton University Press.
Geuss, R. (2010). *Politics and the imagination*. Princeton University Press.
Geuss, R. (2012). Economies: Good, bad, indifferent. *Inquiry*, *55*(4), 331–360.

Geuss, R. (2014). *A world without why*. Princeton University Press.
Geuss, R. (2016). *Reality and its dreams*. Harvard University Press.
Gilabert, P. (2012). Comparative assessments of justice, political feasibility, and ideal theory. *Ethical Theory and Moral Practice, 15*(1), 39–56.
Gilbert, A. (1992). Marx's moral realism: Eudaimonism and moral progress. In McCarthy (Ed.), pp. 303–328.
Goldman, E. (2016). *Anarchy and the sex question: Essays on women and emancipation, 1896–1926*. PM Press.
González-Ricoy, I. (2014). The republican case for workplace democracy. *Social Theory and Practice, 40*(2), 232–254.
Gordon, U. (2018). Prefigurative politics between ethical practice and absent promise. *Political Studies, 66*(2), 521–537.
Gourevitch, A. (2015). *From slavery to the cooperative commonwealth: Labor and republican liberty in the nineteenth century*. Cambridge University Press.
Graeber, D. (2009). *Direct action: An ethnography*. AK Press.
Graeber, D. (2013). *The democracy project: A history, a crisis, a movement*. Allen Lane.
Graeber, D. (2015). *The Utopia of rules: On technology, stupidity, and the secret joys of bureaucracy*. Melville House.
Gray, J. (1986). Marxian freedom, individual liberty, and the end of alienation. *Social Philosophy and Policy, 3*(2), 160–187.
Green, M. (1983). Marx, utility, and right. *Political Theory, 11*(3), 433–446.
Gregor, A. J. (1968). Marxism and ethics: A methodological inquiry. *Philosophy and Phenomenological Research, 28*(3), 368–384.
Hahnel, R. (2005). *Economic justice and democracy: From competition to cooperation*. Routledge.
Hahnel, R. (2012). *Of the people, by the people: The case for a participatory economy*. Soapbox Press.
Hahnel, R. (2015). *Green economics: Confronting the ecological crisis*. Routledge.
Hahnel, R. (2021). *Democratic economic planning*. Routledge.
Hall, E. (2015). Bernard Williams and the basic legitimation demand: A defence. *Political Studies, 63*(2), 466–480.
Hall, E. (2017). How to do realistic political theory (and why you might want to). *European Journal of Political Theory, 16*(3), 283–303.
Hamilton, A., Madison, J., & Jay, J. (2003). *The federalist: With letters of Brutus*. Cambridge University Press.
Hamilton, L. A. (2003). *The political philosophy of needs*. Cambridge University Press.
Han, L. (2020). *Studies of the Paris manuscripts: The turning point of Marx*. Springer.
Harvey, D. (2011). *The enigma of capital: And the crises of capitalism* (2nd ed.). Oxford University Press.

Harvey, D. (2015). *Seventeen contradictions and the end of capitalism* (Reprint ed.). Oxford University Press.
Hayek, F. (1945). The use of knowledge in society. *American Economic Review, 35*, 519–530.
Hayek, F. (1960). *The constitution of liberty*. University of Chicago Press.
Hayek, F. (1973). *Law, legislation, and liberty* (Vol. 1). University of Chicago Press.
Hayek, F. (1976). *Law, legislation, and liberty* (Vol. 2). University of Chicago Press.
Hayek, F. (1978). Coping with ignorance. *Imprimis, 7*, 1–6.
Hayek, F. (1979). *Law, legislation, and liberty* (Vol. 3). University of Chicago Press.
Hayek, F. (1988). *The fatal conceit: The errors of socialism.* In W. W. Bartley (Ed.), *The collected works of F. A. Hayek* (Vol. 1). University of Chicago Press.
Hardt, H. (2000). Communication is freedom: Karl Marx on press freedom and censorship. *Javnost—The Public, 7*(4), 85–100.
Henrich, J., Heine, S. J., & Norenzayan, A. (2010). The weirdest people in the world? *Behavioral and Brain Sciences, 33*(2–3), 61–135.
Herbst, P. G. (1962). *Autonomous group functioning: An exploration in behaviour theory and measurement*. Tavistock Publications.
Hodges, D. C. (1964). Marx's ethics and ethical theory. *The Socialist Register, 1*, 227–241.
Hodges, D. C. (1966). The young Marx—A re-appraisal. *Philosophy and Phenomenological Research, 27*(2), 216–229.
Holloway, J. (1997). A note on alienation. *Historical Materialism, 1*(1), 146–149.
Holloway, J. (2010). *Crack capitalism*. Pluto Press.
Honig, B. (1993). *Political theory and the displacement of politics*. Cornell University Press.
Honig, B., & Stears, M. (2011). The new realism: From modus vivendi to justice. In J. Floyd & M. Stears (Eds.), pp. 177–205.
Hsieh, N.-H. (2008). Workplace democracy, workplace republicanism, and economic democracy. *Revue de Philosophie Economique, 9*, 57–78.
Hsieh, N.-H. (2012). Work, ownership, and productive enfranchisement. In M. O'Neill & T. Williamson (Eds.), *Property-owning democracy: Rawls and beyond* (pp. 149–162). Wiley Blackwell.
Hudis, P. (2013). *Marx concept of the alternative to capitalism*. Haymarket Books.
Hunt, R. (1974). *The political ideas of Marx and Engels, volume 1: Marxism and totalitarian democracy, 1818–1850*. Macmillan.
Hunt, R. (1984). *The political ideas of Marx and Engels, volume 2: Classical Marxism 1850–1895*. Macmillan.

Husami, Z. I. (1978). Marx on distributive justice. *Philosophy and Phenomenological Research, 8*(1), 27–68.
Huws, U. (2003). *The making of a cybertariat: Virtual work in the real world*. Monthly Review Press.
Huws, U. (2014). *Labor in the global digital economy: The cybertariat comes of age*. Monthly Review Press.
Igoin, A. (1977). De l'ellipse de la théorie politique de Spinoza chez le jeune Marx. *Cahiers Spinoza, 1,* 213–228.
Israel, J. (1971). *Alienation: From Marx to modern sociology*. Allyn & Bacon Inc.
Jaeggi, R. (2005). *Entfremdung: zur Aktualität eines sosialphilosophischen problems*. Campus.
Kain, P. J. (1988). *Marx and ethics*. Clarendon Press.
Kain, P. J. (1992). Aristotle, Kant, and the ethics of the young Marx. In McCarthy (Ed.), pp. 213–242.
Kamenka, E. (1969). *Marxism and ethics*. Macmillan.
Kamenka, E. (1972). *The ethical foundations of Marxism* (2nd ed.). Routledge & Kegan Paul.
Kasmir, S. (1996). *The myth of Mondragon: Cooperatives, politics, and working-class life in a Basque town*. State University of New York Press.
Kasmir, S. (2018). Cooperative democracy or competitiveness? Rethinking Mondragon. *Socialist Register, 54,* 202–223.
Katz, C. (1994). The socialist polis: Antiquity and socialism in Marx's thought. *The Review of Politics, 56*(2), 237–260.
Kelly, P. (2011). Rescuing political theory from the tyranny of history. In J. Floyd & M. Stears (Eds.), pp. 13–37.
Kouvelakis, S. (2003). *Philosophy and revolution: From Kant to Marx*. Verso.
Kropotkin, P. (1995). *The conquest of bread and other writings*. Cambridge University Press.
Kropotkin, P. (1997). *The state: Its historic role*. Freedom Press.
Kropotkin, P. (2013). *Mutual aid: A factor in evolution*. Dialectics.
Kuvaas, B. (2009). A test of hypotheses derived from self-determination theory among public sector employees. *Employee Relations, 31*(1), 39–56.
Lane, M. (2011). Constraint, freedom, and exemplar: history and theory without teleology. In J. Floyd & M. Stears (Eds.), pp. 128–150.
Larmore, C. (2013). What is political philosophy? *Journal of Moral Philosophy, 10*(3), 276–306.
Larrabure, M. (2013). Human development and class struggle in Venezuela's popular economy: The paradox of 'twenty-first century socialism.' *Historical Materialism, 21*(4), 177–200.
Lebowitz, M. (2003). *Beyond capital: Marx's political economy of the working class*. Palgrave Macmillan.

Lebowitz, M. (2010). *The socialist alternative: Real human development.* Monthly Review Press.
Lebowitz, M. (2012). *The contradictions of real socialism: The conductor and the conducted.* Monthly Review Press.
Lebowitz, M. (2013). The state and the future of socialism. *Socialist Register, 49,* 345–367.
Lebowitz, M. (2020). *Between capitalism and community.* Monthly Review Press.
Leipold, B. (2015). Political anarchism and Raz's theory of authority. *Res Publica, 21*(3), 309–329.
Leipold, B. (2020). Marx's social republic: Radical republicanism and the political institutions of socialism. In K. Nabulsi, S. White, & B. Leipold (Eds.), *Radical republicanism: Recovering the tradition's popular heritage* (pp. 172–193). Oxford University Press.
Leipold, B. (2022). Chains and invisible threads: Liberty and domination in Marx's account of wage-slavery. In A. de Dijn & H. Dawson (Eds.), *Rethinking liberty before liberalism.* Cambridge University Press.
Leiter, B. (2015). Why Marxism still does not need normative theory. *Analyse & Kritik, 37*(1), 23–50.
Leopold, D. (2007). *The young Marx: German philosophy, modern politics, and human flourishing.* Cambridge University Press.
Leval, G. (2018). *Collectives in the Spanish revolution.* PM Press.
Levine, D., & Tyson, L. A. (1990). Participation, productivity and the firm's environment. In A. Blinder (Ed.), *Paying for productivity: A look at the evidence* (pp. 203–214). Brookings Institution.
Lohmann, G. (1986). Marx's *capital* and the question of normative standards. *PRAXIS International, 6*(3), 353–372.
Löwy, M. (2005). *The theory of revolution in the young Marx.* Haymarket Books.
Lukács, G., & Livingstone, R. (trans.). (1974). *History and class consciousness: Studies in Marxist dialectics.* Merlin Press.
Lukes, S. (1985). *Marxism and morality.* Clarendon Press.
Lukes, S. (2004). *Power: A radical view* (2nd ed.). Palgrave.
Lynch, M. F., La Guardia, J. G., & Ryan, R. M. (2009). On being yourself in different cultures: Ideal and actual self-concept, autonomy support, and well-being in China, Russia, and the United States. *The Journal of Positive Psychology, 4*(4), 290–304.
Lynd, S., & Grubacic, A. (2008). *Wobblies and Zapatistas: Conversations on anarchism, Marxism and radical history.* PM Press.
McBride, W. L. (1975). The concept of justice in Marx, Engels, and others. *Ethics, 85*(3), 204–218.
McCarney, J. (1990). *Social theory and the crisis of Marxism.* Verso.
McCarthy, G. E. (Ed.). (1992). *Marx and Aristotle: Nineteenth-century German social theory and classical antiquity.* Rowman & Littlefield.

McGovern, A. F. (1988). The young Marx on the state. In Wood (Ed.), pp. 166–193.
MacIntyre, C. (2009). *Alasdair MacIntyre's engagement with Marxism: Selected writings, 1953–1974*. Haymarket Books.
McLellan, D. (1970). *Marx before Marxism*. Penguin.
McLellan, D. (1971). *The thought of Karl Marx: An introduction*. Macmillan.
McMurty, J. (1978). *The structure of Marx's world-view*. Princeton University Press.
Mack, E. (2011). Nozickian arguments for the more-than-minimal state. In R. M. Bader & J. Meadowcroft (Eds.), *The Cambridge companion to Nozick's Anarchy, state, and Utopia* (pp. 89–115). Cambridge University Press.
Marangos, J. (Ed.). (2011). *Alternative perspectives of a good society*. Palgrave Macmillan.
Martin, B. (2008). *Ethical Marxism: The categorical imperative of liberation*. Open Court.
Maslow, A. H. (1970). *Motivation and personality* (2nd ed.). Harper & Row Publishers.
Matheron, A. (1977). Le *Traité théologico-politique* lu par le jeune Marx. *Cahiers Spinoza, 1,* 159–212.
Melman, S. (1958). *Decision-making and productivity*. Basil Blackwell.
Menke, C. (2010). Neither Rawls Nor Adorno: Raymond Geuss' programme for a 'realist' political philosophy. *European Journal of Philosophy, 18*(1), 139–147.
Mészáros, I. (1972). *Marx's theory of alienation* (3rd ed.). Merlin Press.
Mészáros, I. (1986). *Philosophy, ideology and social science: Essays in negation and affirmation*. Wheatsheaf Books.
Mészáros, I. (1995). *Beyond capital: Towards a theory of transition*. Merlin Press.
Mészáros, I. (2011). *Social structure and forms of consciousness, volume II: The dialectic of structure and history*. Monthly Review Press.
Mészáros, I. (2014). *The necessity of social control*. Monthly Review Press.
Mill, J. S. (1989). *'On liberty' and other writings*. Cambridge University Press.
Miller, D. (Ed.). (2006). *The liberty reader*. Edinburgh University Press.
Miller, R. W. (1983). Marx and morality. *Nomos, 26,* 3–32.
Miller, R. W. (1984). *Analyzing Marx: Morality, power, history*. Princeton University Press.
Miller, R. W. 1992. Marx and Aristotle: A kind of consequentialism. In McCarthy (Ed.), pp. 275–302.
Mintz, F. (2013). *Anarchism and workers' self-management in revolutionary Spain*. AK Press.
Moggach, D. (Ed.). (2006). *The new Hegelians: Politics and philosophy in the Hegelian school*. Cambridge University Press.
Montesquieu, C. (1998). *Montesquieu: The spirit of the laws*. Cambridge University Press.

Mouffe, C. (2006). *The return of the political.* Verso.
Murayama, K., Matsumoto, M., Izuma, K., & Matsumoto, K. (2010). Neural basis of the undermining effect of monetary reward on intrinsic motivation. *Proceedings of the National Academy of Sciences of the United States of America, 107,* 20911–20916.
Musto, M. (2010). Revisiting Marx's concept of alienation. *Socialism and Democracy, 24*(3), 79–101.
Nasser, A. G. (1975). Marx's ethical anthropology. *Philosophy and Phenomenological Research, 35*(4), 484–500.
Ness, I. (Ed.). (2014). *New forms of worker organization: The syndicalist and autonomist restoration of class-struggle unionism.* PM Press.
Ness, I. (2016). *Southern insurgency: The coming of the global working class.* Pluto Press.
Ness, I., & Azzellini, D. (Eds.). (2011). *Ours to master and to own: Workers' control from the commune to the present.* Haymarket Books.
Newey, G. (2010). Two dogmas of liberalism. *European Journal of Political Theory, 9*(4), 449–465.
Nielsen, K. (1988). Marx on justice: The Tucker-Wood thesis revisited. *The Toronto Law Journal, 38*(1), 28–63.
Nilsen, H. F., & Jordheim, H. (Eds.). (2014). *Politisk Frihet.* Res Publica.
Nozick, R. (1974). *Anarchy, state and Utopia.* Basic Books.
Nussbaum, M. (1992a). Nature, function, and capability: Aristotle on political distribution. In McCarthy (Ed.), pp. 175–212.
Nussbaum, M. (1992b). Human functioning and social justice: In defense of Aristotelian essentialism. *Political Theory, 20*(2), 202–246.
Nussbaum, M. (2003). Capabilities as fundamental entitlements: Sen on social justice. *Feminist Economics, 9*(2–3), 33–59.
Nussbaum, M. (2011). *Creating capabilities: The human development approach.* Belknap.
Oikonomakis, L. (2015). Why we still love the Zapatistas. *ROAR Magazine,* 114–131.
Ollman, B. (1976). *Alienation: Marx's conception of man in capitalist society.* Cambridge University Press.
Ollman, B. (1977). Marx's vision of communism: A reconstruction. *Critique, 8*(1), 4–41.
Ollman, B. (2003). *Dance of the dialectic: Steps in Marx's method.* University of Illinois Press.
Padgett, B. L. (2007). *Marx and alienation in contemporary society.* Continuum.
Parsons, H. L. (1971). *Humanism and Marx's thought.* Charles C. Thomas Publisher.
Peffer, R. G. (1990). *Marxism, morality, and social justice.* Princeton University Press.

Peirats, J. (2011). *The CNT in the Spanish revolution: Volume 1*. PM Press.
Peirats, J. (2012a). *The CNT in the Spanish revolution: Volume 2*. PM Press.
Peirats, J. (2012b). *The CNT in the Spanish revolution: Volume 3*. PM Press.
Pettit, P. (1999). *Republicanism: A theory of freedom and government*. Oxford University Press.
Pettit, P. (2006). The republican ideal of freedom. In D. Miller (Ed.), pp. 223–242.
Phillips, L., & Rozworski, M. (2019). *The people's Republic of Walmart: How the world's biggest corporations are laying the foundation for socialism*. Verso.
Philp, M. (2012). Realism without illusions. *Political Theory, 40*(5), 629–649.
Piven, F. F., & Cloward, R. (1993). *Regulating the poor: The functions of public welfare*. Vintage.
Plamenatz, J. (1975). *Karl Marx's philosophy of man*. Clarendon Press.
Plekhanov, G. (1898). *On the role of the individual in history*. Available online: http://www.marxists.org/archive/plekhanov/1898/xx/individual.html
Polanyi, K. (2001). *The great transformation: The political and economic origins of our time*. Beacon Press.
Postone, M. (1996). *Time, labor, and social domination: A reinterpretation of Marx's critical theory*. Cambridge University Press.
Prinz, J. (2016). Raymond Geuss' radicalization of realism in political theory. *Philosophy & Social Criticism, 42*(8), 77–796.
Prinz, J., & Rossi, E. (2017). Political realism as ideology critique. *Critical Review of International Social and Political Philosophy, 20*(3), 334–348.
Raekstad, P., & Gradin, S. (2020). *Prefigurative politics: Building tomorrow today*. Polity Press.
Raekstad, P. (2013, July 30). Review of the people, by the people: The case for a participatory economy. *Marx and Philosophy Review of Books*. Available online: http://marxandphilosophy.org.uk/reviewofbooks/reviews/2013/792
Raekstad, P. (2015). Two contemporary approaches to political theory. *International Critical Thought, 5*(2), 226–240.
Raekstad, P. (2016). Human development and social stratification in Adam Smith. *The Adam Smith Review, 9*, 275–294.
Raekstad, P. (2017a). Review of Marx's Inferno: The political theory of capital, by William Clare Roberts. *Disputatio, IX*(44), 127–130.
Raekstad, P. (2017b). The democratic theory of the early Marx. *Archiv für Geschichte der Philosophie, 99*(4), 443–464.
Raekstad, P. (2018). Human development and alienation in the thought of Karl Marx. *European Journal of Political Theory, 17*(3), 300–323.
Raekstad, P. (2018). Realism, utopianism, and radical values. *European Journal of Philosophy, 26*(1), 145–168.
Raekstad, P. (2018). Revolutionary practice and prefigurative politics: A clarification and defence. *Constellations, 25*(3), 359–372.

Raekstad, P. (2020a). Adam Smith: Radical neo-roman and moderate realist. *Archiv für Geschichte der Philosophie, 103*(1), 70–92.

Raekstad, P. (2020b). Realism, utopianism, and human rights. *Political Studies Review, 18*(4), 542–552.

Raekstad, P. (2020). The present and future of political realism. *Res Publica, 26*(2), 293–297.

Raekstad, P. (forthcoming a). The model of the legislator: Political theory, policy, and realist utopianism. *Contemporary Political Theory*.

Raekstad, P. (forthcoming b). The radical realist critique of Rawls: A reconstruction and response. *Critical Review of International Social and Political Philosophy*.

Rawls, J. (1999). *A theory of justice* (Revised Edition). Belknap.

Rawls, J. (2001). *Justice as fairness: A restatement*. Belknap.

Rawls, J. (2005). *Political liberalism* (Expanded Edition). Columbia University Press.

Reiman, J. (1991). Moral philosophy: The critique of capitalism and the problem of ideology. In T. Carver (Ed.), pp. 143–167.

Riley, P. (1983). Marx and morality: A reply to Richard Miller. *Nomos, 26*, 33–53.

Roberts, W. C. (2017). *Marx's Inferno: the political theory of capital*. Princeton University Press.

Roberts, W. C. (2018). *Marx's social republic: Political not metaphysical* (13 p). (Unpublished Manuscript).

Robeyns, I. (2005). The capability approach: A theoretical survey. *Journal of Human Development, 6*(1), 93–117.

Rossi, E. (2010). Review: Reality and imagination in political theory and practice: On Raymond Geuss's realism. *European Journal of Political Theory, 9*(4), 504–512.

Rossi, E. (2012). Justice, legitimacy and (normative) authority for political realists. *Critical Review of International Social and Political Philosophy, 15*(2), 149–164.

Rossi, E. (2014). *Facts, principles, and politics* (SSRN Working Paper). Available online: http://papers.ssrn.com/sol3/papers.cfm?abstract_id=2378366

Rossi, E. (2019). Being realistic and demanding the impossible. *Constellations, 26*(4), 638–652.

Rossi, E., & Sleat, M. (2014). Realism in normative political theory. *Philosophy Compass, 9*(10), 689–701.

Rothbard, M. (1977). Robert Nozick and the immaculate conception of the state. *Journal of Libertarian Studies, 1*(1), 45–57.

Rudy, D., Sheldon, K. M., Awong, T., & Tan, H. H. (2007). Autonomy, culture, and well-being: The benefits of inclusive autonomy. *Journal of Research in Personality, 41*, 983–1007.

Ryan, C. C. (1980). Socialist justice and the right to the labour product. *Political Theory, 8*(4), 503–524.
Ryan, R. N. (1995). Psychological needs and the facilitation of integrative processes. *Journal of Personality, 63*(3), 397–427.
Ryan, R. N., & Deci, E. L. (2006). Self-regulation and the problem of human autonomy: Does psychology need choice, self-determination and will? *Journal of Personality, 74*(6), 1557–1586.
Ryan, R. N., & Deci, E. L. (2020). Intrinsic and extrinsic motivation from a self-determination theory perspective: Definitions, theory, practices, and future directions. *Contemporary Educational Psychology, 61*(101860).
Rækstad, P. (2010). Marx fra demokrati til kommunisme. *Rødt!: Marxistisk Tidsskrift, 39*(4), 90–99.
Rækstad, P. (2011a). *Class and state in the political theory of Adam Smith: A chapter in the history of a neglected strand of political thought* (107 p) (Master's Thesis). University of Oslo.
Rækstad, P. (2011b). Deltakende demokrati – en sosialisme for fremtiden. *Rødt!: Marxistisk Tidsskrift, 40*(3), 116–126.
Rækstad. (2012a). "Menneskelig utvikling og menneskelige behov"/"Human development and human needs" as part of the seminar on "growth, wealth and happiness—Are they connected?" (together with Roar Eilertsen and professor Ove Jakobsen). *The Welfare Conference 2012a*, Oslo.
Rækstad, P. (2012b, August 7). Den Radikale Opplysningen. *Klassekampen* (pp. 12–13).
Sabio, O. (2015). *Rojava: An alternative to imperialism, nationalism, and Islamism in the Middle East (an introduction)*. Published independently at www.lulu.com.
Saito, K. (2017). *Karl Marx's ecosocialism: Capitalism, nature, and the unfinished critique of political economy*. Monthly Review Press.
Sangiovanni, A. (2008). Justice and the priority of politics to morality. *The Journal of Political Philosophy, 16*(2), 137–164.
Sayers, S. (1989). Analytical Marxism and morality. *Canadian Journal of Philosophy, Supplementary Volume, 15*, 81–104, reprinted in Sayers 2007b, pp. 111–129.
Sayers, S. (1994). Moral values and progress. *New Left Review, 204*, 67–85, reprinted in Sayers 2007b, pp. 130–148.
Sayers, S. (2007a). Marxism and morality. *Philosophical Researches* (9), 8–12.
Sayers, S. (2007b). *Marxism and human nature*. Routledge.
Sayers, S. (2011). *Marx and alienation: Essays in Hegelian themes*. Palgrave Macmillan.
Schacht, R. (1971). *Alienation*. George Allen & Unwin Ltd.

Schröder, E., & Storm, S. (2020). Economic growth and carbon emissions: The road to "hothouse earth" is paved with good intentions. *International Journal of Political Economy, 49*(2), 153–173.
Schweickart, D. (1996). *Against capitalism*. Westview Press.
Sen, A. (1984a). Well-being, agency and freedom: The Dewey lectures 1984. *The Journal of Philosophy, 82*(4), 169–221.
Sen, A. (1984b). *Resources, values and development*. Basil Blackwell.
Sen, A. (1987). *The standard of living (the Tanner lectures)*. Cambridge University Press.
Sen, A. (1992). *Inequality reexamined*. Clarendon Press.
Sen, A. (1999). *Development as freedom*. Oxford University Press.
Sen, A. (2010). *The idea of justice*. Penguin.
Sen, A. (2012a). Values and justice. *Journal of Economic Methodology, 19*(2), 101–108.
Sen, A. (2012b). A reply to Robeyns, Peter and Davis. *Journal of Economic Methodology, 19*(2), 173–176.
Sichel, B. A. (1972). Karl Marx and the rights of man. *Philosophy and Phenomenological Research, 32*(3), 355–360.
Sitrin, M. (2012). *Everyday revolutions: Horizontalism and autonomy in Argentina*. Zed Books.
Sitrin, M., & Azzellini, D. (2014). *They can't represent us!: Reinventing democracy from Greece to occupy*. Verso.
Skinner, Q. (1998). *Liberty before liberalism*. Cambridge University Press.
Skinner, Q. (2006). A third concept of liberty. In D. Miller (Ed.), pp. 243–254.
Skinner, Q. (2008). *Hobbes and republican liberty*. Cambridge University Press.
Sleat, M. (2010). Bernard Williams and the possibility of a realist political theory. *European Journal of Political Theory, 9*(4), 485–503.
Sleat, M. (2013). *Liberal realism: A realist theory of liberal politics*. Manchester University Press.
Smith, A. (1976). *An Inquiry into the nature and causes of the wealth of nations*. Oxford: Oxford University Press.
Soenens, B., Park, S.-B., Vansteenkiste, M., & Mouratidis, A. (2012). Perceived parental psychological control and adolescent depressive experiences: A cross-cultural study with Belgian and South-Korean adolescents. *Journal of Adolescence, 35*, 261–272.
Soenens, B., & Beyers, W. (2012). The cross-cultural significance of control and autonomy in parent-adolescent relationships. *Journal of Adolescence, 35*, 243–248.
Soper, K. (1981). *On human needs: Open and closed theories in a Marxist perspective*. Harvester Press.
Soper, K. (1987). Marxism and morality. *New Left Review, 163*, 101–113.

Sowell, T. (1963). Karl Marx and the freedom of the individual. *Ethics, 73*(2), 119–125.
Spinoza, B. (1996). *Ethics*. Penguin.
Springborg, P. (1981). *The problem of human needs and the critique of civilisation*. George Allen & Unwin.
Strangers in a Tangled Wilderness (Ed.). (2015). *A small key can open a large door: The Rojava revolution*. Combustion Books.
Swain, D. (2012). *Alienation: An introduction to Marx's theory*. Bookmarks.
Swain, D. (2019). *None so fit to break the chains: Marx's ethics of self-emancipation*. Brill.
Swain, D. (2019). Not not but not yet: Present and future in prefigurative politics. *Political Studies, 67*(1), 47–62.
Tabak, M. (2012). *Dialectics of human nature in Marx's philosophy*. Palgrave Macmillan.
Tabak, M. (2020). *Marx's philosophy of revolution and freedom: A critical reconstruction*. Self-published.
Taylor, R. (2014). The new PKK: Unleashing a social revolution in Kurdistan. ROAR Magazine. Available online: https://roarmag.org/essays/pkk-kurdish-struggle-autonomy/.
Thomas, A. (2014). Sen on Rawls's "transcendental institutionalism": An analysis and critique. *European Journal of Political Theory, 13*(3), 241–263.
Thompson, M. J. (2019). The radical Republican structure of Marx's critique of capitalist society. *Critique, 47*(3), 391–409.
Trist, E. L., Higgin, G. W., Murray, H., & Pollock, A. B. (1963). *Organizational choice: Capabilities of groups at the coal face under changing technologies*. Tavistock Publications.
Tucker, R. C. (1970). *The Marxian revolutionary idea*. George Allen & Unwin Ltd.
Tucker, R. C. (1972). *Philosophy and myth in Karl Marx*. Cambridge University Press.
Valentini, L. (2011). A paradigm shift in theorizing about justice? A critique of Sen. *Economics and Philosophy, 27*(3), 297–315.
Valentini, L. (2012). Ideal vs. non-ideal theory: A conceptual map. *Philosophy Compass, 7*(9), 654–664.
Van de Sande, M. (2015). Fighting with tools: Prefiguration and radical politics in the twenty-first century. *Rethinking Marxism, 27*(2), 177–194.
Van de Veer, D. (1973). Marx's views of justice. *Philosophy and Phenomenological Research, 33*(3), 366–386.
Van der Linden, H. (1984). Marx and morality: An impossibly synthesis? *Theory and Society, 13*(1), 119–135.
van Ree, E. (2020). Productive forces, the passions and natural philosophy: Karl Marx, 1841–1846. *Journal of Political Ideologies, 25*(3), 274–293.

Vansteenkiste, M., & Ryan, R. M. (2013). On Psychological growth and vulnerability: Basic psychological need satisfaction and need frustration as a unifying principle. *Journal of Psychotherapy Integration, 23*(3), 263–280.

Vansteenkiste, M., Neurinck, B., Niemiec, C. P., Soenens, B., De Witte, H., & Van den Broeck, A. (2007). On the relations among work value orientations, psychological need satisfaction and job outcomes: A self-determination theory approach. *Journal of Occupational and Organizational Psychology, 80*, 251–277.

Vansteenkiste, M., Ryan, R. M., & Soenens, B. (2020). Basic psychological need theory: Advancements, critical themes, and future directions. *Motivation and Emotion, 44*(1), 1–31.

Vrousalis, N. (2010). G. A. Cohen's vision of socialism. *Journal of Ethics, 14*(3–4), 185–216.

Vrousalis, N. (2012). Jazz Bands, camping trips and decommodification: G.A. Cohen on community. *Socialist Studies, 8*(1), 141–163.

Vrousalis, N. (2021). The capitalist cage: Structural domination and collective agency in the market. *Journal of Applied Philosophy, 38*(1), 40–54.

Wahl, A. (2011). *The rise and fall of the welfare state*. Pluto Press.

Walker, P. (Ed.). (1979). *Between labor and capital*. South End Press.

Walliman, I. (1981). *Estrangement: Marx's conception of human nature and the division of labor*. Greenwood Press.

Weber, M., Lassman, P., & Speirs, R. (ed.). (1994). *Weber: Political writings*. Cambridge University Press.

White, P. (2015). *The PKK: Coming down from the mountains*. Zed Books.

White, S. (2011). The republican critique of capitalism. *Critical Review of International Social and Political Philosophy, 14*(5), 561–579.

Wilde, L. (1998). *Ethical Marxism and its radical critics*. Macmillan.

Wilkinson, R., & Pickett, K. (2010). *The spirit level: Why equality is better for everyone*. Penguin.

Williams, B. (1980). Political philosophy and the analytic tradition. Reprinted in Williams 2006, pp. 180–199.

Williams, B. (2004). *Truth and truthfulness: An essay in genealogy*. Princeton University Press.

Williams, B. (2006). *Political philosophy as a humanistic discipline*. Princeton University Press.

Williams, B. (2008). *In the beginning was the deed: Realism and moralism in political argument*. Princeton University Press.

Wolff, J. (1991). *Robert Nozick: Property, justice and the minimal state*. Stanford University Press.

Wolff, J. (1992). Playthings of alien forces. *Cogito, 6*(1), 35–41.

Wolff, J. (2003). *Why read Marx today?* Oxford University Press.

Wolff, J. (2011). *Ethics and public policy: A Philosophical inquiry*. Routledge.

Wolff, J., & de-Shalit, A. (2007). *Disadvantage*. Oxford University Press.
Wood, A. W. (1972a). Marx's critical anthropology: Three recent interpretations. *The Review of Metaphysics*, 26(1), 118–139.
Wood, A. W. (1972b). The Marxian critique of justice. *Philosophy and Public Affairs*, 1(3), 244–282.
Wood, A. W. (1979). Marx on right and justice: A reply to Husami. *Philosophy and Phenomenological Research*, 8(3), 267–295.
Wood, A. W. (2004). *Karl Marx* (2nd ed.). London: Routledge.
Wood, J. C. (ed.). (1988). *Karl Marx's economics: Critical assessments* (Vol. 1). Routledge.
Wood, E. M. (2002). The question of market dependence. *Journal of Agrarian Change*, 2(1), 51–54.
Wright, E. O. (1980). Varieties of Marxist conceptions of class structure. *Politics & Society*, 9(3), 323–370.
Wright, E. O. (2010). *Envisioning real utopias*. Verso.
Young, G. (1978). Justice in capitalist production: Marx and bourgeois ideology. *Canadian Journal of Philosophy*, 8(3), 421–455.
Young, G. (1981). Doing Marx justice. *Canadian Journal of Philosophy, Supplementary Volume*, 7, 251–268.
Zibechi, R. (2012). *Territories in resistance: A cartography of Latin American social movements Oakland*. AK Press.

Index

A

Alienation
  first theory of, 7–9, 91, 103, 109, 120
  from labour/production, 63, 119, 128, 146, 151
  from others, 11, 63, 119, 147, 151, 195, 200
  from product of labour, 63, 119, 122, 133, 200
  from species-being, 11, 63, 119, 143, 146, 151, 206
Amoralism, 227, 229, 237–239, 261
Authority, 99, 136, 137, 162, 179
  On Authority, by F. Engels, 139

C

Capital, 122, 127, 132, 137, 140, 143, 148, 163, 164, 201, 203, 241
Capitalism, 1–12, 21–23, 31, 41–43, 45, 50, 53, 58, 62–65, 70, 79, 85, 86, 88, 91, 92, 104, 105, 108–110, 112, 119–121, 123–132, 135–138, 140, 143, 145, 147, 150–152, 156, 157, 159, 161, 162, 164, 165, 168–170, 172–174, 180, 183, 187–191, 195, 198, 200, 202–211, 213–219, 221, 222, 226–246, 249, 250, 253–256, 258–260
Communism, 2, 22, 171
Communist society, 168
Contradictions (of capitalism), 4, 11, 23, 41, 131, 151, 195, 198, 199, 204, 205

D

Democracy, 4, 7–11, 70, 82, 84, 87, 89–101, 103, 105, 107–109, 155, 156, 172, 213, 253
Division of labour, 5, 11, 131, 136, 137, 139, 156, 158, 161–163,

165, 167, 168, 172, 174–176, 180, 183, 190, 214, 217
Domination, 1, 2, 5, 7, 8, 40, 58, 59, 61, 62, 89, 97, 101, 120, 125, 127, 128, 130, 137, 140, 148, 149, 159–164, 190, 200, 201, 207, 208, 216, 217
  impersonal domination, 5, 61, 62, 129–131, 140, 158, 159, 161, 180, 189, 190, 203, 214
  personal domination, 61, 62, 130, 131, 158, 161, 167

E

Engels, F., 93, 105, 111, 112, 128, 137, 139, 150, 155, 157, 158, 161, 165, 196, 197, 209

F

Freedom, 1, 2, 4–7, 9–12, 21, 25, 26, 40, 45, 46, 49, 50, 52, 54, 57–64, 70, 79, 83, 84, 91–93, 96, 97, 111, 119, 130, 140, 141, 146, 151, 155, 157, 160, 163, 166, 170, 172, 182, 189, 195, 198, 204, 207–210, 213, 214, 216, 221, 229, 233, 236, 238, 239, 241, 243, 253–256, 259, 260

H

Hayek, Friedrich, 10, 156, 172, 183, 186–188, 190
Human nature, 7, 10, 37, 40, 49, 51, 52, 55, 56, 58, 87, 109, 141, 147, 189, 221, 222, 228, 232, 233, 244, 253–258, 260

M

Markets, 5, 42, 58, 59, 61, 110, 129, 131, 158–161, 166, 167, 169, 180, 183, 186–190, 201, 214, 215, 217
Marx, K., 1–12, 21–43, 45, 49–70, 79–101, 103–109, 111, 112, 119–152, 155–175, 180, 182–184, 187, 188, 190, 191, 195–207, 209, 210, 213–219, 221–224, 226–260
Method (of political theory)
  agent-centred, 10, 109–112, 195, 206, 213
  realisation-oriented, 9, 108, 112, 213
  realist, 2, 3, 7, 9, 10, 12, 23, 104, 207, 209, 213, 214
Moralism, 7, 209, 222, 233, 236, 238–241, 243, 252–254, 256, 258

N

Nature, 10, 11, 21, 22, 24, 29, 33, 49–51, 53–55, 57, 58, 65, 69, 79, 80, 86–88, 109, 132, 134, 137, 138, 140, 142–144, 146, 149, 151, 156, 164, 169, 170, 173, 197, 198, 200, 205, 207, 208, 213, 215, 217, 221, 224, 226, 228, 238, 240, 248, 249, 252, 254, 256, 258–260
  human nature, 50, 51, 58

P

Planning, 5, 61, 131, 158–161, 166, 175, 178, 183–188, 190, 214, 217

R

Realism, 2–5, 23, 111, 207, 209, 214

Republicanism, 2, 92
Revolution, 4, 5, 10, 12, 39, 84, 100, 106, 108, 110, 150, 175, 190, 191, 196, 199, 200, 203–205, 207, 231, 235, 236

S
Socialism, 2, 4, 8, 10–12, 22, 23, 41–43, 70, 91, 92, 95, 104, 105, 111, 112, 139, 152, 155–158, 161, 162, 165, 166, 168–175, 180, 182, 183, 187, 188, 190, 195, 197, 200, 202–204, 207, 209, 214, 217, 218, 229, 235, 237, 246, 253
Socialist society, 2, 11, 22, 156, 157, 162, 167, 168, 170, 172, 183, 190, 196, 217–219, 242, 245, 260

W
Weber, Max, 10, 156, 172, 173, 175–177, 180, 181, 188, 190

The manufacturer's authorised representative in the EU is Springer Nature Customer Service Centre GmbH, Europaplatz 3, 69115 Heidelberg, Germany. If you have any concerns regarding our products, please contact ProductSafety@springernature.com

Printed and bound by CPI Group (UK) Ltd, Croydon, CR0 4YY

23/03/2026

02076663-0006